DEVILS RIVER
Treacherous Twin to the Pecos, 1535-1900

DEVILS RIVER
Treacherous Twin to the Pecos, 1535-1900

Patrick Dearen

TCU Press
Fort Worth

Copyright © 2011 by Patrick Dearen

Library of Congress Cataloging-in-Publication Data

Dearen, Patrick.

Devils River : treacherous twin to the Pecos, 1535-1900 / Patrick Dearen.
p. cm.
Includes bibliographical references and index.
ISBN 978-0-87565-423-2 (pbk. : alk. paper)
1. Devils River Valley (Crockett County-Val Verde County, Tex.)--History. 2. Frontier and pioneer life--Devils River Valley (Crockett County-Val Verde County, Tex.) I. Title.
F392.D47D43 2011
976.4'875--dc22
2010027658

TCU Press
P. O. Box 298300
Fort Worth, Texas 76129
817.257.7822
http://www.prs.tcu.edu

To order books: 800.826.8911

Designed by fusion29, Fort Worth, Texas

*For Glen Sample Ely, PhD, who first suggested this book.
Thanks, compadre, for all your friendship and generosity.*

CONTENTS

Author's Note ix

CHAPTER 1   *A River Unique* 11
CHAPTER 2   *Spanish Attempts at Conquest* 15
CHAPTER 3   *Blazing the Devils Trail* 22
CHAPTER 4   *Dead Man's Pass* 34
CHAPTER 5   *By Mail Coach and Hoof* 43
CHAPTER 6   *An Army Post at Second Crossing* 56
CHAPTER 7   *The San Antonio to San Diego Mail* 62
CHAPTER 8   *Indian Trouble* 68
CHAPTER 9   *Gray Replaces Blue* 81
CHAPTER 10 *The Devils Indian War* 88
CHAPTER 11 *Black Seminoles to the Rescue* 98
CHAPTER 12 *Avenging in Mexico* 107
CHAPTER 13 *Last of the Arrows* 114
CHAPTER 14 *Coming of the Southern Pacific* 122
CHAPTER 15 *The Big Cattle Drift* 130
CHAPTER 16 *Horn, Fleece, and Drouth* 134
CHAPTER 17 *Badmen Rise Up* 143
CHAPTER 18 *A Potential for Sudden Death* 148
CHAPTER 19 *Fang, Claw, and Buffalo Hides* 157
CHAPTER 20 *The Devil's Brood* 164

Epilogue 172
Notes 173
Bibliography 199
Index 209
About the Author 223

AUTHOR'S NOTE

I produced this work with the assistance of a J. Evetts Haley Fellowship Award granted to me in 2006. Administered by Nita Stewart Haley Memorial Library in Midland, Texas, with funding received from Summerlee Foundation, the fellowship allowed me to dig deeply into the Haley Library's remarkable holdings in search of material related to the Devils River.

I wish to thank the Haley Library Board of Trustees and the Summerlee Foundation for their vital roles in making this book a reality. I also express my gratitude to United Daughters of the Confederacy, Texas Division, for permission to use material from the Texas Confederate Museum Collection in the Haley archives.

I would like to single out the following Haley Library personnel for their tireless support in my long and involved quest: Jim Bradshaw, Pat McDaniel, Nancy Jordan, Susie Chambers, and Glenna Gifford. Each one truly made my exhaustive research all the more enjoyable and rewarding.

CHAPTER 1

A RIVER UNIQUE

Rio San Pedro . . . the Devils River . . . a place deemed unfit for Saint Peter, but a proper abode for the fallen Lucifer.

The very name of this ninety-four-mile sister river of the Pecos in Southwest Texas conjures up specters of doom and judgment, death and hell.[1] From sixteenth-century Spanish explorers to the American trailblazers of the 1840s, from antebellum stage drivers and cattle drovers to post-Civil War venturers and stockmen, the Devils River country posed a two-edged threat worthy of Satan. There was man with an evil as old as Cain, and there was the land, drawn straight out of Dante's *Inferno,* and one was as merciless and deadly as the other.

In 1861 Confederate soldier John E. Hart proclaimed this area the "rockiest and roughest country on Earth,"[2] but early travelers seldom limited their comparisons to the world of the living. In 1849, westbound emigrant Robert Eccleston associated the Devils with the Styx, the river of the dead in Greek mythology.[3] Six years later, J. D. B. Stillman pondered whether the Devils was a "damned river . . . consigned to the Prince of Darkness," and kept a "sharp look out for all sorts of evil ones."[4] In 1861, William Heartsill had no doubts about the river's correlation to perdition. "His 'Satanic Majesty,'" wrote this rebel soldier, "must be in full and undisputed possession of all this region."[5] By 1894, with the lives of the innocent and guilty alike burned so indelibly in the Devils' banks, the *San Angelo Standard* branded the river the "Brimstone Branch."[6]

Draining 4,305 square miles, this tributary of the Rio Grande originates in Schleicher, Crockett, and Sutton counties as a series of intermittent draws that grow in prominence as they trend south. Major watercourses include the Dry Devils River, which forms eight miles west of Eldorado and squirms for sixty-

Dry Devils River just above its confluence with Granger Draw. Photograph courtesy of Patrick Dearen.

three miles; Granger Draw, a forty-eight-mile arroyo rising a dozen miles west of Eldorado; and Buckhorn Draw, which winds forty-two miles from northeast Crockett before joining Granger.

In the shadow of 200-foot hills in Sutton County's southwest corner, the Dry Devils merges with Granger at an elevation of 1,860 feet to spawn the Devils River. A mere forty-three crow-flight miles west lies the Pecos, rushing south along a parallel course. Soon the Devils enters Val Verde County and the rivers swing even closer, engaging in a snake-track dance a mere seventeen to thirty miles apart. Slashing through increasingly precipitous country, the twins reach journey's end twenty-five miles from one another at the Rio Grande and United States-Mexico border.

Devils River canyon, an inverted ridge with relief sometimes greater than 500 feet, boasts of thirty-two minions, including seventy-three-mile Johnsons Run out of Crockett. The theme of gloom and punishment is perpetuated by the names of several other Devils River tributaries: a second Dry Devils River, this one bearing southwest forty-nine miles from its Edwards County wellsprings, and equally descriptive Dark Canyon, Dead Man's Creek, and Big Satan Creek.[7]

Situated at the meeting place of three ecological regions—Edwards Plateau, Chihuahuan Desert, and Tamaulipan Thornscrub—the Devils River area exhibits characteristics of each, yet never so definitively as to compromise its uniqueness. Imagine Hill Country woods lining a stream splashing through a Trans-Pecos wasteland subject to a subtropical, semi-arid climate with annual precipitation of

The Devils River one-third mile below its origin.
Photograph courtesy of Patrick Dearen.

The wooded Devils bottomland in stark contrast to the bordering hills.
Photograph courtesy of Patrick Dearen.

seventeen inches. Only then can one appreciate the Devils as a river apart.[8]

The country's threefold nature bred almost contradictory portraits by early observers, who either condemned its rugged character—"wild with deep and tortuous canyons" and an "impetuous" river, said the October 26, 1889 *San Angelo Standard*—or praised the stream for its "infinite beauty and picturesqueness," as did Edward Fitzgerald Beale in 1857.[9] The flora, as well, generated both scorn and admiration. "It has been said with more truth than poetry that everything here bears a thorn," wrote emigrant Robert Eccleston in 1849.[10] Yet six years later the greenery that graced the river's middle stretches cast such a spell on J. D. B. Stillman that he noted its contribution to the river's "wild beauty."[11]

In 1898, the *Dallas News* eloquently captured this dichotomy of awful terror and sublime charm:

"The Devil's river . . . penetrates lines of lofty hills and precipitous defiles, through deep canyons and mountain gorges, now and then emerging from this wilderness of grand scenery into small but fertile valleys. . . ."[12]

Fed by springs as well as run-off, the Devils of early days had perhaps the most consistent flow of any river in Texas. Measurements between 1901 and 1903 established that the stream had the state's greatest minimum discharge—380 to 480 cubic feet per second.[13] At times, serenity gave way to chaos, and the Devils lived up to its name by way of fiendish torrents that roared through its gorge at rates as great as 597,000 c.f.s.[14]

This, then, is the river known as the Devils—the pulsing artery of unyielding badlands at the time of the first European incursion—and for centuries it would pose challenges that helped hew the character of the American Southwest.

CHAPTER 2

SPANISH ATTEMPTS AT CONQUEST

By the sixteenth century, the Devils River country already had nurtured Indians for millennia. They gathered its edible plants, hunted its canyon lands, fished its waters, sheltered in its overhangs. In 1535, though, as a scraggly party of European castaways approached from the Texas Gulf Coast, the curtain rose on a culture clash that would endure for 350 years.

Across a country thick with piñon pines the Spaniards trudged, Cabeza de Vaca and three companions hoping to reach a Spanish settlement beyond a vast, uncharted wilderness. Their route is debatable, but an eighteen hundred-square mile band of Texas piñons immediately east of the Devils intrigues historians as well as botanists. Generally confined to Trans-Pecos mountains, these drouth-resistant pines unaccountably blanket the watershed hills of the Frio, Nueces, and southernmost Dry Devils rivers—a biologically lost forest that gives clues to a route lost to history. Spanning sixty miles from the Frio on the east to the Dry Devils on the west, and thirty miles from north to south,[1] the nut-bearing piñons gave sustenance to early Indians—perhaps including peoples encountered by Cabeza de Vaca.

"In that country are small pine trees, the cones like little eggs," he wrote of one region, "but the seed is better than that of Castile, as its husk is very thin, and while green is beaten and made into balls, to be thus eaten. If the seed be dry, it is pounded in the husk, and consumed in the form of flour."[2]

Forging on into the sunset, the castaways marveled at a "great river coming from the north."[3] This reference supports the notion that theirs were the first non-Indian footprints on the Devils' banks, for it is the kind of description one might make of the Pecos after fording the Devils and bridging the divide between the waterways.

Fifty-five years later in 1590, the Spaniard Gaspar Castaño de Sosa and 170 men, women, and children embarked northward from central Coahuila, Mexico, in quest of suitable country to colonize. After Castaño reached the Rio Grande near present Del Rio September 9, Juan Perez de los Rios scouted ahead for the Rio Salado, or Pecos, up which Castaño hoped to travel. Impassable terrain prevented Juan Perez from gaining the Pecos, but he returned with news of a heretofore unnamed river fronted by treacherous rock.

For only the second time, perhaps, the eyes of Europeans had beheld the Devils.

Unsure whether *carretas* (ox carts) and livestock herds could cross this "River of Rocks," or Rio de las Lajas, Castaño authorized two subsequent scouts, the second of which discovered a potential ford. On October 2, Castaño's *carretas* rumbled to the site, likely at the mouth of San Pedro Creek. The colonists spent a day or more negotiating the crossing, then made the arduous climb to the divide between the Devils and Pecos and pushed on to the northwest.

Zigzagging across a broken tableland for the next three weeks, the Castaño party spent a rainy October 16 on the upper Devils or perhaps its tributary, Johnsons Run. Finally on October 26, the colonists reached the Pecos below the mouth of Live Oak Creek and left the Devils country behind.[4] Nevertheless, Spain's role in the River of Rocks was only beginning.

In early April 1674, Franciscan friar Manuel de la Cruz and five Indians crossed the Rio Grande north into Texas below present Del Rio. Four and a half days before, they had set out from the mission Santa Rosa de Santa Maria in Coahuila, where Manuel had ministered to several hundred Indians, including 512 Guyquechales. Due to a smallpox epidemic, the Guyquechales had left the mission and gone north. They had never returned, and now Manuel had come in search, despite the threat of an unknown land.

Three days and approximately forty-seven miles north of the Rio Grande, the Manuel party reached "a mountain range" known to the Indians as Dacate. Here, Manuel's zeal for the Great Commission was tested, for he encountered a friendly Indian who warned of hostiles ahead. Undaunted, the friar and his companions pressed on and took refuge for three days in an arroyo, likely the Devils River.

Manuel dispatched a scout, who returned to report that Boboles were in camp 15.6 miles up the same drainage. Traveling all night, Manuel reached the camp and learned that he was within 20.8 miles of the Guyquechales whom he sought. Sending a messenger to the latter band, Manuel quickly discovered that his missionary efforts back at Santa Rosa had born fruit—the Guyquechale leader arrived before sunset with an extraordinary show of support for the friar.

"Knowing . . . the danger I was in," related Manuel, " . . . [he brought] for my protection ninety-eight archers arrayed in their war paint. . . . All came prepared for battle, well provided with arrows."

They would need every feathered missile, for scouts soon reported that 180 hostiles were en route to slay the friar. With a combined force of 147 warriors, the Guyquechales and Boboles prepared to leave Manuel with the women and children and engage the enemy. The friar, however, continued to show his mettle and refused to stay behind, asserting that he would not desert his "sons and brothers" even if it meant death.

Manuel's allegiance had a powerful affect.

"Now we can see that you love us," the Indians told him, "and you may rest assured that we would rather die than desert you."

Emboldened, the Guyquechales and Boboles marched with the friar throughout the night to position for attack. As the warring forces discovered one another at sunup, the Guyquechales and Boboles began to panic in the face of superior numbers. Manuel, though, held fast to his faith and lifted up a crucifix. God surely would come to their aid, he exhorted the converts, for they were defending His law against enemies who persecuted "this Master who died for us on the Cross."

With a great cry, the encouraged Guyquechales and Boboles brandished their bows and proceeded to rout the enemy in a fierce battle that left seven hostiles dead. Returning victorious to the friar, the converts kissed the crucifix in acknowledgment of their deliverance by God.

Manuel and the war party returned to the Bobole camp amid celebration, then both bands marched to the Guyquechales' *rancheria,* two days to the southeast. Another victory observance ensued, this time involving an assembly 673 strong, and Manuel gained assurance that the tribes would accompany him back to the mission in Coahuila.

The next day, after three weeks in the Devils country and elsewhere in present Val Verde, Kinney, and Maverick counties, the friar forded the Rio Grande and re-entered Coahuila.[5]

A year later, two other Franciscan missionaries dared the same region of the Devils. Manuel's superior, Juan Larios, and Father Dionisio de San Buenaventura crossed the Rio Grande into Texas on May 11, 1675, with twenty-one Boboles, an Indian governor, and ten soldiers commanded by Fernando del Bosque. Bosque's orders were to scout the "Sierra Dacate" and determine if the Indians wished to be converted and settle in pueblos so that Franciscans could instruct them in religious matters.

Within a week, the expedition struck a "small river" that Indian guides called "Dacate"—evidently the Devils. Here, the Spaniards met up with a Geniocane Indian chief, who led them to a Geniocane *rancheria* cradled in a hill-defined arroyo 20.8 miles north.

For the next several days, the Franciscans preached to the receptive Geniocanes, then proceeded north with their escort on May 25. Approximately thirty-six miles distant, the Spaniards made camp at "a small arroyo with heavy timber, between some knolls and hills," a description that could fit many locations in the Devils country. Finally on May 29, the expedition turned back for Coahuila.[6]

Rivaling the Spanish for possession of seventeenth-century Texas were the French, whose first highlighted push into the region would come when René Robert Cavelier, Sieur de La Salle landed at Matagorda Bay on the Texas Gulf Coast on February 20, 1685.[7] Remarkably, however, when Dominguez de Mendoza had led a Spanish expedition east across Texas the year before, he had encountered Jediondo Indians sporting a French flag along the lower Pecos.

Mendoza continued into the sunrise as far as the confluence of the Colorado and Concho rivers, then returned via a more southerly route that took him across the upper Devils drainage on May 19, 1684.

"The watering places have been formed of rain water," Mendoza noted in his journal. "All the country is timbered and has very good pastures, and all the land is pleasant."[8]

Sixteen years later, Spaniards established the first mission and military outpost in the region. Presidio de San Juan Bautista, located on the Rio Grande thirty-five miles downstream of Piedras Negras, Coahuila, and within 100 miles of the Devils, would serve as a vital staging ground for succeeding expeditions into Texas.[9]

In the early eighteenth century, Apache raiders from north of the Rio Grande swooped down into Coahuila with increasing frequency, hindering Spanish colonization and missionary efforts. The situation led Coahuila Governor Blas de la Garza Falcon to consider a location upstream of San Juan Bautista for another fort in late 1735. From a camp on the San Diego River in Coahuila fifteen miles south of present Del Rio, he ordered his son, Captain Miguel de la Garza Falcon, to explore the Rio Grande as far upriver as possible.

With thirty mounted soldiers and ten Indian guides, Miguel set out January 4, 1736, and crossed the Rio Grande into Texas the next day. Battling a snowstorm and terrain so rugged that it claimed many of his horses, Miguel traversed the Devils and Pecos country and penetrated 100 miles into a land unknown. Finding the Rio Grande route impassable beyond the present Dryden area, he turned back on January 8 and reached his father's camp three days later.[10]

Apaches continued to bedevil northern Mexico during the succeeding decades, despite missionaries' wishes to convert the tribe and occasional overtures of interest from the Indians themselves. With the feared Comanches encroaching on Apacheria from the north, Apaches had strategic reasons to consider mission life under Spanish protection, but Spain's policy of subjugating Apaches through force and enslavement was a stumbling block.[11] Between 1775 and 1783, tensions led to a series of military campaigns against Apaches in the Devils country and elsewhere.

The first came in 1775, when three Spanish units converged in Texas. One commander, Coahuila governor Jacobo de Ugarte y Loyola, started upstream from San Juan Bautista on September 22 with more than 180 men. Ugarte's intent was to push the Apaches back from the Rio Grande and drive them west toward other forces ready to crush.

After entering Texas and reconnoitering abandoned Presidio de San Saba near present Menard, Ugarte marched back into Coahuila to secure fresh horses from Presidio de Aguaverde on the San Diego River. Resuming the campaign October 16, Ugarte again forded the Rio Grande and set his sights on the Devils, by now known to the Spanish as the San Pedro or "Saint Peter."

He marched to the Devils headwaters, veered west, and set up stakes near the Pecos October 31. From this base, he dispatched contingents far up the Pecos and toward the Concho River wellsprings. After fruitless searches, the parties rejoined Ugarte, who proceeded to backtrack through the Devils country.

On December 22, as a small advance patrol led by Ramon Marrufo neared the confluence of the Devils and Johnsons Run near what would become known as Juno in 1886, a skulking band of Lipan Apaches began raining arrows. Even as thundering hooves signaled the approach of fifty reinforcements under Lieutenant Juan Bautista de Elguezabal, two soldiers and an Indian auxiliary fell. All Bautista could do was avenge their deaths, killing three Lipans and wounding three more before the hostiles scattered.

Ugarte chose to march on to the Devils mouth and establish camp before ordering Lieutenant Alejo de la Garza Falcon back to pursue the Lipans. On December 26, Garza Falcon pushed out with 100 soldiers and thirteen Indian auxiliaries.

They first traced the Rio Grande to San Felipe Springs at modern-day Del Rio, then turned north to the Devils country. Searching the river and hills for the next several days, they discovered fresh tracks and other Lipan signs. On January 2, 1776, Garza Falcon's scouts captured two Indians, a man and a woman, but the prisoners denied knowledge of the hostiles' whereabouts.

The next day, Garza Falcon reached the site of the December 22 ambush and found the scalped body of the Indian auxiliary. After burying him, the Spaniards took up the Lipans' trail and rode upon a recently abandoned *rancheria* with 280 tent sites. Tracks clearly led away toward the San Saba and Nueces rivers, but Garza Falcon soon gave up the chase and rendezvoused with Governor Ugarte at Presidio de Aguaverde in Coahuila.[12]

Despite Ugarte's months-long campaign across the Rio Grande frontier and into the reaches of the Devils, Apaches remained as great a threat as ever.

On November 23, 1777, forty–eight-year-old Juan de Ugalde replaced Ugarte in Coahuila, and eighteen months later this new governor organized the first of his four offensives against the Mescalero Apaches, a band his chronicler would condemn in 1783 for their "perfidy, malice, and ingratitude." A knight in the Order of Santiago, Ugalde had seen action against the Austrians, Moors, and Portuguese, but now he faced an enemy who could strike quickly and vanish into the fastness of the Devils and elsewhere.

His strategy was to foster division between Lipan Apaches and their Mescalero brothers. A Lipan chief, Xaviercillo, had assured the Spaniards that his people would join them in war against the Mescaleros. Putting Xaviercillo to the test as he set forth May 3, 1779, Ugalde supplemented his force of 141 soldiers and four officers with four Lipan captains and an unspecified number of Lipan warriors. Another twenty soldiers and eighty civilians composed a separate unit led by Lieutenant Don Jose Muzquiz.

During the next forty-one days, Ugalde's command sought out Mescaleros in the unyielding country of the Devils and Pecos. By the end of the operation June 12, the Spaniards had attacked two Mescalero camps, killed seven warriors, and taken numerous prisoners.

Ugalde again focused his attention on the Devils when he launched a second surge on November 11, 1781. For seventy-four days his army of 169 soldiers and five officers chased Mescaleros across the wilderness of the Devils and Pecos, and on three occasions the Spaniards skirmished hostiles. In one fight, the governor himself led an advance foot patrol to the front line and was instrumental in capturing seven prisoners and a number of horses.

In another desperate moment, Ugalde and seventeen men were negotiating a high, narrow pass on foot when the *whoosh* of arrows signaled an attack. Whirling, they found themselves outnumbered three to one, but they unleashed a withering return volley with their firearms. In face of the Spaniards' greater firepower, the thirty Mescalero bowmen and their confederates could only retreat into the hills.

With his supplies depleted and his horses exhausted after crisscrossing the Devils and Pecos rivers five times, Ugalde had no choice but to return to his Coahuila base on January 23, 1782.[13]

Although Governor Ugalde twice had taken aggressive action against Mescaleros in the Devils region—and would do so two more times at other locations—his campaigns had no effect in checking bloodshed in the settlements. On the contrary, with Spanish troops absent, Mescalero raids actually had increased.[14] Still, Mescaleros faced not only Spanish arms but Comanche, a dilemma that eventually fostered a fragile peace between Spaniards and Apache groups that included Mescaleros.

In fall 1787, soon after several Mescalero bands relocated to Coahuila, Ugalde agreed to provide an escort for Mescaleros seeking buffalo on the Devils, a region not frequented by Comanches. Setting out from Santa Rosa with almost ninety soldiers on November 25, 1787, the Mescaleros reached the buffalo grounds and hunted without incident for several weeks. On December 20, unidentified riders appeared in the distance, generating doubled sentries but little alarm in the adjacent camps of the Mescaleros and Spaniards. In a shrouding fog the following dawn, however, Comanches stormed the Mescaleros, who fought back but lost several horses before repelling the attack.

When the fog broke later that morning, the Spaniards moved against the Comanches, who offered little resistance and surrendered. The soldiers, obviously confident that their show of force would serve as a deterrent, allowed the Comanches to ride away.[15]

The event served as a stark example of Spanish willingness to forge a lasting peace with Mescaleros and their fellow Apaches. Nevertheless, Spain's fight against Apaches on the Devils was a struggle that Spain would never win, for 1821 marked the end of its dominion over a river that Apaches would continue to haunt for decades.

CHAPTER 3

BLAZING THE DEVILS TRAIL

Through fifteen years under the Mexican flag and another nine under the banner of the Republic of Texas, the Devils was a no man's land, shunned even by the military. With no continuity of government, even the records of three centuries of sporadic exploration were little known to a new generation. Few white men could speak firsthand of the river's mysteries, and when they did, their knowledge might have been forged in a crucible of terror.

Such were the circumstances that surrounded the nine-month sojourn of a woman and her two children on the Devils and elsewhere in 1839 and 1840. The ordeal began in Bastrop County in spring 1839, when emigrant John Webster headed northwest for present Burnet County with his wife, thirteen-year-old son, and young daughter Virginia. In deference to the threat of Indians, they traveled in a four-wagon company that included thirteen other men.[1]

The force would not be enough, for war-mongering Comanches now constituted the largest tribe in Texas. With a total population of 11,000, they generally operated in scattered bands but could muster a single force of 500 warriors, twice that of Lipan Apaches.[2]

Six miles shy of the North San Gabriel River, the Webster party sighted a large Comanche war party in the sunset and turned back. They pushed the wagons hard into the dark and sustained a broken axle, but they effected repairs and desperately pressed on.

As day broke over Brushy Creek near present Leander on June 12, the emigrants formed the wagons into a small fort and braced for onslaught. They met the Comanches' initial charge with a hail of lead, then reloaded and fired again. The siege wore on throughout the day, claiming wagoner after wagoner until the outcome was inevitable. At ten PM, the last man fell, and fierce, painted warriors dragged Mrs. Webster, her son, and four-year-old Virginia away into captivity.

"That awful day still haunts my memory," Virginia noted three-quarters of a century later. ". . . It was a horrible sight to see all the brave and good men fall at the hands of the savage demons."

The Comanches eventually separated the captives, and for the next eight months mother and children saw each other only three times—at Enchanted Rock in Llano County, in Santa Fe, New Mexico, and finally, in February 1840, at the head of the Devils River where the bands gathered to consider a treaty with the Texans. Under the terms, the Comanches were to deliver all captives to San Antonio.

But Mrs. Webster, who had experienced for herself the cruelties of these warriors, wasn't so sure. Here in the Devils country she already had witnessed the execution of six white prisoners, all of them girls. Furthermore, she had overheard talk that every captive might be similarly killed.

Pilfering a small amount of dried buffalo tongue, Mrs. Webster escaped into the Devils wilderness with young Virginia.

Stealing through night after night and subsisting only on jerky, roots, and raw fish, they traversed the Devils country and finally took refuge under a live oak far to the east.

"We were so weak and so near starved to death," Virginia recalled, "that Mother had almost given up, to lie down and die, and I was too weak to cry."

They had no idea that a road lay only 200 yards away—and San Antonio but three miles—until a train of Mexican *carretas* rumbled by and freighters rescued them. About six days later, the Comanches delivered Mrs. Webster's son to the city and reunited the three.[3]

A nightmare worthy of the devil himself was over, but the river would pull many more innocents into its hell in times to come.

After the Republic of Texas joined the United States in 1845, San Antonio grew rapidly, bolstered by ambitious businessmen who dreamed of opening a trade route with the Mexican state of Chihuahua. Only 150 miles from the Alamo city, however, loomed the first of many formidable obstacles—the Devils. But all its unknowns did not deter John C. Hays as he set out to blaze a trail west for Presidio del Norte and El Paso on August 27, 1848.

Thirty-one-year-old Hays, who had gained a reputation for fearlessness in his days as a Texas Ranger, first marched northwest to Camp Llano, where Captain Samuel Highsmith and thirty-five Rangers joined the riders. Thirteen years Hays' senior and a fellow Mexican War veteran, Highsmith similarly had distinguished himself in military matters, particularly as an Indian fighter. Texas could boast of few men more qualified to lead this expedition that included politician and rancher Samuel Maverick and ten Delaware Indians.

Proceeding generally southwest, the men struck what Highsmith described as "an exceedingly rugged and dry country" that would test their limits after reaching the mouth of Devils canyon September 21. They rode upstream the next day, found a ford, and crossed. In need of water on the twenty-third, recorded Maverick, they struggled down a "horrid ravine" to the riverbank and camped.

For a brutal day thereafter, they struggled on foot and led their horses up the Devils' gorge, then climbed the divide between the river and the Pecos September 25. A day later, ravaged by thirst, men and horses finally reached the latter stream.

For four weeks expedition members staggered on west, more dead than alive in face of moonscape. ". . . From the mouth of the Devil's River up the Rio Grande, as far as San Carlos, a town forty miles south of Presidio del Norte," wrote Hays, "is one constant succession of high broken mountains, destitute of timber and water." Finally, on October 22, they stumbled upon Fort Leaton five miles east of Presidio del Norte.

The men laid up nine days to recuperate and acquire horses, mules, and provisions, then started back for San Antonio by way of a more northerly route that would take them up the Great Comanche War Trail. They reached the Pecos November 10, turned downstream to Live Oak Creek, and veered east. Along the upper Devils drainage on November 25, Rangers and citizens separated, with Highsmith returning to Camp Llano and Hays to San Antonio.

After three and a half months, the Hays-Highsmith expedition was over. One man had been lost, the victim of desert madness, but the torturous trek continued to wreak vengeance even after survivors reached the settlements. On January 11, 1849, just thirty-one days after the Rangers arrived at Camp Llano, a weakened Highsmith succumbed to influenza.[4]

Prior to this first significant exploration of the Devils by Americans, the river had still been formally known as the San Pedro, or "Saint Peter." An often-told story, however, holds that Hays took one look at the forbidding land through which it flowed and exclaimed, "Saint Peter, hell! It looks more like the devil's river to me."[5] Indeed, the first published usage of the name Devil's (or Devils) River came in late 1848 when the *Western Texian* printed Hays' December report to Texas Ranger Colonel P. Hansborough Bell, which Bell had forwarded to the newspaper December 14. Wrote Hays:

"Owing to the difficulties we had in extricating ourselves from the deep ravines and mountains which encompass it for many miles from its mouth, we named it Devil's River."[6]

Hays' statement seems beyond challenge, yet a study of Samuel Maverick's journal of the expedition suggests that the men may have only reaffirmed the name "Devil's" rather than coined it. His entry upon reaching the waterway September 21 was straightforward: "Mouth of Devil's river. 14 [miles]."[7] The casual way he noted the stream's name seems unusual for a river never before known by that designation until that very day. Add to this Hays' claim that he and his fellow riders named the river *only* after experiencing difficulty upstream, and it's clear that the two men's accounts contradict one another in regard to the party's first use of the word *devil's*. Certainly, the immediacy of Maverick's daily journal trumps Hays' recollections of twelve weeks, especially considering the grueling survival episode Hays had endured.

Possibly, the "Devil's" appellation was already known to certain party members. One legend holds that a grieving Indian chief cried out "The Devil's River!" after watching his daughter and her lover leap from a cliff and die in its waters.[8] A less romantic account maintains that Mexican wagoners put the name into play by exclaiming, *"El Rio San Pedro es el diablo!"* (The San Pedro River is the devil!) after experiencing disaster in crossing.[9]

Although cartographers began referencing the stream as Devil's as early as 1852,[10] the name San Pedro lingered alongside it on many maps until 1860.[11] Thereafter, Devils (with or without an apostrophe) became the term of choice, not only on maps but in popular usage and historical records.

Even as Hays and Highsmith wandered the Chihuahuan Desert in search of a route to Chihuahua in fall 1848, word of a vast gold strike in California reached Texas and the East. In December, President James K. Polk fired the imagination of the nation when he spoke of the find to Congress,[12] and by January the notion of heading west to California had exceeded mere fancy. Recognizing the necessity of developing a wagon road from Texas settlements to El Paso and other points west, the US Army dispatched Lieutenant William H. C. Whiting and his junior officer, William F. Smith, from San Antonio on February 12, 1849.

Twenty-four-year-old Whiting, with a small escort and a guide from the Hays-Highsmith expedition, cut trail across the head gullies of the Devils and reached El Paso April 12.[13] Meanwhile, emigrant caravans already were forging their own way west, the quest for gold carrying them reportedly to where even the US Army had yet to go—the lower Devils country. By mid-March, one such wagon train had embarked from Victoria and another from San Antonio, a staging ground that by late April saw almost daily departures by emigrant parties.[14] So undaunted were "forty-niners" that a guide along a route through northern Mexico pointed to an unscalable cliff and observed, "If California was on top, Americans would reach it, in spite of walls or anything else."[15]

Whiting headed back from El Paso April 19 in search of a better course than that which had brought him from San Antonio. He traced the Rio Grande downstream to the Quitman Mountains, then bore generally east to the Pecos and

Pecan Springs in 2009. Photograph courtesy of Patrick Dearen.

marched with its flow. At what would become known as Lancaster Crossing near present Sheffield, he forded the river. Here, provisions in the charge of Henry Skillman caught up with Whiting, and soon the replenished expedition struck out across the divide.

Dropping into a Devils tributary May 12, Whiting and his command reached the river the following day and found "a still and beautiful lagoon of clear blue water" lined by abandoned frames of Comanche lodges. They followed an Indian trail down the intermittent stream, pausing only to shoot rattlesnake after rattlesnake, and camped at a pool beneath a lofty red bluff. On May 14, they continued on to the westernmost bulge of the Devils' canyon and burst upon "a magnificent pecan grove which enclosed a bright blue lagoon"—Pecan Springs, which marked the head of the river's permanent flow.

The next morning Whiting ascended the bordering bluff in order to cut across a great bend and avoid the virtually impassable canyon that had so tormented the Hays-Highsmith expedition. In the undulating high country, they gave chase to five bears and felled them all, thereby replenishing their depleted stores.

On May 16 Whiting sent Smith, Skillman, and scout Richard Howard on ahead for San Antonio, then led his remaining command southeastward. Later that day, Whiting descended into a gorge with perpendicular walls of limestone riddled with caves, one of them rich with Indian rock art. A muleskinner, Francisco, identified the canyon as "a famous Comanche pass" to which he once had pursued raiders who had struck the Mexican village of San Fernando. Whiting dubbed this deeply etched ravine "Painted," which in turn would lend its name to the large cave so impressively decorated.

Past a brief, elevated stretch, the riders picked their way down to the canyon of the Devils and discovered a ford that would become known as First Crossing, for it marked the point at which westbound travelers first intersected the river. The site, approximately five miles above the mouth of the Devils, lay at the stream's confluence with San Pedro Creek. For Whiting, heading into the sunrise, this "exceedingly good" ford signaled the end of hundreds of miles of hurdles in a nonetheless promising trace.

By the time he reached San Antonio May 25, he had established his return course from El Paso as a viable route for wagons. As later refined, the so-called Lower Road extended 673 miles and would stand as one of the most important trails in westward expansion.[16] Yet like its sister road the Upper, blazed across West Texas on a latitude well north of the Devils the same year, it would also be known for its treachery.

Moving swiftly, the US Army in early June ordered Lieutenant Colonel J. E. Johnston to lead a topographical party west along the Lower Road. His junior officers included Lieutenant William F. Smith, who was now familiar with the route;

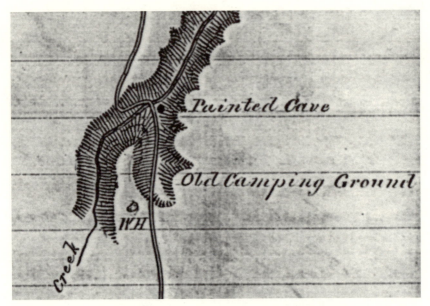

Painted Cave in 1869. Journal of Lieutenant Colonel Thomas B. Hunt, National Archives.

Major Jefferson Van Horne, who would command a work crew; and Captain S. G. French, U.S. Army Assistant Quartermaster, in charge of the provision wagons. The full party consisted of six companies of the Third Infantry, almost 275 wagons, and 2,500 animals.

At the same time, emigrants converged on San Antonio and readied to strike out for California. Among them was Thomas B. Eastland, who had arrived by ship at Port Lavaca May 20. His group of thirty or so, loosely attached to a large emigrant caravan directed by John C. Hays, left San Antonio June 6 to overtake Colonel Johnston's slower-moving command. Two days later the Freemont Association of New York, consisting of thirty-nine wagoners who also had disembarked at Port Lavaca, prepared to follow with their own vehicles. Other gold-seekers, such as a company of Mississippians, prepared to set out from San Antonio with nothing but pack mules.

From a point on the Frio River eighty-two miles down-trail from San Antonio on June 13, Lieutenant Colonel Johnston started toward the Devils River with surveyor Richard Howard, a First Infantry escort, and twenty laborers to open the road for the trailing military and civilian wagons. By late June, the crew had cleared 160 miles of trail to San Felipe Springs. Situated at present Del Rio, the largest of these springs along San Felipe Creek formed a pool twenty-eight feet deep and fifty feet across—an ideal place to water and rest before striking out across another eleven miles of barrens for First Crossing on the Devils.

San Felipe Springs today. Photograph courtesy of Patrick Dearen.

On June 29, Eastland and his companions caught up with the road engineers at the ford, a site rumored to be rife with horrible difficulties.

"Here we expected to find his Satanic Majesty in the shape of rugged mountains and impassible [sic] ravines," he wrote.

Nevertheless, he found the location breathtaking for its "beautiful, immense cliffs of rock on all sides." He was also impressed by the work of the Army, which had cut a good approach road "that an expert wagoner could drive down *without locking.*"

To Eastland's eye, the stream was about 100 yards wide, a strong surge of water coursing over smooth rock. Only fifteen inches deep, it presented no problems for the emigrants' wagons. The same was not true for the horses, however, as Eastland's pony slipped and spilled the forty-niner.

Whether or not First Crossing was truly representative of the Devils remained for Eastland to determine, but the river's reputation for insidiousness filled other emigrants with dread of their own. Robert Eccleston, who bore west from San Antonio with the Freemont Association ten days behind Eastland, dwelled on this looming "River Styx"—River of the Dead—as far back up-trail as Turkey Creek, sixty-two miles distant.

Eastland and his fellow wagoners, following on the heels of the road engineers, proceeded to a spring thirteen miles beyond Painted Cave on July 3, and on to California Springs another two and a half miles farther five days later. As they lingered on the tableland, waiting for the Army crew to do its work ahead, the trailing Freemont company finally reached First Crossing. Eccleston's impressions differed from Eastland's most dramatically in the ford's width, which the Freemont wagoner estimated at somewhat more than 100 feet. Eccleston was

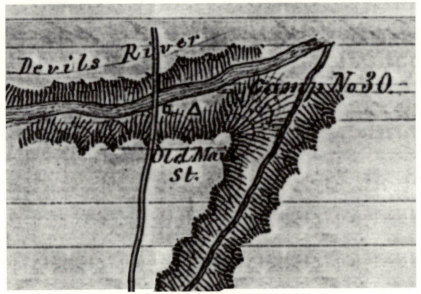

First Crossing in 1869. Journal of Lieutenant Colonel Thomas B. Hunt, National Archives.

also less smitten by the location's esthetic qualities.

"The only good thing that can be said of this place," he wrote, "is that we had plenty of good water to drink and a fine place to bathe."

On July 12, the Freemont Association, which had dwindled to thirty-four persons, overtook the Eastland party and learned that a rider returning from the road gang had encountered an Indian that day. Although the warrior had made peaceful overtures, the frightened man had fled with his horse at full gallop.

In another incident, Henry Skillman led a military escort single-file around a canyon bend and came face-to-face with an Indian at the head of a band. Even as the Indian's confederates fled, Skillman threw up his rifle and forced the leader to hold his ground. Questioning him in Spanish, Skillman learned that these were friendly Tonkawas and let them go their way.

On July 17, the Eastland wagoners bolted ahead of the stationary Freemont company by accomplishing nineteen miles over the new road. All the way from First Crossing, they had roughly paralleled the river's upstream course to the north-northwest. Now, after bypassing a series of great, canyon-riddled bends in favor of a more direct and practicable route, they descended a north-trending defile that funneled the wagons down into the Devils' forested valley, where Second Crossing awaited only a mile upstream. Situated midway along the river's squirming track toward the Rio Grande, this vital ford lay thirty-eight miles by road from First Crossing.

Approximately a mile upstream of the Devils' mouth in 1918 or 1919.
Whitehead Memorial Museum, Del Rio, Texas.

Only minutes into the eight-and-a-half-mile course between Second Crossing and Pecan Springs, the wagoners halted and made camp. Two days later, the Freemont party and military provision wagons also traced the ruts to this paradise a mere 300 vertical feet beneath a wasteland fit for hell.

Remaining separated for practical reasons as the days ensued, the emigrant companies tested each new section up the sinuous Devils soon after the Army crew hewed it out. No matter the engineers' efforts, however, the trace continued to be demanding.

"A very rugged road, running along the River bottom," noted Eastland on July 19. Indeed, this stretch immediately upstream of Second Crossing required travelers to cross the intermittent river seven or eight times, six at locations with water. The way proved especially troublesome for the Army's provision wagons, some of which broke down.

On the night of July 22, Indians stole two mules and four horses from the Army. After daybreak, searchers found one of the horses dead, the victim of an arrow—a reminder to the emigrants that a military escort did not necessarily ensure safety.

"The Indians are now about us," penned Eastland. ". . . This will at least have the effect to make the night guard more vigilant. . . ."

Where the river widened into a small, natural reservoir that would become known as Beaver Lake, twenty-two miles upstream from Second Crossing, East-

Beaver Lake in 2009. Photograph courtesy of Patrick Dearen.

land and his companions camped July 27 and waited for the engineers to complete a trail out across the divide between the Devils and Pecos. The pool, fringed by live oaks, willows, and mesquites, was an exquisite site, even for a river of singular characteristics.

"We are encamped in a beautiful Valley surrounded by an hundred Hills rich in fine Grass, enough for thousands of Animals," described Eastland. "In the midst of the Valley is a beautiful lake of pure water fed by many springs running out of the neighboring hills."

The Freemont wagoners had pitched tents only a mile away, and on July 28 they welcomed their fellow forty-niners to an evening of worship amid campfires in a circle of wagons. The service had a powerful impact on Eastland, facing as he was an unknown wilderness in his quest for a faraway land.

"To hear many voices joining in songs of praise to God, then the effective prayer, and then the word of God proudly and manfully defended . . . " he wrote. "I will not soon forget 'the sermon of the Valley' preached in the 'stilly night,' the dark Hills shutting out all save the starry Heavens above & the bright moon."

As dusk fell over both emigrant camps the next day, a black bear ambled down a hill toward the Freemont wagons. When several armed men gave chase, the bear veered toward the neighboring company. Alerted, Eastland and his companions opened fire, their third shot felling the animal. The kill meant fresh meat, but it also preempted a potential stampede by the herds.

Ten hours apart on July 30, the emigrant wagon trains started out of the Devils valley for the Pecos, eighty-three miles distant. Although a few often-dusty water holes and the equally unreliable Johnsons Run lay within a hard day's travel of Beaver Lake, the next sure water loomed at Howard's Spring—a dead man's march of more than forty miles. Such was particularly true on this day, when a searing sun spiked afternoon temperatures to 114 degrees shortly before the Freemont caravan rolled away from the lake.

Four weeks and 250 miles later as Davis Mountains rocks tortured the oxen's hooves and quaked the Freemont wagons, Eccleston reflected back on the Devils and condemned its trace as the worst they had endured.

On September 8, Lieutenant Colonel Johnston and his command completed the road to El Paso and yielded the way on west to the determined forty-niners. After recruiting fresh animals, he headed back for San Antonio October 11 by way of the Upper Road with twenty-five men and two Delaware Indian guides. Upon reaching the Pecos in bitter cold, he reconsidered his route and marched downstream to intersect the warmer Lower Road.

At Beaver Lake, Johnston, Richard Howard, and ten men veered east in hope of finding a shorter and less rugged route to San Antonio. For the succeeding sixty miles, all the way to the western branches of the Nueces, they found but a waterless track.[17]

With the Devils confirmed as the better course, the river in 1850 would witness continued migration west, reconnaissance of its mouth by boat, and Indian depredations that would serve as grim reminders that warrior tribes would not yield this land easily. ●

CHAPTER 4

DEAD MAN'S PASS

As the spring of 1850 approached, the gold bug flared again and afflicted men such as J. Frank Bowles, who left home in Belton and fell in with a California-bound caravan. He never anticipated that the Devils was about to assert its sovereignty so insidiously.

Drouth raged as the wagons bore toward the river, and when the emigrants gained First Crossing they found the stream distressingly low. They set up camp for an extended respite, rested their animals, and speared catfish trapped in crevices in the river's rock bed. For three days, fate obliged, but on day four, they suddenly found their own reason to curse this stream as Lucifer's abode.

Cholera erupted and claimed seven lives, including Bowles' friend and partner.

"I helped to bury him on the bank of Devil's River, and placed large rocks over the grave to keep the wolves from uncovering and eating the body," recalled Bowles many years later.

There was no time for mourning. With the dead buried, the wagoners pushed on immediately to distance themselves from the scene of the outbreak.[1]

Such a story of abrupt tragedy would be repeated again and again on the Devils, where nature and hostiles seemed bound in an unholy conspiracy against uninvited intrusion. Military might was useless against acts of God, of course, but at least the US Army kept the Lower Road well-rutted in face of Indians with evil intent.

In mid-July, two huge military supply caravans splashed across First Crossing en route to El Paso from Fort Inge, a Lower Road post gracing the Leona River eighty-five miles east of the Devils. The trains, commanded by Brevet Major John

T. Sprague, included 450 civilians, 175 soldiers, 340 wagon teams, and 4,000 animals. Although Sprague required the processions to travel apart to avoid competition for water and forage, he could not accommodate the demands of a country as rugged as the Devils.

"The poor cattle suffered much from being so tenderfooted," wrote Ben Coons upon reaching Second Crossing in charge of 130 Sprague wagons July 16. "The sharp flint rock soon ruins their hoofs and wherever they go a trail of blood is left behind."

Not only had Coons lost more than forty oxen on the approach to the ford, but many of the wagons had broken down. Most troubling, the ordeal had brought out the worst in the teamsters, one of whom had plunged a butcher knife into another's breast.

"I . . . found . . . [the victim] stretched near the side of [the] wagon and close by him a pool of blood," related Coons, who tended the man while other teamsters seized the perpetrator and tied him to a wagon.

Fortunately, the knife had penetrated only two inches, but a follow-up attack might have finished matters. "He is bold and desperate," Coons said of the culprit. "I believe he will kill the fellow as soon as I let him loose."

Opposing factions squared off in support of one actor or the other, threatening the fragile harmony of the entire train. Wisely, Coons turned the assailant over to the military escort—which itself showed signs of discord as day broke over Second Crossing.

During the night, the rear guard from Company E, Eighth Infantry, had stolen a keg of liquor from Coons' baggage wagon. Now the soldiers were roaring drunk, forcing the livid lieutenant in charge to lash them to wagons and trees and raise their ire.

"Mutiny was the consequence," related Coons, "and in my presence several of the men threatened to shoot the officer if he did not release them."

That this was indeed a country ruled by evil was not lost on Coons.

"There seems to be something in the air of Texas—very well adapted to the growth of rascality and meanness," he lamented.[2]

Just under three weeks later on August 4, 100 emigrant wagons bound for California forded the river at likely Second Crossing under the direction of Parker H. French, an unscrupulous entrepreneur who had acquired provisions in San Antonio by forging bank drafts. By now, drouth had reduced the river to "a small brook, which we could step across," related Michael Baldridge, company secretary. Nevertheless, driftwood in treetops "thirty or forty feet high" provided dramatic evidence that awesome floods sometimes raged.

In a span of fifteen miles, the Parker wagons crossed the Devils seventeen times, and although the emigrants soon climbed from its valley, they could not easily escape the dark angel who ruled it. As they struggled across a thirsty land on August 6, prairie fires surrounded them like the flames of hell.

"Awful and sublime to behold," described caravan member William Miles.[3]

While wagon trains rumbled west on the Lower Road, Captain Harry Love and a twelve-man crew started up the Rio Grande from Ringgold Barracks at present Rio Grande City to determine the border river's navigability. Their keel boat, fifty feet long and sixteen feet wide, drew only eighteen inches of water, a necessity considering that the stream was at its lowest recorded stage.

For more than four months they rowed, skirting the Devils' mouth and squeezing through canyon after canyon before impassable falls turned them back on July 15. Although they negotiated 1,014 miles, the last forty-seven by skiff, Love pinpointed the confluence of the Devils as the head of steamboat navigation. In the 617 miles between the Devils and Ringgold Barracks, only Kingsbury Falls in present Maverick County hindered passage.

Based on Love's report, Brevet Major W. W. Chapman suggested the Army construct a channel through the falls and establish a military post at the mouth of the Devils. El Paso-bound provisions could then be shipped as far as the Devils by steamboat and from that point westward by wagon—potentially "judicious economy," observed Chapman, noting the "immense expense" of a full overland trip from Port Lavaca to El Paso.

The post, he added, also would enable the Army "more faithfully to perform our treaty stipulations with Mexico," a reference to the Treaty of Guadalupe Hidalgo that climaxed the 1848 Mexican War. Under its terms, the United States was responsible for ending raids in Mexico by Indians from American territories.[4]

The prospect of navigating the Rio Grande by steamship would come up again after the Boundary Commission's 1854 inspection of the Rio Grande by boat. Although issues related to border rather than transportation would inspire the commission's downriver journey past the Devils' confluence, party member William H. Emory would write that "at some distant day, no doubt, the navigation will be extended up as high as the mouth of Devil's river."[5]

As events proved, however, the steamboat port at the mouth of the Devils was just as fanciful as any hope of soon subduing warrior tribes, who continued to commit atrocities on both sides of the border in 1850. In June, fifteen Lipans raided San Juan de Endes, Mexico, thirty miles southwest of present Eagle Pass, and kidnapped a nine-year-old boy and his six-year-old sister. Villagers quickly rallied, and the children's father and twenty other men set off in pursuit.

They dogged the band day and night from landmark to landmark—the mouth of the Devils, First Crossing, Painted Cave. Sunset on the second day found the Mexicans in yet-unnamed Dead Man's Pass, where the Lower Road slashed through ominous hills at the very summit of the divide. In this three-quarter-

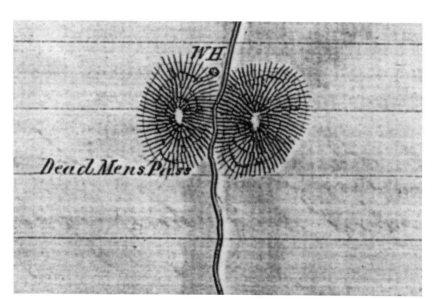
Dead Man's Pass in 1869. Journal of Lieutenant Colonel Thomas B. Hunt, National Archives.

mile-long gorge, where sharply rising battlements squeezed close, they rested their horses before resuming the chase. Scouts soon returned with promising news—the war party was camped at a body of water near Second Crossing, twelve and a half miles beyond Dead Man's.

Advancing through the night, the Mexicans dismounted a mere 300 yards from the Lipans and readied for battle despite their meager arms. Leaving four men to guard the saddle stock, the other seventeen crawled toward the sleeping Indians, pinned them against the river, and opened fire at first light.

Caught unawares, the Lipans never put up a fight. Bolting for the river, they either broke upstream at water's edge to leave a bloody trail, or plunged in to swim across under a hail of whizzing balls. Tom Collins, an American riding with the Mexicans, sent one Lipan to the river's bottom with a carefully placed shot.

As the gun smoke subsided, the men of San Juan de Endes searched the camp and found the children alive and well. Four days later, brother and sister were home, the beneficiaries of a rare rescue along a river seldom known for happy endings.[6]

August brought more Indian trouble to the region. In a nighttime attack on a California-bound caravan thirty-five miles from present Eagle Pass, a war party wounded one or two emigrants and seized forty horses. When word reached Fort Duncan, situated adjacent to Eagle Pass, soldiers set out to wreak vengeance and recover the stock.

Dead Man's Pass in 2009. Photograph courtesy of Patrick Dearen.

Tracking the Indians to the Devils' eastern watershed, they heard gunfire across a cedar-fringed valley and charged. Unknown to the Duncan soldiers, Company C of Fort Inge's Second Dragoons had chanced upon the raiders while campaigning against hostiles in their Devils country stronghold.

"The Indians were right between us and the Dragoons," related Jesse Sumpter, who was with the Duncan contingent. "That caused the Captain to deploy us to the right so as to get out of the range of the Dragoons' shots. As soon as we got around so that the Indians saw us, they broke for the cedar bluff which was close by."

The Duncan soldiers opened up with a fierce volley that bloodied several Indians, although all but a woman escaped. Another Indian casualty, a warrior shot from his mule by a Dragoon, continued to unleash arrows from where he sat until he died in a storm of rifle balls.

While soldiers rounded up the stolen horses, a Duncan hospital steward dressed the woman's wounds. The captain in charge then placed her on a mule and released her to rejoin the band.[7]

Despite the Army's success in the skirmish—one of the earliest US Army-Indian engagements in the Devils region—dominion over this land would come at a great price to both soldiers and civilians. A case in point was the saga of several men with Brevet Major John T. Sprague's supply train, which pulled into El Paso September 7. A week later, the wagons turned back for San Antonio under infantry escort. By the time the caravan reached the Devils, a number of teamsters were low on rations and decided to press on, leaving the soldiers camped at Beaver Lake.

Sunset found thirteen men with five wagons at soon-to-be-named Dead Man's Pass. Another eight men, six horseback and two afoot, traveled ahead of the party, and as lead wagoner John L. Mann spied a distant figure in the road, he took it for one of the men without mounts.

Little did he know that hostiles had laid a trap, and that the figure was an Indian who had just relayed the relative positions of teamsters and riders to warriors lurking on either side.

As Jerry Priest and a mentally ill blacksmith, both on foot, preceded Mann's wagon into the ambush, Indians sprang up from thick bear grass that lined one side of the road. Priest whirled to the opposite hill and found equally savage warriors swooping down on horseback.

"Indians!" he cried, running for the wagons.

The unaware blacksmith was the first to die, dropping where he stood to a shot in the breast. Then an ox in Mann's team went down, halting the wagon, and Mann could only run for the gun in its bed. Unable to find the weapon, he fell back with Priest to the next vehicle.

Confusion reigned. Most of the men abandoned their teams and concentrated at a single wagon, from which they answered the flying arrows and singing lead with a fusillade. A veteran Indian fighter named Brown stood at a wagon wheel and coolly squeezed off rifle shot after rifle shot, one of them cutting down a mounted warrior thirty yards away. Then a ball struck Brown in the heart, and he became the second teamster to die. Charles Blawinsky, fighting alongside him, caught a slug below the chest and fell writhing. Seeing that Blawinsky was still alive, other teamsters dashed out and dragged him to cover.

With the situation growing ever more dire, Nick Andres dived into a wagon bed to use the wall as protection. The moment he lifted his rifle to meet a charge, a ball exploded into his throat and the hostiles claimed a third life.

An elderly teamster, whose name has escaped history, grabbed Andres' weapon to help repel yet another charge and took a bullet in the knee. Two other men, John Crowder and Emory Givins, sustained arm wounds, while Mann, who had seized a fallen comrade's weapon to defend himself, avoided death by mere inches when a rifle ball whizzed through his hair.

As the fight wore on into the blackness of midnight and beyond, the wounded Blawinsky's agony intensified and he finally succumbed—the fourth teamster to perish. Meanwhile, the survivors positioned three wagons abreast to form a makeshift fort and inflicted a heavy toll of their own, felling Indian after Indian until the war party backed off at two AM. Four hundred yards away, the warriors brazenly built fires and roasted beef from Mann's wagon.

The teamsters remained vigilant, and at daybreak they found the fire rings abandoned. With no hostiles apparent, Charley Hill climbed the adjacent knoll to scout the area, only to face a charge by mounted warriors.

"The Indians are coming again, boys!" he cried, taking gunfire as he fled.

They chased him to the wagons, then four of the warriors turned their horses northward up the road while the others retreated out of rifle range.

The standoff continued until nine AM, when seven advance horsemen with a Mexican *carreta* train rode up from Second Crossing. Upon hearing the teamsters' harrowing account, one rider spurred his horse back to hasten the caravan while the others helped the Americans better prepare for assault. Wheeling the wagons about, they formed a compact triangle and stacked rocks between the spokes as a breastwork.

When *carreta* boss Jim Fisk arrived with the train and assessed the situation, he dispatched a messenger for the soldiers at Beaver Lake. The rider met the troops just above Pecan Springs, and the officer in charge immediately ordered half his command forward. The soldiers marched relentlessly, not knowing the fate of the survivors, and burst upon the scene after dark to learn that the Indians had long-since fled.

The next day, the soldiers set off in vain pursuit while the teamsters buried their dead on the west side of the road. The pile of rocks that marked the mass grave would remind every succeeding traveler of the fragility of life in this pass known thereafter as "Dead Man's."[8]

The Mexican *carretas* were likely traveling the Chihuahua Trail that shared ruts with the Lower Road across the Devils country. This trade route, the culmination of efforts highlighted by the Hays-Highsmith expedition of 1848, linked the Texas ports of Lavaca and Indianola with Chihuahua, Mexico, a populated region isolated from Mexican coastlands by mountain and desert.

From central Chihuahua, the ruts followed the Rio Conchos northeast to its confluence with the Rio Grande at Presidio del Norte. Crossing into Texas, it continued on the same general heading to the distant Pecos. Here, a branch turned downstream and eventually intersected the Lower Road that connected it to the Devils and points east.

Coursing to and fro through the Devils country for the next three decades, freighters used a variety of vehicles, particularly *carretas* and mule-drawn wagons that resembled prairie schooners. Each two-wheeled *carreta,* fashioned completely of wood, could carry 5,000 pounds in a bed fifteen feet long and six feet wide. As a team of oxen pulled the cart through the Devils country, the action of the seven-foot wheels turning on the axle—wood against wood without lubrication—created a screech like the wails of the damned. If the load was great, friction produced smoke, necessitating that freighters insert a prickly pear leaf between wheel and axle to quell a potential fire.

As serviceable as a cart was, a schooner exceeded its capacity by a ton or more, due to a solid axle that supported a bed twenty-four feet long, four and a half feet wide, and five and a half feet deep. Designed for the demands of a rugged trail, the vehicle had seventy-inch rear wheels and fifty-eight-inch front wheels, each rimmed by iron tires six inches wide. Teams generally consisted of ten grass-fed mules (although some freighters preferred fourteen), while a typical train included a dozen wagons, twenty-three men, and 150 spare mules.[9]

The drouth that plagued the Devils in 1850 spread like a blight throughout West Texas and wreaked a toll. US Army troops in El Paso, with diminished capacity to subsist off the land, eventually exhausted their provisions. When word reached Washington, DC, by early January 1851, Quartermaster General Thomas S. Jesup shipped a large supply of stores by sea for wagons waiting at Indianola.

Recognizing the demands of the long, overland trek through a bleached-bones wilderness to El Paso, Jesup selected Assistant Quartermaster S. G. French to lead the undertaking. Captain French already had endured an expedition to El Paso in 1849 and was not anxious to repeat the ordeal—especially "over a now barren country, destitute of water and grass"—but he knew that his familiarity with the route would be invaluable.

On May 7, French started from San Antonio with the last contingent of a caravan that soon totaled 150 wagons and more than 1,000 animals. Upon reaching Fort Inge, he added fifty First Regiment infantrymen, a strong enough deterrent against Indians to induce a number of emigrants to join the procession.

From the Nueces to the reaches of the Devils and on to the Trans-Pecos mountains, French rode a land seared by hell's own sun.

"The hills that before were clothed in verdure now are bare," he wrote. "Valleys that seemed to vie in fertility with the most favored appear sterile; and plains where two years ago the tall grass waved like fields of wheat now are rocky and barren."

Certain stretches in particular seemed to bear witness to perdition's judgment.

"Where the prairie had been swept over by the fires of the previous summer," observed French, "the surface of the earth was still black and covered with ashes."

On the night of May 23, Heaven's floodgates unexpectedly opened up as the wagoners slept in their tents along the very river named for Heaven's nemesis. Startled into wakefulness by the crack of lightning, the men faced a sheet-like torrent driven by roaring winds that no canvas could withstand. Forced into the open, they could only suffer through the raging storm until it abated.

At noon the next day, French checked the adjacent ford and noted only a minimal rise in water level. Still, his experience told him that heavy rains in the upstream watershed could change matters quickly. Already, a wall of turbid foam could be roaring his way.

He ordered the baggage wagons across first, but as soon as they gained the far bank, a rise of several feet cut them off from the main caravan. The stranded wagoners had to wait almost two days before the waters subsided enough for French and the others to join them.

On June 24, the supply wagons rolled into El Paso, culminating a seven-week journey. After a thirteen-day stay, French returned via the Lower Road, this time traveling the stretch through the Devils without incident. By the time his mule teams plodded into San Antonio August 9 and completed the round trip, his night guards had fired twice at supposed Indians—a warning to succeeding stage drivers that not all obstacles along a route both parched and drenched were environmental.[10]

CHAPTER 5

BY MAIL COACH AND HOOF

Undaunted by the challenges of an eleven hundred-mile route,[1] Henry Skillman entered a bid in 1851 to provide mail service between San Antonio and Santa Fe, New Mexico. As a member of both the 1849 Whiting expedition that pioneered the Lower Road, and the subsequent Johnston expedition that developed it, Skillman was an ideal choice.

Born in New Jersey in late 1813 or early 1814, he grew up in likely Kentucky. A courier on the Santa Fe Trail by 1842, he later freighted goods between El Paso del Norte and Santa Fe, thus familiarizing himself with the route up the Rio Grande. With the Mexican War raging in 1847, Skillman marched to Chihuahua City, Mexico, with Colonel Alexander P. Doniphan, and distinguished himself in the Battle of Sacramento. Subsequently, he served as a scout in Colonel Sterling Price's invasion of Chihuahua.

Forged by the backcountry and tested by fire, Skillman understood as well as any man the demands of the San Antonio-Santa Fe route—a fact not lost on postal authorities. On November 1, 1851, the government awarded Skillman a contract that would extend through June 30, 1854.

For $12,500 a year, Skillman's line was to depart San Antonio the first day of every other month and negotiate the Devils en route to San Elizario, fifteen miles southeast of El Paso. Arriving on the nineteenth, the mail would continue up the Rio Grande a day later and reach Santa Fe on the last day of the month. San Antonio-bound mail would depart San Elizario bi-monthly on the twelfth, again challenge the Devils, and gain the Alamo city at month's end.[2]

To captain the escort for the first run, Skillman selected thirty-four-year-old William "Bigfoot" Wallace, an accomplished frontiersman whose exploits even-

Fort Clark and Las Moras Springs in 1869.
Journal of Lieutenant Colonel Thomas B. Hunt, National Archives.

tually would merit him folk hero status. A giant for his day—six feet, two inches and 225 pounds—the Virginia native had immigrated to Texas to avenge his brother's death at Goliad in the 1836 Texas Revolution. Six years later, Wallace fought against Mexican general Adrian Woll, who had stormed San Antonio, and subsequently marched with Alexander Somervell's retaliatory expedition that captured Laredo.

In December 1842, Wallace invaded Mexico with the Mier Expedition, only to surrender with his fellow Texans to superior Mexican forces. Joining in a mass escape on February 11, 1843, he was quickly recaptured, along with 175 other Texans. As punishment, Mexican authorities forced every man to draw from an earthen jar containing 159 white beans and seventeen black beans—white for life, black for death. Wallace drew white and survived, but seventeen of his comrades went before a firing squad March 25.

Six months later, Mexican officials cast Wallace and the other survivors into the dungeons of Perote Prison in the state of Vera Cruz. Finally released, he made his way back to Texas, rode with the Texas Rangers under John C. Hays, and fought in the Mexican War. In the course of his many adventures, he had gained the sobriquet "Bigfoot"—not in acknowledgment of unusual foot size, but because he had killed an Indian of that nickname in a hand-to-hand fight.[3]

Wallace knew what it took to survive and he knew the frontier—essential attributes in escorting mail through the Devils country in this demanding year of 1851. With a Concord coach pulled by six spirited mules and guarded by Belgian

Las Moras Springs today. Photograph courtesy of Patrick Dearen.

immigrant Dedrich Dutchover, E. P. Webster, and sixteen other men, Wallace and Skillman accomplished the baptismal run without incident. In a December vote of confidence, the US Army adopted the line as its official courier between Santa Fe and San Antonio.[4]

Crafting advertising copy on December 6, Skillman listed passenger rates to the Alamo city: $100 from El Paso and $125 from Santa Fe, with a baggage allowance of forty pounds per person. He also stressed his familiarity with this route that had but a single forty-mile waterless stretch—evidently the section between Beaver Lake and Howard's Spring.[5] A year later, postal officials increased his yearly subsidy to $28,000 to accommodate monthly departures by four-horse coaches from both San Antonio and Santa Fe starting in January 1853.[6]

In 1854, Frederick Law Olmsted took note of the westbound mail party as it passed through Fort Inge, the last point to change teams until faraway El Paso. The caravan consisted of two heavy wagons and a passenger ambulance, each pulled by four mules. One spare mule per vehicle followed the churning wheels. A mounted guard of six men, each drawing forty dollars a month, carried Sharps rifles and Colt repeaters.

The expressmen generally camped from ten PM until four AM, then started down-trail without breakfast. Twice a day—at eight AM and after three PM—they halted to graze the mules and eat.[7] A relentless and perilous journey all the way to and from Santa Fe, it required both physical prowess and mental toughness. Regular mail runs in 1852 did not change the Devils' identity as a "wild dangerous place... almost given to the Indians," Major General Zenas R. Bliss recalled.[8] To protect this section of the Lower Road, the US Army established a fort at *Las Moras* Springs forty miles east of First Crossing on June 20, 1852. Initially christened Fort Riley, the post was renamed Fort Clark July 15. Clearly, as Brevet Lieutenant Colonel W. G. Freeman later noted, Las Moras Springs was a "point of primary importance... from its salient position looking both to the Rio Grande and Indian frontiers."[9]

After desperate moments on September 9 in the walled pass of Painted Canyon just west of First Crossing, Bigfoot Wallace could testify firsthand to the Indian threat on the road. Westbound with the mail coach and five or eight men, the veteran Indian fighter was on guard as they stopped at Painted Canyon's water hole to noon. At daybreak, they had seen Indian smoke signals in the distance, and later the stage had crossed a fresh trail of fifteen to twenty horses. Now, surrounded by brushy bluffs ideal for ambush, Wallace was more uneasy than ever.

Still, rest was essential after an all-night push, so the men watered and hobbled the animals, downed a quick lunch, and positioned the coach against a quarter-acre of thick chaparral that would give a measure of security as they napped. Wallace alone stayed awake, heeding a sixth sense that told him trouble was on the way. Rifle in hand, he took a sentinel's post on a small knoll fifty or sixty yards from the coach.

A deer bounded by, unaccountably alarmed, sending Wallace over to awaken Ben Wade; something was amiss, and he needed help bringing in the stock. The two men proceeded to tie the animals to the chaparral, then Wade again lay down to resume his nap.

His ear to the ground, Wade was the first to hear the drum of hooves. He sprang up, alerting the others in time for the men to shoulder rifles from the chaparral and take aim. As two dozen mounted Comanches thundered in with arrows whistling and bullets exploding, the mail party responded with a fusillade that felled four warriors, perhaps including a chief. One Comanche slug struck an iron wagon tire and fragmented, wounding Adolph Fry in the chest.

Withdrawing, the Indians dismounted and returned on foot to surround the small thicket of chaparral that concealed the mail party. As their blood-curdling cries echoed from the bluffs, Wallace sent half his men to defend the thicket's far side while he and the others protected the coach.

Three times, or maybe four, the Indians charged, once so successfully that the mail party had to engage them at close quarters. One warrior would have buried an arrow in Wallace's back from only six feet away had not Wade dropped the Indian with a timely shot. Before the mail party could repel the horde, another feathered missile drove through a man's arm and pinned him against a prickly pear stand.

Now, the wounded and the able men alike took cover under the coach and waited. Flat on the ground but vigilant with rifles, they held their position long enough to lure one Comanche into the open, then four more—five warriors side-by-side seventy yards away.

Four men took aim, and four Comanches fell dead to a sudden boom. The fifth Indian scampered to safety. After fifteen or twenty minutes of inactivity, the mail party watched as hidden Comanches cast loops from the distant brush and dragged away their dead and wounded.

Believing the Indians had withdrawn, Wallace ordered the coach harnessed while he assessed the situation from the small knoll. From four hundred yards down-canyon, a second war party approached. Now, the situation seemed ominous indeed, for fully forty warriors were astride horses.

Still, Wallace held his ground, and when the Comanches came within 100 yards, he defiantly showed himself. The horsemen immediately stopped, and a presumed chief advanced alone another thirty or forty yards. They exchanged words in Spanish, and Wallace knew enough about Comanche psyche to exhibit all the bravado he could.

Even when the chief called him a sneaking coyote and squaw and asserted that he was too cowardly to continue his journey, Wallace kept up his bluster. Not only would he and his men dare the road, he replied, but they would camp that night at California Springs "in spite of the whole Comanche nation!"

Turning his back on the chief, Wallace fearlessly walked back to the coach.

The ploy worked. The Comanches, convinced the men would press on, evidently rode for California Springs to plot an attack. Three warriors alone remained behind to spy on the mail party, which had no intention of riding into another gauntlet.

After a thirty-minute wait to create separation from the main body of Indians, Wallace and his men lashed their animals hard for First Crossing and Fort Clark. Two of the Indians raced their ponies away to inform the war party, but the third followed the coach at a distance for seven or eight miles.

It was a rattling trek back to Clark for a coach with three imbedded arrows and two wounded men, but the fort's flags welcomed them to safety the next morning. Unable to get an escort west from Clark, Wallace fell back another forty-two miles to Fort Inge and tried again with a similar result. Finally the undaunted frontiersman, vowing to "fight it out" with the Indians, hired his own guards and delivered the mail to El Paso.[10]

Both the US Army and Texas Rangers recognized the Devils as a refuge for hostile tribes, and while Ranger captain Owen Shaw and fifty Texas Mounted Volunteers reconnoitered the river and elsewhere in January 1853,[11] Philip St. George Cooke dispatched federal troops from Fort Terrett, situated forty-six miles east-northeast of the Devils' head. Cooke's aim was to pin marauding Lipan

Apaches between Company A of the Second Dragoons, advancing southeast toward the Guadalupe River, and two Eighth Infantry mounted companies that would block their escape to the Devils or Mexico.

Caught in the vise at the head of the Guadalupe on January 12, the Lipans nevertheless outmaneuvered the soldiers and fled. G Company of Second Dragoons pursued, capturing eighteen warriors and more than 100 ponies, but the majority of the band escaped to the Nueces and possibly on to the Devils,[12] as much a place of sudden death as ever.

Bigfoot Wallace and the express party, making another run through the Devils country in April, left behind a shallow grave to affirm this river's insatiable lust for tragedy. As the barreling coach raised dust, guard Ben Sanford let his mule drop off the pace. He heard the twang of a bowstring from a nearby Spanish dagger, and a split second later an arrow ripped into his flesh.

Critically wounded, he managed to gig the mule up abreast of the coach and cry out that an Indian had killed him. The coach driver immediately pulled rein, and Wallace ordered guards to avenge the attack even as caring hands placed the bleeding man inside the stage. Although Wallace managed to remove the arrow, he had little reason to doubt Sanford's self-prognosis.

The guards returned after a fruitless search, and Wallace had no choice but to push on. The coach delivered a jarring ride at best, but the journey was sheer torture for someone in Sanford's condition. On into sunset and throughout an agonizing night, he clung to life, then mercifully died the following day.

Wallace buried him beside the road—yet another lonely cairn, perhaps, to testify to this land's evils—then put the scene behind him to the crack of a whip and lunge of the team.[13]

The ultimate fate of Sanford's grave is unknown, but Indians sometimes exhumed an enemy and left a desecrated corpse on display, perhaps as a macabre warning. Julius Froebel, venturing east on the Chihuahua Trail two months after Sanford's death, never expected such a horrid greeting as his caravan forded Lancaster Crossing on the Pecos and set sights on the "notorious" Devils ahead. Still, a haunting visage would burn into his memory long before trail's end.

Two four-mule coaches in a well-guarded mail party passed the wagons at Lancaster, giving Froebel an opportunity to reflect on a "true picture of wild American life." He noted a striking contrast in the passengers, all of whom were heavily armed men except for a three- or four-year-old girl.

"It was touching," wrote Froebel, "to see how these rough, bearded men, with their pistols and daggers, supplied the place of a mother's care to the tender little creature."

As Froebel's caravan rolled toward the Devils, the land displayed signs that the withering drouth of the early 1850s was but a memory. Beyond Live Oak Creek,

The Devils River above Second Crossing in 1854. William H. Emory, Report on the United States and Mexican Boundary Survey, 1857.

the highlands undulated with "fresh young grass," while the descent to the Devils was like entering "another world." On the steppe above, the cacti and yucca of a desert ruled, but the bottom land cradled oaks, walnuts, and wild plums, and yielded dramatic evidence of torrential rains: Across the valley from mountain to mountain, floods had deposited a bulwark of stones and jumbled boulders. Amazed at this manifestation of "fearful power," Froebel was no less awed by the driftwood that clung to the upper branches of trees, an indication of the incredible height to which flood waters had surged.

As graves piled with stone pointed the way, the caravan snaked downstream through the Devils' defile and climbed the tableland between Second and First crossings. Logistics demanded that the wagoners halt for the night on these gulch-rent heights, but conditions at their spot of choice gave them pause. Not only were there fresh horse tracks and a recent Indian camp, but also repulsive human remains.

"The grave of some traveller had been opened near the road, the half decomposed body thrown out, [and] the head set upon a pole," recorded Froebel. Furthermore, wagon boards that had constituted the coffin now formed an indistinguishable pattern in the road.

The next day, Froebel found nothing in Painted Canyon to lift the morbid pall that had descended on the land.

"This is ... one of the most gloomy localities I ever saw," he wrote of the gorge, "so barren and inhospitable as to produce the most painful impressions." Even the lower Devils at the mouth of Painted Canyon, he added, exuded "much the same gloomy character."

First Crossing alone, to Froebel's eye, held the "classic beauty of a wilderness," considering its "broad crystal" waters, "noble trees wreathed by vines," and towering cliffs of rock. Even here, however, stood a stark monument to a despicable crime, if caravan hearsay was true.

Years before, an informant told Froebel, runaway slaves had taken refuge at First Crossing in a hut of branches, whose ruins and chimney still stood. Hunger forced them to consider the unthinkable—cannibalism—and while one man slept, the others fell on him and did what survival demanded. Subsequently, passersby discovered the charred remains, and the perpetrators turned themselves in to the law.[14]

The account is difficult to verify, but escaped slaves sometimes did flee to the Devils. Bigfoot Wallace, camped on the river with the westbound mail party one day, encountered a half-starved slave who had escaped from his master in Louisiana. Captured by Indians, the fugitive had broken free again and was barefoot and almost naked by the time Wallace took him in. Wallace transported the runaway to El Paso and back to San Antonio and collected a $200 bounty from the owner.[15]

Early in 1854, the US Army acted to extend its presence west along the Lower Road and dispatched Second Lieutenant Samuel H. Reynolds and a First Infantry detachment to establish a post approximately 150 miles from Fort Clark. On April 1, the infantrymen broke camp near California Springs, marched to a point "near the head of Rio San Pedro" the next day, and set up the Devils' first semi-permanent military outpost.[16] Named for Lieutenant Jacob E. Blake, a topographical engineer who died in the Mexican War,[17] Camp Blake was actually fifty or so miles nearer Clark than advised.

Although Blake's exact location is debatable, evidence points to the vicinity of Beaver Lake, a coveted oasis that long had nurtured passing military parties. Not only was the lake generally considered the river's head, thus echoing the description in Camp Blake's post return for April, but on June 6 a traveler would delineate a "Devils River Station" (presumably Blake) at the final watering point before the road struck out for Howard's Spring—an accurate characterization of the Beaver Lake area. Furthermore, a subsequent diarist placed the post near a "water hole" that, like Beaver Lake, lay upstream of a long stretch of river with four or five dry crossings.[18]

Initially, Lieutenant Reynolds commanded thirty-seven enlisted men, but his force dwindled to thirty-four in May and thirty-one in summer,[19] a season that fostered more indications of the Army's commitment to protecting the Lower

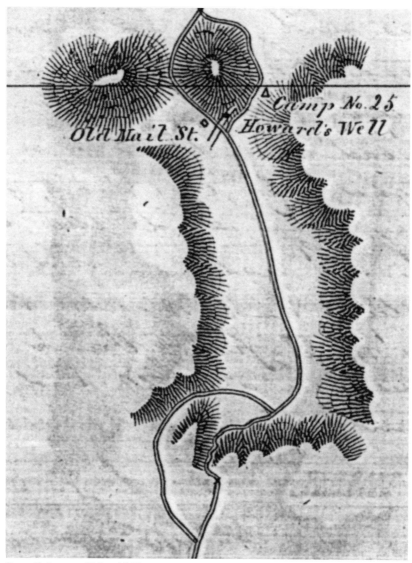

Howard's Spring or Well in 1869.
Journal of Lieutenant Colonel Thomas B. Hunt, National Archives.

Road. In July, companies A & H, Eighth Infantry, occupied a second encampment downstream on the Devils. This temporary outpost, Camp on the San Pedro, likely lay just above Second Crossing,[20] thereby creating short-lived deterrents at two strategic points along the river.

Still, the service of these scattered infantrymen was not without danger in

1854, as violence spiked up and down the Lower Road. Where bone-dry hills of the Pecos watershed guarded an unforgiving canyon and Howard's Spring—a seemingly inexhaustible pool in a deep crevice that split the rock bed of Howard Draw[21]—Indians attacked mail parties twice.[22] By ambush, Indians killed two Blake soldiers.[23] At Second Crossing, a man took the life of a fellow traveler after mistaking him in the dark for a hostile.[24]

Even peril couldn't suppress ambition, however. Ever since 1849, cowmen had targeted beef-hungry miners in the gold fields with drives down the California Cattle Trail, yet another trace that shared the Lower Road through the Devils country. Now in 1854, cattle drives were at their peak, drawing from a reservoir of free-ranging longhorns in the Texas brush country. The 1,500-mile journey exacted the best from both men and animals, but a Texas beef could net between $6 and $100 in an ever-fluctuating California market.

The drive of five to six months required four cowhands for every 100 cattle, although with so many emigrants eager to join a westbound procession, additional drovers sometimes worked for necessities alone. In 1854, Frederick Law Olmsted encountered a "California cattle-train" of 400 beeves and twenty-five cowhands, only a few of whom drew wages. The demands of this most-hazardous of cattle trails were evident in their choice of mounts and weapons, as well as in their abundance of provisions.

"They were all mounted on mules, and supplied with the short government rifle and Colt's repeaters," observed Olmsted. "Two large wagons and a cart, loaded with stores, cooking utensils, and ammunition, followed the herd."[25]

Journals kept by two drovers in 1854 paint vivid portraits of travel through the Devils section of the cattle trail. Michael Erskine started out from a ranch east of San Antonio with 1,054 beeves the last week of April and pointed the herd into First Crossing June 3. After bedding the animals three miles north-northwest of Painted Cave, the drovers pushed the herd hard across the arid bend the next day and reached a location four miles beyond California Springs by sundown. On the fifth, 4,000 flinty hooves deepened fifteen miles of desert trace and gained Second Crossing, an Eden for thirst-crazed beeves.

At eight o'clock the next morning, the longhorns started up the winding canyon splashed green by plentiful grass. Grazing as they marched, they trudged all the way to a good watering spot within four miles of Camp Blake. Here, Erskine decided to lay over and give the beeves a chance to rest and fill their bellies before the long, dry drive to Howard's Spring—a two and a half-day trek which they undertook June 8. Just under five months later, 814 head would arrive at Warner's Ranch in California.[26]

Twelve days behind Erskine's drove, a herd owned by John James of San Antonio negotiated First Crossing and stopped at Painted Canyon's water hole. After

Cow carcass at Yellow Tank near old Yellow Banks water hole in 2009.
Photograph courtesy of Patrick Dearen.

a forced march that ended at California Springs the next day, the drove proceeded through Dead Man's Pass and forded Second Crossing. Following several Indian alarms that evening, drovers likely stayed on edge June 18 as they forged up-canyon with the cattle, whose hooves suffered terribly along a route paved with stones.

On the nineteenth, cowhands urged the beeves past Camp Blake and found only a dry course ahead, forcing a retreat for the night. A half-mile from the post, they bedded the animals and stood guard in shifts against Indians, storms, and a saddlebag-full of other catalysts that could trigger a stampede.

"Most of the men had only hours rest," cowhand James G. Bell said of an ensuing night on the Devils. "The noise of changing guard frequently keeps one awake."

Before daring the forty-plus miles of sun-baked wasteland ahead, the drovers let the longhorns recuperate almost two full days. Their stomachs finally bloated, the beeves marched away June 21 amid choking dust that would only get worse before they attained Howard's Spring and its fleeting stream.[27]

While hooves furrowed the trace along the Devils in 1854, the wheels of mail coaches whirled under new ownership. In March, the federal government accepted David Wasson's bid to take over the San Antonio to Santa Fe Mail from Henry Skillman July 1. For $16,750 a year, Wasson was to provide monthly service in two-horse coaches, but as his agents sought to ready the operation in San

George H. Giddings. N. S. Haley Memorial Library, Midland, Texas.

Antonio, harsh realities set in. Not only did the wilderness route call for four- or six-mule vehicles, but also a sizable escort armed with Sharps rifles and Colt pistols.

Having underbid drastically, Wasson was unable to initiate service without negotiating advances from thirty-year-old San Antonio merchant George H. Giddings, who in turn requested security. Wasson had only the four-year postal contract to offer, which Giddings accepted. With Skillman's line defunct June 30, the new operation started in July as planned with Giddings at the company reins. Another seven weeks would pass before Wasson legally transferred the contract to Giddings, a Pennsylvania native who had lived in San Antonio since 1846. However, not until April 7, 1854, would Giddings enter into an agreement with postal officials, who authorized him to operate the line through June 30, 1858, at an annual compensation of $16,750.

The initial schedule called for departures from both San Antonio and Santa Fe the first day of every month with arrivals twenty-five days later. Giddings' first mail party embarked from San Antonio with a six-mule coach and a seven-man escort, including four mounted guards who drove twenty-six spare mules. With no stations along remote stretches, the expressmen stopped every twenty-five to thirty miles to graze the animals and change teams.

Giddings eventually convinced the federal government to double his annual compensation to $33,500, an amount that would cover expenses for which Wasson had failed to account.[28] Whatever Giddings' budget, he wisely took advantage of Skillman's unparalleled experience and expertise and hired him as a driver.[29]

Another Giddings employee was conductor James M. Hunter, whose mail parties sustained three Indian attacks between 1854 and 1856. One incident occurred at the Devils' head, where hostiles stormed the mail camp in the black of night and tried to stampede the mules. The expressmen seized arms and opened fire, saving the animals and repelling the Indians without loss to either side.[30]

The US Army, in need of faster communication than Giddings could provide, set in motion its own semi-monthly express through the Devils country September 30.[31] Within days, the Army also established Fort Davis along the Lower Road in far West Texas[32] and ordered the First Infantry to abandon Camp Blake.[33] With Camp on the San Pedro also deserted, the Devils again lacked constant troops to thwart the very hostiles whose arrows would draw blood in the mid-1850s.

CHAPTER 6

AN ARMY POST AT SECOND CROSSING

As new Lieutenant Albert J. Myer first entered Indian country marching west on the Lower Road in January 1855, the twenty-five-year-old surgeon understood a reality that few officers voiced.

"The war on this frontier is one of extermination," he wrote, adding that not only did Army troops have orders to take no captives, but to refuse peace overtures "until the [Indian] race is cowed by their punishment."

Judged by the standards of a civilized society that had no empathy for warrior mentality, the actions of the hostiles seemed to justify such a position.

"In the worst sense of the word these tribes are savages," condemned Myer, headed for his new station at Fort Davis. "They are *devils* and the coldest blood must boil at the narration of the manner in which they have treated prisoners who have fallen into their hands—not men alone, taken with arms in their hands, for *they* can but die, but innocent women and children."

Still, the surgeon mustered admiration for these "best horsemen in the world," each of whom could hang over the side of a galloping mount and unleash arrow after arrow from below the animal's neck.[1]

East and west of the Devils that month, warrior tribes displayed their skills in battle and thievery. At the Fort Clark mail station, a band seized a dozen or more mules,[2] while in a January 7 skirmish at still-unnamed Lancaster Crossing on the Pecos, companies A and G of the Regiment of Mounted Riflemen killed seven Comanches.[3]

Aware of the threat to Pacific Railroad surveyors as they traveled the Lower Road in spring, Company I of Fifth Infantry set up a field camp on the Devils April 30. Labeled "Camp on the Rio San Pedro,"[4] this temporary post likely represented a reoccupation of the earlier Camp on the San Pedro near Second Crossing. Still, trouble brewed, giving rise to a May 27 engagement along the river between hostiles and a detachment from Company H, Mounted Riflemen.[5]

Two months later, Army headquarters commanded the Department of Texas to establish a post on Live Oak Creek, seventy-nine miles west of Beaver Lake and four miles shy of the Pecos. As Captain S. D. Carpenter and two First Infantry companies camped on the Devils en route to fulfill the order, an unseen bowman launched an arrow that ripped through a musician. Unable to exact direct retribution, Carpenter could only march on to Live Oak and set up Camp Lancaster as a western deterrent August 20.[6]

Ten days later, Captain Daniel Ruggles and Company A, Fifth Infantry, occupied Camp Palo Blanco, a fleeting field camp evidently located at unreliable Palo Blanco Springs between First and Second crossings.[7] Nevertheless, a series of Army-Indian engagements erupted that very day at the nearby Rio Grande-Pecos confluence. On into September 8 the skirmishes persisted, involving detachments of Company C, Second Cavalry; Company I, First Artillery; and Company B, First Infantry. In yet another battle December 18, Company C of Second Cavalry fought Indians near Fort Clark.[8]

Sometime during this period, cowhands John Dunlap, John Reinhart, and Joseph Richarz (or Richaz) delivered a cattle herd to Camp Lancaster and turned back for Fort Clark. At a Devils River ford—likely Second Crossing—they met three Apaches driving 150 horses in the wake of a rain. Armed with only pistols and confidence, the cowhands charged in an attempt to seize the herd.

To the men's chagrin, however, the change in angle revealed seven more Indians who switched to fresh horses and met them with a counterattack. Frantic, the cowhands wheeled their jaded mounts and sent mud flying from the galloping hooves. When the Apaches failed to pursue, the men reined up and their courage returned.

"Boys," said Dunlap, "I believe the guns of those Indians were wet, and that was the reason they did not fire or charge us. . . . We can go back and clean them up yet."

Spurred on by the prospect of besting so many Apaches and stealing their herd, the glory-seeking men attacked a second time. Once more, the Indians repelled the surge, this time chasing the riders into a thicket and forcing them to prepare for siege. Now as the hostiles fell back to the horses, the relieved cowhands were content to let them go their way.[9]

Throughout the entire region, hostilities only heightened in 1856. In March, Indian marauders took eighteen mules valued at $150 each from the Giddings station at Camp Lancaster,[10] and two months later on the Devils, Lipan Apaches struck a Fort Davis-bound payroll shipment in the charge of Major Henry Hill. In

Camp or Fort Lancaster in 1869.
Journal of Lieutenant Colonel Thomas B. Hunt, National Archives.

answer, Fort Clark captain A. J. Lindsay and Second Lieutenant E. Tracy searched the river with two Mounted Rifles companies,[11] for Lipans and their Mescalero cousins knew the Devils as a sanctuary as well as brood grounds for violence.

"They keep out of sight & commit depredations & murders at times when least expected," noted Colonel J. K. F. Mansfield, who inspected Fort Clark June 1-3. "They are on the Pecos, in the mountains, on Devils river, &c, always concealed & difficult to find."[12]

Marching westward to assess Lancaster, Mansfield met Lindsay and Tracy at First Crossing by week's end and subsequently camped at Second Crossing. A mere five miles upriver that very night, Indians killed one cowhand and seriously wounded another in an attack on a large "cow & calf train" headed for New Mexico. Mansfield found the four remaining drovers so disorganized that he assigned five soldiers to escort the herd to Lancaster.

"But for my timely arrival, and the aid of this post [Lancaster], wrote Mansfield, "these men would have been murdered & their cows & calves, so important to the inhabitants of New Mexico, captured by the Indians."[13]

By now, Clark had an aggregate force of six officers and 240 enlisted men, and Lancaster three officers and 150 men[14]—two posts indispensable in the face of hundreds of miles of wilderness road always exposed to Indian attack. Between these sentinels—at a point near Second Crossing eighty miles from Clark and ninety-eight miles from Lancaster—soldiers continued to tent frequently.[15]

Developments in summer and fall signaled a new Army emphasis on protecting the Devils-to-Pecos section of road. On July 26, the Department of Texas ordered Lancaster to deploy Company B, First Infantry, to the Devils station, where the men were to remain until November 1.[16] By September 29, the tent grounds had earned the designation "Camp Hudson" in military correspondence.[17] Named for Second Lieutenant Walter W. Hudson, who had died of wounds sustained in an 1850 engagement with Indians near Laredo,[18] this encampment evidently lay upriver of the post's later location. When John C. Reid tramped cross-country en route to the Gadsden Purchase that season, he found Captain Charles Gilbert and an infantry company entrenched a mile upstream of Second Crossing at a site he knew as Camp Davis. From this cantonment, apparently Hudson, the troops campaigned against Lipans who had ridden unchecked between the ford and the Pecos.[19]

On August 21, eleven days after B Company received the instructions to march to Second Crossing, Order Number 53 upgraded Lancaster from camp to fort.[20] As these events unfolded, a party of Tonkawa Indians occupied the Texas side of the Rio Grande just downstream of the Pecos confluence and alarmed military officials. On August 14, Assistant Adjutant General D. C. Buell ordered Fort Clark's commander to muster a force and attack the Tonkawas.

Buell suggested a command of forty to fifty men who, with competent guides, should "move secretly and promptly with pack mules" in an effort to surprise the Indians. He further recommended that the detachment follow the Lower Road to California Springs before veering toward the mouth of the Pecos. Realizing that the Tonkawas might attempt to escape toward the Devils, Buell also instructed that the senior officer at the Devils post be alerted.

On August 20, Captain James Oakes rode out from Clark with a contingent that included detachments of First Infantry and First Artillery. In a trio of skirmishes near the Rio Grande-Pecos confluence ten days later, Oakes and his force caught the Indians unawares and wreaked a fearsome toll, killing or wounding eight and driving the others into Mexico.

"The gallant conduct of the troops under circumstances of great hardship and privation is entitled to high approbation," applauded the Headquarters of the Army two and a half months later.[21]

Even as Oakes campaigned against the Tonkawas, he heeded additional orders from Buell to search the deeply chiseled canyon of the extreme lower Pecos for a practicable crossing. Despite the Lower Road's well-established trace, a shorter route to El Paso was of "constant importance," said Buell.[22]

Still seeking to improve the course in late September, the assistant adjutant general ordered simultaneous scouts from both Devils River and Lancaster to explore the highlands between the posts for a better track, not only in respect to distance, but in availability of water. A Hudson detachment was to march west about twenty crow-flight miles to the Pecos gorge and proceed upriver to meet the downstream-trending Lancaster party about October 18. Together, they would reconnoiter Howard's Canyon from its confluence with the Pecos to Howard's Spring.

"The country to be examined is scarcely known at all," Buell noted.[23]

Despite repeated attempts to pioneer a new route across the Devils-Pecos region, geographic and water concerns in this complex of riparian canyon lands and desert heights continued to validate the existing Lower Road as the preferred course.

In his September 29 orders, Assistant Adjutant General Buell also instructed Captain Charles Gilbert, Hudson's commander, to extend B Company's occupation of the camp until the men exhausted provisions in likely mid-November. Thereafter, they were to march east, with wagons creaking along the Lower Road while a detachment explored the unknown canyon bottom between Second and First crossings.[24]

From Clark to Lancaster, violence swelled in succeeding months. Troops engaged hostiles on the Rio Grande near Clark December 18 and again three days later,[25] while a January raid on the Clark stage station cost the Giddings company thirty-five mules valued at $5,250.[26] Howard's Spring marked the site of two Army-Indian skirmishes early in 1857, the first on January 3 and the second twenty-eight days later. The latter fight involved detachments of companies A, C, F, G, and H from Fort Davis' Eighth Infantry.[27]

In apparently a separate incident at Howard's Spring soon afterward, Indians swooped upon a mail party and killed four men, including an Army sergeant who fought on even after suffering a mortal wound. The hostiles scalped three of the men but spared the sergeant's body, choosing instead to decorate his chest with an elegant wreathe bearing his excised heart—a gruesome tribute to his bravery.[28]

In the dusk of a June day, raiders struck the Fort Clark mail station again, this time breaching the corral and making off with another thirty-five mules.[29] Clearly, the events of the past half-year called for additional troops up and down the Lower Road.

"Scarcely a mile of it but has its story of Indian murder and plunder," Lieutenant Edward Fitzgerald Beale lamented. "In fact, from El Paso to San Antonio

Second Crossing and Camp Hudson in 1869.
Journal of Lieutenant Colonel Thomas B. Hunt, National Archives.

is but one long battle ground—a surprise here, robbery of animals there."[30]

To counter the surge, Theodore Fink and Company G, Eighth Infantry, reoccupied Camp Hudson June 7, pursuant to Special Order 57 issued May 4 by the Department of Texas.[31] It was possibly at this time that soldiers eschewed the old tent grounds a mile upstream of Second Crossing in favor of a new location: the yawn of a west-side canyon a half-mile south of the ford. This flat fifty to sixty feet above the river protected soldiers from floods, but also removed the garrison from the shaded bottom land. The camp's exposed position, coupled with encroaching hills of whitewashed limestone that denied breeze and radiated heat, created a suffocating environment that nurtured only cacti, bear grass, and occasional scrub mesquite.

"I think Fort Hudson was the hottest place I ever served at," career officer Zenas R. Bliss later observed. ". . . During the long summer with the thermometer sometimes at 110 or 112 it was terrible."

Nearby, however, the river widened into a 100-by-300-yard pool known as Bull-Head Lake, named for twenty or so bovine skulls that formed a cross on the bank—the work of Indians, believed Bliss.[32]

Within two weeks of arriving, the new Hudson troops commenced a series of scouts that would expend five days by month's end and thirteen more in July.[33] Meanwhile, developments involving the mail line had consequences that would reach as far as the Pacific Ocean. ❖

CHAPTER 7

THE SAN ANTONIO TO SAN DIEGO MAIL

On March 3, 1857, Congress authorized mail service from San Antonio to San Diego,¹ a line unparalleled in length and danger. More than 1,475 miles of trace unfurled westward from San Antonio, yet the greatest stretch without water lay between the Devils and Howard's Spring—for harness mules, a death march of twelve to sixteen hours.²

Three months later, postal authorities awarded a four-year contract to James Birch. For $149,800 per annum, he was to provide semi-monthly expresses that would leave both San Antonio and San Diego on the ninth and twenty-fourth of each month. A through ticket would cost $200, with each passenger allowed thirty pounds of baggage in addition to firearms and blankets.³

Faced with a transcontinental line intimidating in its vastness, Birch soon would seize upon George H. Giddings' experience and hire him as eastern division agent. Spearheading the overall operation was General Superintendent I. C. Woods, who dispatched a lieutenant from New York to San Antonio June 15 to secure the necessary outfit to start the first mail west on July 9.⁴

While preparations were underway, Lieutenant Edward Fitzgerald Beale embarked from San Antonio June 25 with the most exotic of caravans—camels bearing the brand of the US Army. In a test of worthiness, these "ships of the desert" carried almost 600 pounds apiece as they bore west for the Devils and beyond.

Beale reached First Crossing July 3 and made day camp after ascending the west bluff. That evening, his command marched another six hours through showering rain before halting for the night. Awakening to a downpour at three AM on the Fourth of July, the soldiers prodded the camels down-trail under miserable conditions that raised the specter of hypothermia.

"All day long it rained a cold relentless torrent, accompanied with gusts of wind which drove the chilled water through everything," Beale recorded in his journal. ". . . The men sat shivering in dogged silence on their mules, which shivered and humped themselves in return."

On to the summit of Dead Man's Pass the deluge followed, drowning the very highlands whose predominant aridity defined the classic notion of desert. Finally a wagon broke down, necessitating a halt, and just as soldiers managed to start a fire, the rain relented. A meal of bacon, bread, coffee, and brandy rejuvenated the men, and an afternoon sun restored their spirits. The camels, meanwhile, had endured the storm much better than Beale had expected.

On July 5, dark clouds descended again and unleashed showers that once more soaked the men as they marched to Second Crossing. They spent the rest of that day and the next slowly working their way up the valley before pushing on for Howard's Spring late on the sixth.[5]

Three days later, the first San Antonio to San Diego mail left San Antonio by mule in the charge of James Mason. A half-dozen men rode guard over the express, which included additional pack mules bearing provisions, grain, and camping equipment. Riders drove another twenty-seven mules to deploy at strategic locations to accommodate team changes for the next outgoing mail, which would be by wagon.[6] On July 16, while the hooves cut a dusty course on into the sunset, Superintendent Woods hired Henry Skillman as conductor for the second express.[7]

Before Skillman could depart, however, a deadly confrontation underscored the dangers inherent in the Devils. On July 5, twenty-six-year-old Second Lieutenant John B. Hood, who would gain fame as a Confederate general, set out from Fort Mason on an extended scout with twenty-four men from Company G, Second Cavalry. Twelve days later, he struck a three-day-old Indian trail bearing generally south toward the Devils headwaters and took up the chase.

The trace led from water hole to water hole—dry marches of thirty-five to fifty miles that tired their horses. The morning of July 20 found the soldiers seven miles above the Devils' head at yet another watering, where signs indicated a second party had joined the hostiles to form a force thirty to forty strong.

Hood hurried his command on down-trail, the weary horses struggling for hours over bluffs and mountains that paralleled the river at a distance of approximately three miles. Even more demanding than the terrain was a dehydrating sun that burned in the sky, and in late afternoon the quest for water overruled all else. Hood turned his command for the river, but accomplished only a mile before movement on a ridge two and a half miles away caught his eye.

The distance was too great to discern details except for a white flag flying from a group of horses. Hood presumed the signal to be that of reservation-bound

Tonkawas traveling under the security of such a banner by Army permission. He decided to investigate, but the poor condition of his horses forced him to leave several riders behind as he formed a line and cautiously advanced.

Hood and his command of seventeen expended a full hour in gaining the proximity of a small mound rising out of Spanish bayonets, or native yuccas. On its crest, Hood identified ten Indians, five of whom started toward him with the flag. When the parties came within thirty paces of one another, the Indians dropped the banner and ignited a large heap of dry vegetation before the troops. As war cries erupted and the blaze soared thirty feet, a dozen riflemen and eighteen bowmen attacked from Spanish bayonets a mere ten paces away. Simultaneously, eight or ten mounted Indians charged with bent bows or outstretched lances.

Lured into a trap, Hood and his men gave a battle cry and plunged their horses into the middle of the presumed Comanches or Lipans. Hand-to-hand, the soldiers fought, only to face withering fire that momentarily forced them back. Hood proceeded to rally his troops, their six-shooters exploding again and again from close range.

In the ebb and flow of the desperate struggle, Private Thomas Ryan fell, never to rise. A second enlisted man, William Barry, faced a similar end after losing his horse and fleeing into a ravine. Another soldier, likewise deprived of a mount, took three arrows in the back, one piercing a lung. Severe wounds debilitated three additional men, even as Hood himself reeled under an arrow that ripped through his left hand and pinned him to the bridle. As projectiles whizzed and lances clashed all about, the officer broke the shaft below the point and pulled it from his hand, freeing himself to fight on.

Outnumbered six to one by later estimate, the soldiers exacted bloody payment of their own, killing nine to nineteen Indians and wounding another ten or twelve. With their weapons emptied and the hostiles' deadly fire terrifying their horses and thwarting efforts to reload, the men of Company G fell back fifty yards. Dismounting to ready for another assault, the soldiers watched the Indians gather their dead amid howls of mourning—a sign that their losses were as heartfelt as the soldiers'.

An unvoiced truce ensued, and no one was more relieved than Hood. If the Indians had mounted another charge, he would have had but five or six severely dehydrated foot soldiers to fend off scores of warriors.

"We were nigh meeting a similar fate to that of the gallant Custer and his noble band," the officer reflected decades later.

With dusk approaching, the Indians retreated and Hood moved his command to the river. Tortured by thirst, the cavalrymen reached Beaver Lake about ten PM to find a wagon train in camp; Indians had assailed the caravan and absconded with the mules, stranding the wagoners until they could secure more teams from

San Antonio. In desperate need of medical attention for his men, Hood dispatched a messenger for Camp Hudson.

Hudson's commander, Lieutenant Theodore Fink, hurried to Beaver with an Eighth Infantry detachment and a wagon for transporting the casualties. Hood, despite his own wound, returned to the battleground the next day with an infantry escort to bury Private Ryan and search for the missing Barry. Hood found no trace of the soldier, but his study of the area at least provided intelligence that the Indians had scattered.[8]

With a crack of a whip July 19, Bigfoot Wallace had headed out from the Alamo City with an advance supply train for the second San Antonio to San Diego express, which Henry Skillman would start west five days later. Wallace placed a nine-mule relay at Fort Clark and rolled on toward Lancaster, where he was to leave another eighteen mules and turn back.[9] Nevertheless, passage through the Devils was particularly perilous in the wake of the deadly trap that had almost cost Hood his detachment.

On July 25, five days after G Company's brush with massacre, evidently the same Indian band set up an ambush fifteen to eighteen miles north of Hudson. As Wallace brought up the coach a few hundred yards behind the mule herd, hostiles opened fire from chaparral that guarded both sides of the road. The terrified team bolted, wheeling so sharply that the wagon tongue snapped. Set afoot, Wallace leaped from the box and shouted to William Clifford to join him in defending the herd.

Wounded in the arm, Wallace managed to fight his way up-road, but Clifford wasn't so lucky. Surrounded, he made a stand at the wagon and paid with his life. With Wallace's help, the muleskinners turned the herd off-road in the hope of out-distancing the warriors and saving the animals. Still, with Wallace and another man forced to ride double, escape from such a determined foe was clearly impossible. In desperation, the expressmen abandoned the herd to the Indians.

As the survivors made their way back to Hudson, they assessed their casualties: one person killed and another wounded in the arm. Furthermore, they had lost a coach, as many as twenty-two mules worth $3,300, $100 in cash, and hundreds of dollars in personal property.

At Hudson, Wallace found Captain Charles J. Whiting on scout with a Second Cavalry detachment from Fort Clark. Whiting quickly set out in pursuit of the presumed Comanches, and in a skirmish five days later, his men killed two warriors and recaptured most of the mules. Nevertheless, the ordeal had ruined many of the animals for stage use.[10]

In the meantime, Skillman and the second mail party left San Antonio July 24 as scheduled, with plans to meet the eastbound express in Arizona and return with its missives. Oblivious to the events on the Devils, he brought the standard half-dozen guards to protect the coach and nine spare mules.[11] But the dangers ahead were not limited to the Devils, as that very day detachments of the First and Eighth infantries skirmished eighty to 100 Indians about twenty-two miles up the Pecos from Lancaster Crossing. A sergeant and three hostiles lost their lives[12]—added testimony that the summer of '57 was a hazardous season on the Lower Road.

Despite the loss of the relay teams expected at Fort Lancaster, Skillman made good time, negotiating the Devils and Pecos without incident and overtaking the mule-borne first mail in southwestern New Mexico.[13]

Superintendent Woods, desperate for mules and equipment even before learning the fate of Wallace's train, purchased George H. Giddings' entire store of San Antonio to Santa Fe Mail coaches and mules July 29. The two men further agreed to combine services as far west as El Paso. Woods, now confident that he could fulfill James Birch's mail contract, immediately dispatched a caravan of coaches, mules, equipment, and provisions to stock the San Diego line wherever needed, particularly beyond El Paso.

Planning to accompany the party on to California, Woods soon overtook the train. As he proceeded down-trail through a drizzling rain August 2, he met two harried expressmen riding for San Antonio on borrowed mules. Hunched over and shrouded in blankets, the wounded Bigfoot Wallace and his fellow expressman were "all that now remained of a fine outfit," Woods lamented in his journal. Their funereal appearance cast an even greater gloom over their narrative of tragedy and loss on the Devils.

Concerned about the limb that Wallace carried in a sling, Woods left him in the care of a surgeon, then bore on for the Devils with twenty well-armed men. At Hudson on August 6, he found Wallace's wrecked coach, which soldiers had retrieved.[14]

At line's end, Woods was scheduled to meet up with Birch, who sailed from New York for California on the steamship *Central America* August 20. A few days after Woods reached San Diego September 8, however, the *Central America* foundered in a savage storm south of Cape Hatteras, North Carolina. Birch managed to reach a life raft, but a wave swept him away and sealed his doom.[15]

Even as the future of the fledgling mail company came under question, Indian troubles continued to bedevil the operation. From his San Antonio base, Giddings dispatched Bigfoot Wallace and five other men with fifty-four mules valued at $8,100 to stock stations along the line. As the hooves plodded west near Hudson in September, hostiles wrested the entire herd from the drovers.[16]

The US Army, still unable to deter such depredations, temporarily bolstered Hudson's forces with the October 3 arrival of troops from Camp Cooper on the Clear Fork of the Brazos River.[17] Later in the year, several campaigns against Indians originated at both Hudson and Lancaster. On November 28, Second Lieutenant Alex M. Haskell embarked from the latter post to reconnoiter a vast stretch of country between Beaver Lake and Comanche Springs.[18] A Hudson detail that set out December 22 found two-day-old Indian signs ten miles northeast of Second Crossing, and the next day a second Hudson detachment tracked Indians along a four-mile section downstream of the post. A third Hudson contingent, this one on foot, marched to Beaver Lake and back in late December but discovered no evidence of hostiles.[19]

The Army's heightened concern about warrior tribes on the Devils was well-founded, especially if the report of another massacre at Dead Man's Pass is accurate. Sometime in 1858, according to Chihuahua Trail freighter August Santleben, the Amlung family—husband, wife, and three children—and seven other persons died at the hands of Indians in a Dead Man's ambush.[20]

On January 17, 1858, mail superintendent Woods returned to San Antonio from California, only to learn the following day that Birch's widow had revoked his authority October 26.[21] On March 9, the federal government reassigned the mail contract to George H. Giddings, who was to provide service between San Antonio and San Diego until June 30, 1861, for $149,800 per annum.[22] He soon had in place sixty-five men, 400 mules, and fifty coaches.[23]

Still, with an angel of death hovering over the Devils, any hope of a route free of peril rested solely in the hands of the US Army. ✺

CHAPTER 8

INDIAN TROUBLE

In 1858, nothing short of military occupation stood a chance of stemming the tide of violence along the Devils—a realization that spawned important developments on the river.

In spring, Captain Larkin Smith, his junior officer Zenas R. Bliss, and the men of Seven A Company, Eighth Infantry, marched from Fort Davis to Camp Hudson and relieved a First Infantry company. Lieutenant Theodore Fink and G Company, Eighth Infantry, were absent, possibly on scout, but they soon returned and Hudson became a two-company post.[1] Several adobe buildings already marked the ten-acre reservation, but by summer's end the garrison would complete a hospital and erect a barracks and multiple two-room officers' quarters using a lime-gravel mix known as pizet.

"These houses were very comfortable, cool in summer and warm in winter," recalled Bliss, "and could be plastered more easily than the adobe houses, the gravel furnishing a surface for the plaster to adhere to."

A quartermaster's office of canvas supplemented the buildings, while a corral, parade grounds, and gardens graced the outlying area.[2] Despite Hudson's move toward a fully realized post, however, hostiles continued to haunt travelers.

As westbound expressmen approached Dead Man's Pass on the night of May 26, they learned that Indians had been sighted on sentineling hills ten miles ahead. "For 20 miles we looked for a Red Devil in every bush, and expected every moment to hear the wild shout which would likely be the death knell for some of us," passenger Phocion R. Way recorded in his diary.

Fortunately, the heavily guarded stage negotiated the stretch safely and gained refuge for the night at Camp Hudson.

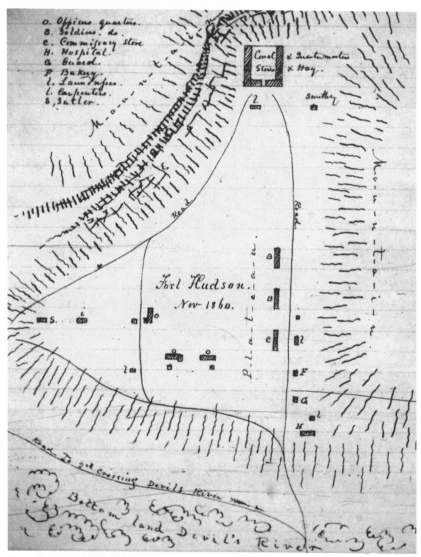

Camp Hudson in 1860. N. S. Haley Memorial Library, Midland, Texas.

"It is far from any habitation, in a barren waste surrounded by hostile Comanches," wrote Way, "but it is a beautiful place."[3]

On June 4, the Department of Texas ordered Hudson and other posts along the mail line to allow the Giddings company to build sheds and corrals "sufficiently near to receive . . . protection."[4] Soon afterward, Giddings looked to the upper

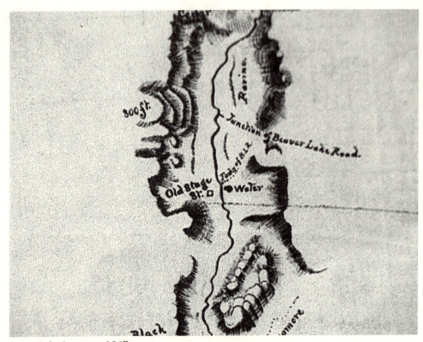

Beaver Lake Station in 1867.
Topographical sketch, Brevet Lieutenant Colonel E. J. Strang, National Archives.

Devils and established a relay station of native rock 200 yards west of sprawling pools of clear water at a cost of $1,000. A hundred yards southeast of the station, which stood just west of the next-to-last crossing for El Paso-bound stages, abundant wood and fine grazing nurtured a popular campground. Although known as Beaver Lake Station, the stand actually lay four road miles downstream near what was later Juno.[5]

During the same period, Giddings also set up stations at Howard's Spring[6] and inside the lower Devils canyon on the west bank of First Crossing. With completion of the latter rock structure,[7] stage drivers could change teams three times as they rolled across the Devils country.

"I kept at each station from Clarke [sic] to San Elizario from 18 to 30 head of stock," Giddings recalled in 1891. ". . . I also had at each station between Clarke and [Fort] Quitman from four to seven well armed men, with a liberal supply of provisions for the men, mail guard, passengers, etc."

Equally vital was forage for the mixed-breed Spanish and Texas mules, reason enough for each station to maintain a store of ten to thirty tons of hay and fifty to 200 bushels of corn.[8]

Whether by mail coach, emigrant wagon, or saddle stock, travelers coursed the Lower Road almost daily with significant amounts of property, yet the US Army continued to struggle with protection.

"It is important that this road be well guarded, *but I have not the force to do it,*" observed Brevet Major General D. E. Twiggs on August 24.[9] On September 17, Twiggs expressed concern that Comanches, Kickapoos, and other hostile tribes might unite in a war against frontier Texas.[10]

Despite warrior activity, small parties sometimes dared the Devils trail without escort. In September the Hudson sutler, whose last name was Dunlop, and his clerk, Ned Gallagher, headed out for Fort Clark and stopped for the night in a hidden ravine thirty miles from Hudson. Awakened by a passing caravan before daylight, they investigated and learned that El Paso-bound wagoners Hall and McComb intended to halt for breakfast down-trail at Yellow Banks, wet-weather pools with discolored water twenty-three miles from Hudson.

Riding on for Clark, Dunlop and Gallagher came face-to-face with a band of Indians near Painted Cave. War cries echoed from the bluffs, and the traders wheeled their mounts and fled toward distant Hudson with eight hostiles pursuing on horseback and five more on foot.

Armed with only six-shooters, the merchants were in dire straits. Gallagher was astride a strong horse that might outdistance the Indians, but Dunlop rode a gotch-eared old mule that resisted his attempts to spur it to greater speed.

As Gallagher pulled away, Dunlop shouted in desperation. "Are you going to leave me, Ned?"

Whirling, Gallagher realized Dunlop's situation. "No! Not as long as there is a hair on my head!" Even as the Indians closed and arrows whizzed by, Gallagher slowed his horse to match the mule's gait.

The race wore on for mile after frantic mile across country slashed by impassable ravines. As hopelessness set in, the traders turned their mounts onto a recently engineered shortcut and gained a critical lead of 300 to 400 yards. Still, Dunlop's mule began to fade, and only after the sutler removed his spur and raked it across the foamy back could he encourage the animal to keep pace.

Thirteen chilling miles carried the men over a final hill and down toward Yellow Banks, where Hall and McComb had fashioned their wagons into a corral typical of encamped caravans. At Dunlop's warning cry, the wagoners secured their mules and gave harbor to the two men.

The Indians initially assumed a position on a nearby hill, then eventually disappeared, inducing the teamsters and two merchants to press on together for Camp Hudson just before sunset. As they approached Dead Man's Pass, the train advanced through the heavy shadows in standard formation—a rider and bellmare leading the spare mules, followed by more riders and then the wagons. As Dunlop and Gallagher took their mounts down into a gully, rifles suddenly boomed from the adjacent darkness.

Yellow Tank near old Yellow Banks water hole in 2009.
Photograph courtesy of Patrick Dearen.

A bullet exploded through the corner of Dunlop's mouth, wrenching out several teeth and ripping his cheek open to the ear. Then his mule went down, pinning the bleeding man to the road. Another rifle blast felled Gallagher's horse, similarly holding him fast against the ground.

At first gunfire, the teamsters began forming their vehicles into a makeshift citadel, but the lead wagon's mules stampeded and veered too sharply, throwing the driver and breaking the wagon's tongue. As the Indians charged the train, the wounded Dunlop crawled out from under his downed mount and turned the spare mules back toward the caravan.

The Indians soon withdrew, apparently content in seizing the broken wagon's ten mules, but the traders and wagoners remained under threat until they reached Camp Hudson.

With no surgeon at the post, the task of sewing up Dunlop's cheek fell upon Captain Albert G. Brackett. Although the wound demanded a lengthy convalescence, Dunlop soon struck out for Clark again. He met with no hostiles this time, but the rigors of the eighty-mile ride opened his stitches and rendered his appearance ghastly by the time he reached the fort.[11]

October brought no respite for the beleaguered Lower Road. On the first, hostiles wounded a Private Hinkley in a skirmish with Hudson's Company K,[12] and an attack on Lancaster Station later in the month cost the mail company eighteen mules valued at $150 apiece. Troops pursued the raiders, but failed to recapture the animals.[13]

The perilous situation across the Texas frontier prompted Department of Texas commander D. E. Twiggs to declare a "crisis" in an October 22 dispatch to Army Headquarters. He beseeched the General-in-Chief to provide him a command of four or five mounted companies in order to "penetrate the Indian country from the El Paso road between Forts Lancaster and Davis."[14] Nevertheless, additional troops were unavailable, and all the Army could do was put out a call for recruits.[15]

On October 23, with stages dusting the new Butterfield Overland Mail line that traced the Upper Road across Texas, postal authorities discontinued Giddings' service between Yuma, Arizona, and Mesilla, New Mexico, the point at which the two lines merged.[16] The action did not affect mail runs along the Devils, but a December 1 report at Hudson of Indians in the Beaver Lake vicinity was a harbinger of things to come.[17]

In January 1859, presumed Comanches burned Beaver Lake Station and absconded with twenty-six mules. Other losses included fifteen tons of hay, seventy-five bushels of corn, provisions, camp and cooking utensils, two muskets, ammunition, a six-horse harness set, and a coach. Monetary damages were significant, totaling $6,637.50, but the theft of the relay teams caused operational issues that forced the Giddings firm to bring in eighteen mules from Fort Clark.[18]

With Comanches striking the Texas frontier and retreating across the Rio Grande border with impunity, Twiggs sought permission January 13 to seize control of northern Mexico, where 700 to 800 warriors had assembled on a lake seventy to eighty miles from the city of Chihuahua.

"The Mexicans are either unable or unwilling to restrain them, so that the evil is growing daily," he wrote, "and if not put a stop to, will result in a suspension of the California overland mail."[19]

In a separate dispatch that day, Twiggs again called for a surge in troops in order to scout the road between forts Lancaster and Davis and pursue "hostile parties into Chihuahua."[20]

Nevertheless, US military operations in Mexico could have instigated an international incident, leading the Secretary of War to notify Twiggs on January 19 that "it is inexpedient to allow the troops in pursuit of the Indians to pass beyond the borders of the United States."[21]

In light of the Secretary's decision, the Department of Texas redeployed First Artillery troops from the lower Rio Grande to Camp Hudson on February 5. The

An early photo of Dolan Falls. Whitehead Memorial Museum, Del Rio, Texas.

arrival of F Company from Ringgold Barracks, and D Company from Fort McIntosh,[22] allowed Hudson commander Brackett to embark on an ambitious scout down the Comanche War Trail into present Brewster County in April. Crossing into Mexico in search of supplies May 3, Brackett and his company defied the Secretary of War (perhaps unknowingly) and attacked Indians in the Sierra del Carmen of Coahuila.[23]

That same month, word reached Fort Clark that marauding Lipans had rendezvoused immediately downstream of Dolan Falls between First and Second crossings. As a cavalry detachment rode for the stronghold, a superior force of Lipans bushwhacked the soldiers about eight miles upstream of the Devils' mouth. In a protracted battle inside the canyon, the troops held their ground and eventually repelled the hostiles.[24]

While Indians raided a vast frontier and soldiers fought back in this perilous year of 1859, Giddings' stages rolled determinedly onward, overcoming repeated setbacks so effectively that the company initiated weekly service through the Devils country that year.[25]

With the US Army still studying the feasibility of camels for transport purposes, Lieutenant William H. Echols and Second Lieutenant Edward L. Hartz arrived at Camp Hudson with twenty-three able camels May 18 and set up stakes half a mile downstream. Testing the animals along the jungled stream, the party relocated to the mouth of a side canyon a short distance above the post on the twenty-fourth and spent another rigorous day challenging adjacent highlands cut by ravines.

On May 26, the expedition embarked in earnest, marching nineteen miles to the head of the river. The next day, Echols and Hartz proceeded west, leaving the Devils behind and setting their sights on Trans-Pecos moonscape. In the succeeding weeks, Hartz repeatedly applauded the camels' performance:

> "June 24. . . . The superiority of the camel for military purposes in the badly-watered sections of country, seems to me to be established."
> "July 14. . . . The performance of the camels was all that could be desired."
> "July 17. . . . The patience, endurance, and steadiness which characterize the performance of the camels during this march is beyond praise."
> "July 23. . . . The camels are capable of going anywhere with their burdens that horses with their riders or mules with their packs can be taken."

By the time the expedition returned to Hudson August 7, the merits of camels over other pack or saddle stock seemed beyond debate. Despite traversing "the most difficult country in northwestern Texas" with heavy packs, inferior forage, and scant water, the camels had arrived back at Hudson "in nearly the same condition in point of flesh, which characterized them in setting out." Meanwhile, several horses and mules had perished, and many others were now emaciated and spent—dramatic testimony to their "inferiority to the camel for this service."[26]

That spring, Army developments had placed Lieutenant Zenas R. Bliss in charge of Hudson, a post at which he had served the year before. The arrival of Captain George Stoneman in summer, however, relegated him to junior officer status. Nevertheless, Bliss continued to command for all but two or three weeks of the next nine months, due to Stoneman's frequent absences on scout with his Second Cavalry company.[27]

During a patrol of the Pecos in the summer of 1859, Stoneman employed five Indian guides who raised the suspicions of Texas Ranger W. R. Henry in an August standoff at First Crossing. Scouting out of Camp Uvalde, Henry and his men struggled west from the Nueces and gained the Devils' waters an estimated ten miles downstream of Hudson. Riding with the river's flow despite challenges posed by "high and rugged mountains" that pressed close on either side, the Rangers managed to reach the vicinity of First Crossing after three days.

Proceeding with another Ranger two miles in advance of the company, Henry halted at the ford and started across on foot. As the water rose to his knees in mid-stream, he discovered five men that he took to be Mexicans a mere ten paces away against the timber on the far bank. Addressing them in Spanish and eliciting

Overlooking the bleak site of Camp Hudson in 2009.
Photograph courtesy of Patrick Dearen.

a response in English, he was taken aback by the realization that they were Indians.

"My first impression was to fire upon them," Henry reported, "but I considered their advantage over me, and at the same time they expressed friendship."

Although the Indians contended that they had served as guides for Stoneman, Henry was far from convinced.

"I told them I was hunting Indians and that if they did not behave themselves I would hang them on the trees," the Ranger related.

Even when the Indians produced an Army officer's letter stating their military duties, Henry remained skeptical. Nevertheless, prudence dictated a peaceful resolution for the moment, and he let them go their way while he pushed back to the main body of Rangers.

"[I] ordered them on the march to overtake them and either hang them on the trees or take them prisoners," wrote Henry. "I did not consider that they had sufficient authority to come in[to] the settlements."

For fifteen miles the Rangers chased the dubious guides east, catching only their hanging dust before overtaking an escort, apparently US Army, who verified the Indians' story.[28]

Bliss, in his two tours of duty at Hudson, came to know the Devils intimately, and decades later he painted a vivid portrait of late-1850s life along the river. Despite almost unbearable heat at times, he found his stay "about as pleasant . . . as I ever had at a Frontier Post," he remembered. "The only draw-back was in the fact that I was alone most of the time, and could not get away from the post on a scout or hunt as often as I would have liked to."

Indeed, the solitude at so isolated an outpost was intense.

"During the two years that I was stationed at Hudson," wrote Bliss, "I saw but four or five people that were not connected with the Post in some way. . . . Our circle of society was not very large, and our opportunity for improvement by mixing with the world, was small."[29]

Dwarfed by the immensity of a vast wilderness, an individual either learned to adjust or went mad. As Bliss marched for Hudson with the Eighth Infantry's Seven A Company in spring 1859, a corporal named Thorpe faced an inner terror far worse than anything the Devils had to offer. The year before, he had panicked while wading across the Pecos at Lancaster Crossing; now, faced with the prospect of fording the Devils, he committed suicide.[30]

In another incident, Bliss asked an elderly soldier named Meehan to shave him, but the man unaccountably fled the room in mid-task. Outside, he seized an ax, cleaved a corporal's shoulder, and escaped to the river bottom. The first sergeant rushed inside to inform Bliss that Meehan was "as crazy as a loon, that he was a raving maniac, and did not know what he was doing." Captured a day or two later, Meehan eventually was committed to an asylum in Washington, DC.

Bliss, having bared his throat before a razor in the hand of a crazed man, counted himself lucky.

"Life on the frontier," he reflected, "is at all times attended with more or less danger, and it sometimes comes in the most unexpected way."[31]

Assuredly, peril was often a man's closest companion on the Devils. When time permitted, Bliss hunted bears, deer, javelinas, turkeys, and ducks, yet this land's two-legged denizens could transform hunters into prey with the twang of a bow string.

"I hardly ever went out, that something did not happen to remind me of the folly of being away from the Post without men enough to make a fight," recalled Bliss.

Fishing in midstream six miles below Hudson one day, Bliss and his lone guard discovered the ten-minute-old tracks of a war party.

"I suppose they crossed while I was fishing above the bend and did not see me," Bliss observed. ". . . Nothing would have been easier than to lie concealed on the bank till I came along, in the water, and then have fired at me and my companion."

Their narrow escape, reflected the officer, "was more good luck than good management."[32]

Until the summer of 1859, the US Army had occupied Camp Hudson without

U.S. Army map showing relative positions of posts Hudson, Clark, Lancaster, and Stockton.
N. S. Haley Memorial Library, Midland, Texas.

ownership rights to the tract. On July 1, however, landowner John James leased to Major D. H. Vinton, Army Quartermaster, 400 acres encompassing the post's existing boundaries and adjacent lands. The agreement specified that James receive fifty dollars a month for up to twenty years and granted the Army a purchase option.[33]

Facing an ever-fluid situation on the frontier, the Department of Texas constantly juggled troops in and out of posts such as Hudson as the need arose.

"We changed stations so often," recalled Bliss," that I do not remember the dates of our departures and arrivals."[34]

Under an August 15 order, soldiers abandoned Camp Van Camp, situated between Horsehead Crossing and newly established Camp Stockton, and marched to Hudson.[35] On September 7, Captain George Stoneman returned to Hudson after a campaign along the Pecos,[36] only to strike out again upon receiving a September 23 directive to address the Indian menace near Eagle Pass. In the same special orders, Brevet Major General Twiggs instructed his quartermaster to hire an express rider to relay the frequent missives to Hudson from Department headquarters in San Antonio.[37]

With so many troops on the move, engagements with hostiles were inevitable. At Howard's Spring on May 7, 1860, a war party overwhelmed a government caravan in the charge of Sergeant Thomas G. Dennin and a Company K detachment from First Infantry. The raiders wounded a civilian wagoner and seized four mules, four oxen, and one horse, yet paid a price with two dead warriors.[38] Less than seven weeks later on June 23, Indians struck Howard's Spring again, besieging the mail station and stealing a horse.[39]

The next day, Brevet Second Lieutenant William H. Echols pushed out from Hudson with yet another camel expedition, this one consisting of twenty animals and their attendants, fifteen pack mules, and thirty-one infantrymen. Echols' twofold purpose was to resume his 1859 reconnaissance of the Trans-Pecos and Big Bend and again test these "ships of the desert" under the most trying of conditions. After a night near Beaver Lake, the caravan trod westward for the Chihuahuan Desert on June 25 and did not return for punishing weeks.[40]

One can only wonder what marauding Indians thought of these strange beasts of burden, but they let them pass unmolested and bided their time. The most gruesome Devils River incident of 1860, however, had nothing to do with warrior societies.

One day as the eastbound mail dropped into the upper canyon and headed downriver, the expressmen sighted a spiral of smoke above a thicket and halted. Such a blatant sign was unlike Indians, who usually practiced stealth, but runaway slaves might not have been so cautious. Lured by $200-a-head bounties, the expressmen crept into the thicket and surprised a Negro man and woman beside a campfire.

The man jumped up to flee, but held his ground in face of a host of six-shooters. From the fire and an adjacent rock wafted the aroma of roasted meat, and the mail party could not resist. Presuming it to be bear meat, they began to partake heartily.

Meanwhile, the slaves remained tight-lipped, refusing to answer questions. When an expressman named Garner searched the brush for their bear gun, he discovered something that sickened every man—the severed head of a Negro.

"You should have seen our faces—some long, some broad, and of changeable colors," coach driver Jack Hodge remembered. "I think I was green. Well, that bear meat didn't stay with us long."

Only now did the woman open up and share the horrific details. With her husband and two other slaves, she had fled their owner at Columbus on the lower Colorado River, only to face starvation in the backcountry. By the time they reached the Devils, they turned to prickly pear for subsistence, and the situation eventually grew so dire that one man staggered away alone in search of food and

Foundation of Beaver Lake Station in 1999.
Photograph courtesy of Joe Allen.

never returned. Finally, the woman and her husband saw no hope but to wait in the road for recapture. The third man, Jim, agreed, but encouraged the couple to wait until morning.

While the woman's husband slept that night, Jim killed the unsuspecting man and then threatened to do the same to her. Compounding his heinous deed, the perpetrator had resorted to cannibalism—an act in which the expressmen had unwittingly participated. Not even the bounties in which Hodge eventually shared would erase the memory.[41]

Warrior tribes of the Devils may have shunned such barbarism, but their outrages continued to fuel cries that they were less than human themselves. In November or December, they swooped upon Beaver Lake Station for the second time,[42] and in January 1861 the stage stand at Howard's Spring again drew fire. In the latter raid, Indians razed the native rock building, destroyed its contents and two coaches, and made off with eighteen mules, wreaking a total loss of $5,725.[43]

Still, the actions of scattered bands of warriors would pale before the conflict that suddenly brewed across a troubled nation.

CHAPTER 9

GRAY REPLACES BLUE

On February 23, 1861, Texas voted overwhelmingly to secede from the United States and align with the Confederacy[1]—an act that helped set the stage for a bitter war whose consequences would reach all the way to the Devils.

A day later, US Army headquarters in San Antonio ordered the evacuation of Camp Hudson and other Lower Road posts west of Fort Clark. W. A. Nichols, Assistant Adjutant-General of the Department of Texas, instructed the garrisons to march for waiting ships at Indianola in orderly fashion—the westernmost post first, followed by each succeeding post two days after the passage of the preceding command.[2] A February 27 modification placed a sense of urgency on the evacuation; now, each garrison would set out "as soon as the means of transportation" arrived.[3]

On March 17, Hudson's troops embarked for the coast, followed two days later by garrisons at Lancaster and Clark.[4] Even as federal soldiers continued the eastward retreat in subsequent weeks, Texas forces bore west through the Devils country to occupy the abandoned posts. The first such contingent included Morgan Wolfe Merrick, who kept a journal of the march to seize the forfeited Fort Davis.[5]

In an interesting instance of cooperation, the Texas company joined a large wagon train headed to Davis to facilitate the removal of the federal garrison. On April 12, the very day that the Civil War erupted at Fort Sumter, South Carolina, the combined parties camped at First Crossing. They gained Howard's Spring soon afterward and reached Fort Davis on the twenty-second.[6]

Another state force, Major Edwin Waller's Second Texas Mounted Rifles, struck out for New Mexico from Camp Leon near San Antonio about June 1. En route, Waller left Captain H. A. Hamner and companies C and H to garrison Fort Clark, then proceeded down-trail with companies A, B, D, and E. At the head of the Devils, Waller received a report that US troops intended to move toward Fort Bliss, situated at El Paso in the shadow of the Franklin Mountains. Waller immediately ordered a forced march to the fort, 448 miles distant.

"We had two or three pack mules and our supply of provisions soon began to fail," wrote Martin Hardwick Hall, one of the mounted riflemen. ". . . Our horses began to fail and almost everyone in the company had to foot it. Some, I supposed, walked over 100 miles. Some days we ate but one meal."

Upon gaining Bliss July 4, Major Waller discovered a Rebel flag already flying.[7]

Although the outbreak of war ended the Butterfield Overland Mail operation between Mesilla, New Mexico, and Tucson, Arizona, the Giddings company acquired Butterfield's stock and briefly undertook service all the way from San Antonio to Los Angeles. Coaches surged through the Devils country only until July, when the Confederate government pulled Giddings' authorization in Texas. Indian raids in Arizona finished off the section west of El Paso by September, but stages would resume traveling the San Antonio-Mesilla route under Giddings' August 28 contract with the Confederacy and continue until August 1862.[8]

With citizen and military forces preoccupied with the Civil War, warrior tribes displayed new vigor in Texas as well as Arizona. In the conflict's early months, as Indian marauders blitzed the Texas settlements and disappeared into the Devils backcountry, Captain W. H. Perry scouted the region with mounted riflemen from the Twenty-sixth Brigade, Texas Militia.[9] Still, before the conflict between North and South would end, the frontier would retreat as much as 100 miles in face of Indian raids that increased "in number and boldness," according to a later government assessment.[10]

With the Lower Road playing a strategic role in military matters, First Lieutenant William G. Jett and a Company B detachment of the Second Texas Mounted Rifles garrisoned Fort Lancaster in the early summer of 1861. The contingent's stay was brief, as Captain William C. Adams and C Company relieved the soldiers July 29.[11]

One hundred seventy-nine miles up the trace to the east, the W. P. Lane Rangers (Company F, Second Texas Mounted Rifles) settled in at Fort Clark by late September. Between these points, Camp Hudson continued to harbor only rattlers and scorpions until orders divided Lane's force October 28 and sent detachments to the Devils country. Within days, twenty-five men occupied Hudson, while another seventy-five Rangers pressed on for Fort Lancaster.[12]

Developments that fall suggested the importance of all three posts in protecting against a potential Yankee invasion from the West. Confederate forces under Lieutenant Colonel John Robert Baylor had seized the Mesilla Valley in southern

New Mexico July 27,[13] but now 2,500 Union soldiers reportedly threatened his tenuous hold. Most alarming, reported Baylor, 2,000 Californians may have been poised to join the Federals, and unless he received reinforcements to stave off the menace, the Lower Road could provide Union passage all the way into the Texas heartland.[14]

Although Baylor's fears did not come to pass, the cloud of possible invasion would shroud the road again before war's end. But even while most Rebel strategists focused on the trace from a defensive posture in 1861, Henry H. Sibley saw in the road a conduit for attacking the far West.

Born in Louisiana in 1816, Sibley graduated from West Point in 1838 and eventually served as a US Army officer in New Mexico Territory. Upon resigning from the Army May 31, 1861, he drew upon his familiarity with New Mexico in persuading Confederate President Jefferson Davis to sanction his plan to seize the West for the Confederacy. Gaining a commission as a brigadier general, Sibley hurried to San Antonio and organized Sibley's Brigade, a 3,200-man force consisting of the Fourth, Fifth, and Seventh Regiments of the Texas Cavalry.[15]

From the start, the bold campaign faced enormous challenges. R. H. Williams, a Frontier Ranger captain during the war, later observed:

"It was a foolhardy scheme to send the flower of our Texan youth on a march like this of 800 miles, into a country where they had no base of operations and could get no reinforcements, and no help, unless they met with complete success."[16]

Nevertheless, in late October Sibley's force began marching west along the Lower Road in carefully planned stages dictated by the demands of nature. The Fourth Regiment set out October 26, the Fifth Regiment November 2, and the Seventh Regiment November 20.[17] Even a single division, however, would have overtaxed meager water sources and scant forage, leading the Fourth Regiment to split into two units at San Felipe Springs.[18]

Diarist John E. Hart reached First Crossing with a contingent November 6 and halted at California Springs the next evening. On the approach to the water hole, provision wagoners had sighted Indians, and that night hostiles stole into camp and tried to stampede the cattle. Officers quickly posted an extra guard, deterring any subsequent attempt.

While Hart's group marched to a point three miles upstream of Hudson November 8,[19] Second Lieutenant Julius Giesecke and the trailing half of the Fourth Texas Cavalry splashed across First Crossing. By the eleventh, the companies had rendezvoused at Beaver Lake, from which they moved out in stages for Howard's Spring.[20]

General Sibley himself departed San Antonio November 18[21] and overtook the Fifth column between First Crossing and Painted Cave on the twenty-third.

Artifacts found near California Well or Springs in 2009.
Photograph courtesy of Patrick Dearen.

For the next several days, the division forged steadily up-trail, then proceeded west from Beaver Lake.[22] Soon, the Seventh Texas Cavalry followed suit, but lagging units of Sibley's Brigade coursed along the Devils through mid-January.[23]

While Sibley's command marched toward its destiny in New Mexico, Texas forces guarded the Devils from a base at Camp Hudson. By the January 17, 1862 publication of the weekly *Camp Hudson Times,* the post was home to the W. P. Lane Rangers and sported a saloon, farrier operation, butcher shop, and drug store. With the Rangers' term of service set to expire in April, the newspaper made a patriotic plea for reenlistment.

"Lincoln's myriads of hireling soldiers are now invading the South from every quarter," said the periodical, "and it behooves every true and loyal Son of the Sunny South to march to the battle field, and if it be necessary, to yield up his life on the altar of our common Country."[24]

When commissary stores ran low in the second week of February, two men pushed out from Hudson to secure provisions from Fort Clark. Meanwhile, the garrison subsisted on half-rations and turned to the land. "Our main dependence is on the crack of the Rifle and its result," Ranger W. W. Heartsill noted in his journal on February 14. Not until March 6 did a commissary train finally arrive.[25]

A few days later, Hudson's troops embraced encouraging developments in the New Mexico war front. On the tenth, an eastbound wagon train passed with Yankee prisoners captured the previous summer by Lieutenant Colonel John Baylor in the Battle of Mesilla. Three days later, the Santa Fe mail rolled in with news that Sibley had routed federal forces from Fort Craig February 21 in south-central New Mexico.[26]

Nevertheless, Sibley's Brigade was on a foredoomed mission. Forging on up the Rio Grande, the troops took Albuquerque and Santa Fe, only to lose their supply train to the First Colorado Volunteers in the March 28 Battle of Glorieta. General Sibley had no alternative but to abandon his goal of western conquest and eventually fall back to Texas.[27]

In the meantime, the majority of the W. P. Lane Rangers at Camp Hudson vowed March 20 to reenlist. Although six days later diarist Heartsill noted that "all the talk in Camp is about home, and how long the days appear to be," the pledged Rangers did not waver upon marching into San Antonio April 11. On the nineteenth, the soldiers signed up to remain in the service of the South for the duration of the war.[28]

By early July, Sibley's Fourth Regiment reached the Devils in its retreat toward the Texas settlements. Julius Giesecke and his confederates camped at Beaver Lake on the fifth and sixth before proceeding downriver and nooning at Hudson July 8. A day later, General Sibley overtook the column between the post and First Crossing, while in his wake trudged unit after unit, strung out for hundreds of miles through the Devils country and Trans-Pecos. By late August, the last of his brigade finally straggled into San Antonio, culminating a ten-month campaign of dreams and failure.[29]

With Confederate troops abandoning their gains in New Mexico, federals quickly filled the void and pushed into El Paso, where they occupied Fort Bliss in August and effectively ended the San Antonio–El Paso stage line.[30] But even as the Texas interior increasingly feared invasion, unionists pondered rumors of another Confederate campaign in the West. By November, a confrontation between opposing forces supposedly loomed at Horsehead Crossing on the Upper Road,[31] and the following month Brigadier General James H. Carleton, commander of the US Army's Department of New Mexico, dispatched troops to Horsehead to quell a reported military operation against El Paso by 6,000 Confederates.[32] No clash resulted, but tensions on both sides remained high.

Indian offenses in 1863 served as a reminder that not all threats wore blue or gray. When Lipan raiders absconded from the Nueces River with two captive women and their infants, L. D. Lafferty and a small party of soldiers pursued. At an unspecified Devils River crossing, the riders overtook the Lipans. After a fierce fight in which Lafferty and another soldier suffered wounds, the Indians escaped with their captives.[33]

At another point in the year, Indians may have claimed the lives of Tom Black and a person named Jones on the Lower Road three miles from Beaver Lake.[34] To the east, meanwhile, troops engaged Indians at or near Fort Clark on August 10.[35]

With Comanches increasingly terrorizing the settlements in early 1864, Texas forces purportedly prepared to campaign against the tribe in the Devils country.[36] Officers delayed the plan, however, when a scouting party returned from the west with news that two companies of California federals were bearing down on Fort Lancaster, and perhaps had already seized it. Frontier Rangers responded immediately, marching to Lancaster to find the report without merit.

Returning to Piedra Pinta, a creek east of the Devils, the Rangers again readied to scout the Devils for Indians. Proceeding to the river and camping successively at Painted Cave, Yellow Banks, and Pecan Springs, the riders found abundant fresh Indian signs. They trailed the war party on beyond the Pecos, where by night they took fire from 150 Comanches. Fortunately the Rangers avoided casualties, but the confrontation forced them to retreat eastward.

By January 22, Confederate regulars went on alert after a detachment from Eagle Pass gathered intelligence that suggested an imminent Yankee advance from El Paso. Colonel John S. Ford, skeptical but cautious, instructed the commanding officer at Eagle Pass to scout as far as the Devils. Additionally, Ford garrisoned Fort Clark with at least one company, a stop-gap measure with almost no chance of succeeding against an enemy force of size.[37]

As the threat of invasion via the Lower Road continued to concern Confederate authorities, Ford submitted a plan on February 8 to fortify "the pass of Devil's River." In light of the dry stretch of more than forty miles between Howard's Spring and Beaver Lake, Ford recommended engaging an advancing enemy from behind a fortification blocking a pass leading to the lake. A successful defense would cut the invaders off from water and turn them away.

Should the Confederates be unable to hold their position, continued Ford, they could fall back to a bulwark of stone and timber erected across the steep-walled

Pecan Spring or Springs in 1869.
Journal of Lieutenant Colonel Thomas B. Hunt, National Archives.

Devils canyon at Pecan Springs. Although the defenders would be subject to pursuit during the miles of retreat, an enemy exhausted by a long, dry march would be unlikely to chase them down before they reached this lower fortification.

To protect the proposed works, Ford recommended not less than 600 men and four pieces of artillery. Even a force of that size, he added, would be inadequate "if assailed with energy and activity."

With the possibility that invading troops might avoid the Devils route and attempt to penetrate the interior of Texas via Horsehead Crossing and the Upper Road, Ford also suggested stationing a small party of scouts on the Concho River.[38]

Although in mid-winter Union General H. W. Halleck had encouraged James H. Carleton to send New Mexico troops to sever trade and communication between Texas and the Territory,[39] no invading Federals would ever test the mid-stretches of the Lower Road.[40] For the Texas heartland, it was fortuitous, as Confederate authorities never acted on Ford's blueprint to fortify the Devils pass. Fifteen months after he presented his plan, the Battle of Palmito Ranch near Brownsville marked war's end,[41] ushering in dark economic days that again would lure travelers to a river more hazardous than ever.

CHAPTER 10

THE DEVILS INDIAN WAR

Struggling under the constraints of Reconstruction in early 1866, a half-dozen Cross Timbers cattlemen considered pasturing their herds in Mexico. About February, Charles Goodnight, C. C. Slaughter, Kit Carter, Richard Joel, Albert Lane, and George Lemley set out from Palo Pinto on an exploratory trip and bore southwest. As the days wore on, Goodnight and Lane decided to seek a market for their cattle and turned back.

Soon afterward, the remaining riders reached the Devils and broke trail single-file through tangled brush. When a low-hanging limb caught Lemley's firearm, the weapon discharged and a ball exploded through Slaughter's shoulder and lodged against his breastbone. He fell, gravely wounded, and all that his companions could do was pull a silk handkerchief through the wound and hope for the best.

One or more men tended Slaughter for nearly a month in a Devils camp before he improved enough to be transported by litter to the nearest settlement. Although Slaughter eventually made it back to Palo Pinto, his wound confined him to his home for almost a year.[1]

In the meantime, on April 24 Bethel Coopwood initiated mail service through the Devils country for the first time since 1862. His coaches rolled between San Antonio and El Paso until mid-November, when the firm of Sawyer, Risher, and Hall assumed operation.[2]

It was a perilous season on the Lower Road, for the Devils region had been without a permanent military presence throughout the latter part of the war and for a year and a half thereafter. Finally on December 12, Captain John A. Wilcox and Company C, Fourth U.S. Cavalry, reoccupied Fort Clark. Within two weeks, a report of hostiles east of the Devils pressed the troops into action. Marching to Mud Creek on the night of December 23, Wilcox and forty men attacked the band and captured twelve horses and two mules.[3]

It is unclear which tribe was involved in the Mud Creek engagement, but the Civil War years had changed the dynamics of the Indian situation in the Devils area. During the conflict, Kickapoos from Kansas and Indian Territory had migrated to northern Mexico and joined other Kickapoo bands previously forced out of Texas. Henceforth, most raids in the Devils country bore the mark of two displaced American tribes, Kickapoos and Lipans, operating out of Coahuila.[4]

Hostiles pushed back hard against a resurgence of travelers in the region in 1867. In late winter or early spring, E. C. Powell and other members of a San Antonio-bound caravan negotiated the stretch from Fort Stockton to Camp Hudson under constant surveillance by Indians.[5] During the same period, warriors stormed the camp of a ten-man mail party on Live Oak Creek near Fort Lancaster. The expressmen, forced to desperate measures, abandoned their flaming stage and retreated on foot toward the Devils. Near Hudson, they met the westbound mail and related their misfortune, then continued their exhausting tramp toward Fort Clark.[6]

On March 9, Second Lieutenant A. Irwin and fourteen enlisted men spurred their mounts away from Clark in pursuit of perpetrators of recent depredations near the post. Overtaking their quarry on the Devils, the soldiers routed the Indians and captured thirty-four horses and mules.

About the same time, a fifty-man contingent under Clark commander John A. Wilcox attacked multiple Indian camps on the Pecos after a chase that began near the Devils on the ninth. In a four-hour fight, the men of Fourth Cavalry dropped twenty to thirty hostiles while suffering minimal casualties of their own—one dead, one missing, and two wounded. Still, Captain Wilcox had no choice but to fall back in face of an overwhelming force reportedly totaling 1,500 Comanches, Apaches, and Kickapoos.[7]

Despite the aggressive approach of Irwin and Wilcox in addressing the Indian problem, civilian authorities quickly realized that the US Army had not deployed the necessary forces to protect the entire Texas frontier.

"The Indians have taken advantage of the absence of the troops from Fort Inge and Fort Clark [while] . . . on scout to the Devil's River and Pecos River," Medina County Judge H. I. Richards wrote Governor J. W. Throckmorton on March 19.

Indeed, three war parties of twenty or more warriors each had crossed the Rio Grande into Texas.

"[They] are at present ravaging . . . [these] parts right down to Bexar County and round the city of San Antonio," Richards lamented, adding that Medina County residents had just buried "one of the victims sacrificed by the . . . negli-

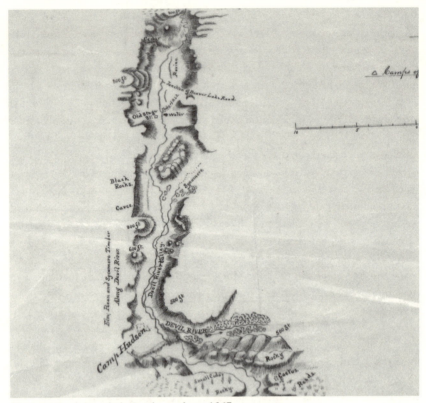

The Lower Road through the Devils corridor in 1867.
Topographical sketch, Brevet Lieutenant Colonel E. J. Strang, National Archives.

gent policy of the U.S. Government."[8]

Only additional soldiers across the region could perhaps deter such incursions. On May 28, Brevet Major William Bayard and companies C and I, Ninth Cavalry, reoccupied Camp Hudson, and fifteen days later, Captain John M. Bacon arrived with a replacement garrison, the Ninth Cavalry's D and G companies.[9] Two hundred sixty miles west on July 1, more troops from the same division revived another Lower Road post, Fort Davis.[10]

On into year's end, the Army's fighting men had ample reason to keep their powder dry. On September 20, a detachment of the Fourth Cavalry's C Company from Fort Clark skirmished Indians near the Devils.[11] Soon afterward, Ben Ficklin took over the mail line, only to meet with a bloody start. Despite a four-man Hudson escort beyond Second Crossing, the first westbound express fell prey to 100 or more Indians at Howard's Spring October 11. Corporal Samuel Wright and Private Eldridge Jones lost their lives, while privates Wardlow Irvin and Albert Johnson sustained serious wounds.[12]

During the same month, 200 Comanches captured George Sharp of the Ninth Cavalry's Company K as he herded US Army stock near the ruins of Fort Lancaster. Before escaping, Sharp would endure a three-year ordeal that would carry him as far afield as Arizona.[13]

A December 26 battle at Lancaster underscored the heightened threat that clouded the region. As the Ninth Cavalry's K Company camped at the ruins, 200 Indians, Mexicans, and white renegades swooped down and stampeded the remuda. Sixty attackers swept through the surprised soldiers, who fought back only to find hundreds of enemy reinforcements lining the surrounding hills and blocking a nearby canyon.

Fortunately for the soldiers, the hostiles were content to withdraw after capturing thirty-two horses and six mules. Company commander William Frohock soon learned that three of his men were missing and presumed dead, while estimates of enemy losses ranged between two and twenty.[14]

As rifle fire echoed in 1867 in a widespread fight for supremacy, nature served notice that it alone was sovereign. In summer, a flood buried the vital well at Howard's Spring under fifteen feet of silt, creating an eighty-six mile march through a waterless hell between the Devils' head and Live Oak Creek.

In November, Lieutenant Francis Dodge and forty-two men from Hudson's D Company, Ninth Cavalry, established a Beaver Lake camp to support detachments charged with re-opening Howard's and digging additional wells on Johnsons Run.[15] The troops also were in a position to deter hostiles, a strategy that led Hudson's commander to post a corporal and seven men of Company G at First Crossing on January 16, 1868.[16] With the Second Crossing post still garrisoned, the US Army now held three vital points along the river.

Nevertheless, this ever-fluid Indian war could modify needs quickly. On February 25, the Department of Texas ordered Company G to Fort Clark and Company D to Fort Stockton, thereby closing Hudson and its two outposts. Transportation issues delayed the evacuation until the second week of April,[17] but as the spring sun swelled into a searing summer orb, the river was no less at the mercy of warrior bands.

The actions of one such party spurred the Ninth Cavalry's M Company into action at Fort Clark on the night of August 3. After an informant related that the Indians were riding for a Rio Grande ford at the mouth of the Devils, two officers and thirty-six men set out in pursuit. Striking the Rio Grande six miles below present Del Rio, the troops searched the region but found no trace of the hostiles.[18]

Meanwhile, wagoners bore westward along a Lower Road haunted by warriors. Purportedly, Isaac Parker Metcalf and B Company of the Second Texas

Rangers rode upon a grisly scene four or five miles from the Devils' head in August or September. If one accepts Metcalf's questionable recollections, the bodies of thirty-six emigrants told a horrific story of massacre approximately four days earlier. Headed for California, the wagoners had passed through Jacksboro and Fort Worth before falling into the ruts of the Lower Road and coming under siege.

The task of burying the mutilated bodies fell to Company B.

"One man would hold a shovel of burning tar so we could breathe the smoke and stand it—the stench was awfully bad," Metcalf remembered. "The pregnant women had been cut open and their babies removed and then left lying upon their breasts. The men had their privates cut off."

The Rangers tracked the Indians far out upon the lower South Plains before losing the trail.[19]

Too late to help the emigrants, the Ninth Cavalry again occupied the camp at Beaver Lake late in the year.[20] The garrison's stay was temporary, however, and dangers persisted as the Lower Road lured cattle droves and freighters to the Devils country in 1869. Henry Taylor of the Sabinal River valley made it through safely with a California-bound herd,[21] but a six-wagon caravan belonging to the San Antonio firm of Adams and Wickes was not as fortunate.

On the afternoon of May 26, 150 Indians surprised the wagoners between the Devils and Johnsons Run. The freighters put up fierce resistance and dropped a pair of warriors, but the onslaught was too great. The band captured all seventy-seven of their mules before withdrawing, leaving the men to commit a Mexican teamster to a shallow grave.[22]

Twelve days after the attack, detachments of companies G, L, and M, Ninth Cavalry, battled Indians along Johnsons Run and on the Pecos.[23] Hostiles remained unchecked, however, and another Adams and Wickes train took fire June 20 near Howard's Well, as the spring was now better known. One teamster died before the war party vanished in the dust of 150 stampeding mules.[24]

Indians evidently struck with impunity along both sides of the border in 1869, for sometime that year Mexican national troops conducted a retaliatory raid into Texas. Crossing the Pecos "opposite Hudson" (presumably across the divide from the post), the troops killed an unspecified number of Indians and captured stock before retreating into Mexico.[25]

When Brevet Lieutenant Colonel Thomas B. Hunt passed through the Devils country in late November with the eastbound Fifteenth Infantry Regiment, he found the mail stations abandoned and Camp Hudson in ruins. Forty-nine miles beyond the old post, however, the houses and fields of San Felipe del Rio greeted him as he neared San Felipe Springs,[26] an indication that the frontier was gradually creeping toward the Devils.

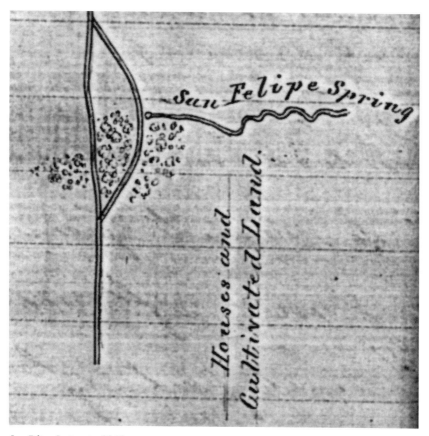

San Felipe Springs in 1869.
Journal of Lieutenant Colonel Thomas B. Hunt, National Archives.

The next month, August Santleben initiated freight service from the port of Indianola to Chihuahua City and points between. The Devils section played no small role in his eleven-year, 50,000-mile odyssey through "a wild and uninhabited country, over routes that were continually beset by savage Indians . . . and by equally lawless men."[27] Indeed, as Santleben's wagons coursed the Lower Road near Beaver Lake in 1870, a war party descended and set sights on his spare mules. By roping the lead bell mare, the Indians induced the entire herd to follow as they made their getaway.[28]

A bell mare again proved the focal point that year when approximately 135 hostiles assailed an Adams and Wickes caravan in the charge of a man named Gruington (or Brewington) at Santa Nina Waterhole, situated along the Lower Road between Beaver Lake and Johnsons Run. During the first wave, the band's captain

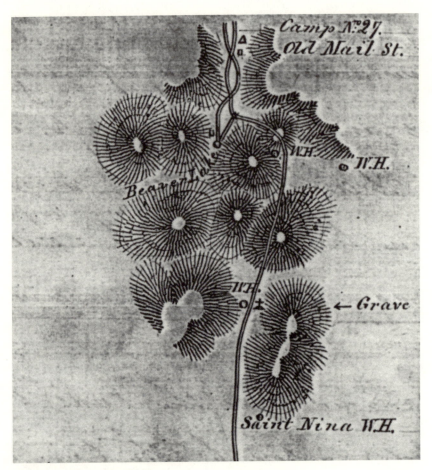
Beaver Lake and vicinity in 1869.
Journal of Lieutenant Colonel Thomas B. Hunt, National Archives.

shouted instructions in Spanish to capture the mare, an act that would facilitate the theft of the mules. Through the fog of battle, he finally realized that the mare was staked and ordered it killed.

Still, the animal stood, holding the mule herd in place, until the leader dashed in and slashed the bell strap. Jingling the bell and gigging his horse, he led the mules away through a fusillade of bullets. Only when sagebrush seized the raider's braids did Gruington realize that this freckled chief was actually a white man with red hair.[29]

With the Devils country providing a conduit to and from safe haven in Mexico for marauders, the US Army and Texas Rangers scouted the river repeatedly in 1870. In January, twenty federal mounted troops rendezvoused with an Army major in the Beaver Lake vicinity and proceeded to search for hostiles.[30] Between January 3 and February 6, detachments of the Ninth Cavalry and Twenty-fourth Infantry engaged Indians during scouts along the Rio Grande and Pecos.[31] With the approach of summer, Fort McKavett commander William Rufus Shafter considered the troublesome Devils and Pecos and planned his own campaign.

"Indians have always been found there and are there now without doubt," observed the thirty-four-year-old Michigan native June 27.[32]

On August 12, while Lieutenant Colonel Shafter solicited troops and supplies, Captain Charles B. Gaskill and a Twenty-Fifth Infantry detachment pushed out from Fort Clark to patrol the Nueces River area. The next day, Gaskill's command fell into the fresh trail of a war party and commenced pursuit.

Following the meandering trace 155 miles, the infantrymen crossed an upper Devils drainage on the seventeenth and faced a sixty-mile stretch of arid country extending north. Their water dwindling, the soldiers had no alternative but to abandon the chase and retreat to Beaver Lake. On August 25, Fort Clark's streaming flag welcomed them back, culminating a 315-mile quest for elusive wisps that had faded into the land.[33]

Three days earlier, Lieutenant Colonel Shafter had embarked from Fort McKavett with 120 men and four officers from the Ninth Cavalry's F and M companies. Corpulent yet vigorous, Shafter utilized Beaver Lake as a staging ground for an extended scout to the Pecos country, where he found only months-old Indian trails and abandoned camps. His five-week expedition ended with his return to McKavett September 26.[34]

Autumn brought a series of additional scouts for raider ghosts in the Devils' den. After Indians kidnapped Clint and Jeff Smith from Cibola Creek, Texas Ranger Captain John Sansom dispatched a state force from Fort Clark to Red's Water Hole—an otherwise unidentified point on the Devils—in a vain attempt to recover the boys.[35] At Fort McKavett on December 4, Shafter ordered two officers and twenty-five men to the wellsprings of the Devils and Llano in a fruitless attempt to intercept a large party of supposed Comanches; on the first of December, the band had killed a man twenty miles below the post.[36]

Eighty miles to the south-southwest on December 5, fifty or so Indians approached within two miles of Fort Clark and prompted Major Zenas R. Bliss to order pursuit. Despite the Twenty-Fifth Infantry's best efforts, the marauders escaped into Mexico by way of a Rio Grande ford near the Devils' mouth.[37] In yet another scout, Texas Rangers combed the Devils mountains for days before returning to Fort Inge in Uvalde County in early December.[38]

Although the US Army and Texas Rangers failed repeatedly to engage hostiles directly, their efforts disrupted the free movement of warrior tribes back and forth from Mexico. Forced to constant vigilance, the hostiles could only rely on stealth, guile, and chance to avoid patrols. Still, military authorities clearly were frustrated, denied as they were the right to pursue raiders into sovereign Mexico territory.

"The tribes protected by the Mexicans have a secure base of operation of two hundred and fifty miles long," Ranger Captain H. J. Richarz reported from Fort Inge on December 9, a day after learning that Indians had killed his son and another Ranger. ". . . If it was not for this cursed international law, I know very well what to do to clean out these bloody savages on the other side of the Rio Grande."[39]

In the winter of 1871, the troubling situation led the US Army to station troops on the Devils again. On January 28, a lieutenant, ten men of E Company, Ninth Cavalry, and fifteen men of I Company, Twenty-Fourth Infantry, struck out from Fort Clark with thirty days' rations to guard First Crossing.[40] The picket held the site on into spring, a season in which the Department of Texas ordered reinforcements to the region.

On May 1, Company I, Twenty-Fourth Infantry, left Clark for Howard's Well, where the soldiers were to alter the channel of Howard Draw to protect the spring from flood. Additionally, they had orders to improve the Lower Road where it ascended and descended three hills between Howard's Well and Beaver Lake. On their return journey to Clark, the company commander was to instruct the First Crossing picket to repair the road at the ford and between Dead Man's Pass and Camp Hudson, once more a site of importance.[41]

On April 28, the Department of Texas had designated Hudson a permanent Clark sub-post for the purpose of guarding the road, conducting regular scouts as far afield as Howard's Well, and keeping the trail between Howard's and Clark in good repair. Taking steps to fulfill the order twenty days later, Captain Samuel Pettie rode out of Clark with an officer and thirty-eight men of Company F, Twenty-Fifth Infantry, and twenty-one men of Company C, Ninth Cavalry. Reaching Hudson's ruins with thirty days' supplies May 23, they set about reviving the post, a development that rendered a guard at First Crossing no longer necessary. The picket abandoned its position and arrived back at Fort Clark May 28.[42]

In another sign of resolve that month in face of increasing hostilities, the Army garrisoned Fort Lancaster as a permanent sub-post of Fort Stockton.[43]

Patrolling a land so rugged as the Devils was demanding, prompting frequent redeployments at Hudson, which Clark's post return for June referred to as a fort rather than a camp.[44] On July 18, Captain A. E. Hooker and fifteen men of E Company, Ninth Cavalry, along with an officer and forty-nine men from C Company, Twenty-Fifth Infantry, relieved the Hudson garrison.[45] Replacing C Company on September 9 was the Twenty-Fifth Infantry's F Company, which spent the rest of September repairing the road and the post's public quarters.[46] Company H of the same regiment arrived at Hudson October 6 and relieved F Company the following day.[47] On November 13, First Lieutenant Andrew Geddes and Company A, Twenty-Fifth Infantry, as well as four men from E Company, Ninth Cavalry, supplanted the Hudson garrison and assumed the task of constructing additional quarters.[48]

Ninety-eight miles northwest at the region's western sentinel, the January 7, 1872 withdrawal of two officers and a surgeon reduced Fort Lancaster to a mere eight men.[49] Hudson's troop strength held steady that month, however, with Captain D. D. Van Valzah commanding the Twenty-Fifth Infantry's D Company and two Ninth Cavalry privates who served as messengers.[50] Nevertheless, Hudson's days were numbered.

On February 7, the Department of Texas ordered the camp abandoned after less than nine months as a Fort Clark sub-post. Complying, Van Valzah and D Company headed out for Clark February 21,[51] once more leaving the Devils country at the mercy of a hostile faction who soon would commit an outrage indicative of a people emboldened. ✦

CHAPTER 11

BLACK SEMINOLES TO THE RESCUE

As freighter Anastacio Gonzales and his caravan camped at Howard's Well April 20, 1872, approximately 140 Kiowas and Comanches (and perhaps renegade Mexicans) laid siege under the leadership of Kiowa chiefs White Horse and Big Bow.

In a brutal display of violence, the band massacred at least nine caravan members, including a woman and her one-year-old grandchild. Only the chance arrival of Lieutenant Colonel Wesley Merritt and Ninth Cavalry troops bound for Clark saved the child's mother from captivity and two more teamsters from terrible death—warriors had lashed the men to wagon wheels and set the vehicles afire.

On into dusk, Captain Michael Cooney and companies A and H chased the perpetrators in an attempt to wreak vengeance and recover government stores seized from the train. Nine to ten miles from Howard's Well, the cavalrymen overtook the band, only to face withering fire that mortally wounded Lieutenant F. R. Vincent. Outnumbered and short on rounds, the soldiers had no recourse but to fall back and allow the war party to escape.[1]

In light of such an atrocity, military strategists could only persevere and hope for the best. With Major Zenas R. Bliss and companies F and I, Twenty-Fifth Infantry, set to march from Clark to Fort Stockton with thirty-three wagons in May, Merritt had already ordered Captain Lewis Johnson of the Twenty-Fourth Infantry to secure 9,000 pounds of forage from Clark and make advance drops along the route. Johnson was to deposit one-third of the grain at First Crossing and the remainder at Camp Hudson. To protect these supply depots, Merritt also had instructed Johnson to post guards with thirty days' rations.[2]

Undaunted by the recent violence at Howard's Well, Bliss and his command wagoned past First Crossing and reached Hudson in early May. The major had supervised part of the post's original construction and took note of its deterioration, despite Hudson's months as a Clark sub-post.

"The adobe buildings were nearly all down, but the pizet [lime-gravel] buildings still had the walls standing," he recalled. "The shingles and wood work generally had been burned or carried off by passing trains."

Bliss and the two Twenty-Fifth Infantry companies proceeded past desecrated Howard's Well and reached Fort Stockton without incident May 20.[3] Reflecting on the gauntlet between the Devils' head and Fort Lancaster decades later, Bliss grimly observed that it had "been the scene of more Indian fights and massacres than any other part of the road, of the same length."[4]

On into summer, the Devils continued to be a hotbed of Indian activity. At Fort Concho, ninety-five miles northeast of the river's head, Major John P. Hatch received information that a large horde of Indians with "several thousand head of horses" was at Beaver Lake. Hatch considered the July 19 report credible in light of the fact that the most recent animals stolen from the Concho area had cut a trail toward the Devils.[5]

After Indians struck the Fort Clark region repeatedly in August, furious citizens threatened to take it upon themselves to raid the Kickapoo village in Mexico and torch the establishments of Coahuilan merchants who protected the tribe.[6] The Army, as well, was growing increasingly frustrated with an enemy who gained harbor in a country off-limits to US forces, as a mid-autumn scout illustrated.

Captain Michael Cooney, who had led the charge against the band responsible for the Howard's Well massacre, rode north from Fort Clark November 17 with a first lieutenant, a guide, and thirty men of Company A, Ninth Cavalry. From the west fork of the Nueces, the cavalrymen bore toward the Devils through gulch-riddled mountains that challenged both men and animals. Reaching the Devils' canyon November 21, the patrol struggled along the rim for several hours before managing a descent and discovering a recently deserted Indian camp.

Marching downriver, Company A sighted four Indians approaching with eight horses or mules. Soldiers quickly spurred their mounts forward, forcing the hostiles to abandon the animals and race away into a falling night.

Unable to ascend the ridge in darkness, Cooney and his command camped on the river and negotiated the west bluff the next morning. Searching out the Indians' trail, the men pushed their jaded animals down the trace and struck the Lower Road about two miles south of California Springs. Here Cooney met a Lieutenant Valois, who also was scouting out of Fort Clark. By now, Cooney's horses were sorely in need of rest, forcing the captain to make camp while Valois and his command pressed on down the raiders' trail.

Artifacts on a Camp Hudson ruin in 2009.
Photograph courtesy of Patrick Dearen.

When darkness overtook Valois, he too stopped for the night, but his men resumed the chase at daybreak and tracked the Indians to the Rio Grande. The banks on either side told the story of a band that had crossed and made camp just inside Mexico a mere day before. Valois had no choice but to stare in chagrin into a land forbidden and ride back to inform Cooney.

By the time the latter officer returned to Fort Clark November 27, his command had made a profitless march of approximately 250 miles through a land intimidating in nature.

"My animals suffered greatly from the roughness of the country and want of grass," Cooney reported on November 28. "The men also suffered and were forced to lead and pull the horses over at least half the distance travelled." Still, he added, the men in his charge had never complained and "would feel compensated for all if they could only get a brush with the Indians."[7]

During the second week in April of 1873, a triumvirate of military leaders met at Fort Clark to consider methods of not only achieving that ambition, but ending raids out of Mexico once and for all. Fourth Cavalry commander Ranald S. Mackenzie, a thirty-two-year-old New York native who recently had taken station at Clark, gained a secret directive from Secretary of War William W. Belknap and Lieutenant General Philip H. Sheridan, the Army's chief strategist in the Indian Wars.

"I want something done to stop these conditions of banditry, killing, etc., etc., by these people across the [Rio Grande] river," Sheridan told Mackenzie, who had commanded troops in several Civil War battles. "I want you to *control* and *hold down* the situation, and to *do it in your own way*. . . . Let it be a campaign of *annihilation, obliteration* and *complete destruction*."

Astounded by the implications, Mackenzie pressed Sheridan. "Under whose orders and upon what authority am I to act?"

"Damn the *orders!*" roared Sheridan, pounding the table. "Damn the *authority*. You are to go ahead on your own plan of action, and your authority and backing shall be Gen. [President Ulysses S.] Grant and myself."[8]

Taking Sheridan at his word, Colonel Mackenzie proceeded to plan a US Army raid on Kickapoo and Lipan strongholds in northern Mexico. Vital to his invasion would be the Black Seminole Scouts (or Seminole Indian Negro Scouts) under the command of Lieutenant John L. Bullis.

The Black Seminole Indians gained identity as a people in the seventeenth century, when runaway slaves found sanctuary with the Seminole Indians in Florida. Although tribal members considered the negroes their bond servants, they allowed them to live in adjacent communities under self-rule, subject only to a yearly tribute. The Seminole Wars of the early nineteenth century, however, led to ill will between the two groups and their eventual joint relocation to Indian Territory.

When the Seminoles accepted Creek Indian rule in 1845, the Black Seminoles found their autonomy threatened. Four years later, many of the negroes fled to Coahuila, Mexico, where they battled hostile Indians and familiarized themselves with the land. In 1870, the US Army convinced eleven Black Seminoles to serve as scouts and Indian fighters out of Fort Duncan in exchange for government support of their clan. Additional Black Seminoles joined the unit the following year,[9] and on August 7, 1872, seventeen of the scouts transferred to Fort Clark, a

Ranald S. Mackenzie.
N. S. Haley Memorial Library, Midland, Texas.

development that induced another five Black Seminoles to enlist at Clark that very month.[10]

The squadron quickly earned high praise. "These negroes had all the habits of the Indians," recalled Zenas R. Bliss, who served at both Duncan and Clark. "They were excellent hunters and trailers, and splendid fighters."[11]

At Fort Clark on March 6, 1873, Lieutenant John L. Bullis assumed command of the Black Seminole Scouts, a fighting force that would distinguish itself in twenty-six expeditions during the next eight years. Born in New York in 1841, Bullis joined the One Hundred Twenty-Sixth New York Volunteer Infantry in 1862 and honed his combat skills in the Civil War. After a period as a civilian, he accepted an appointment as a second lieutenant in the US Army in 1867.

A small, wiry man with face burned red by the sun, Bullis had a pit bull mentality that belied his size. No matter the odds, he displayed fierce aggression and unwavering determination, a combination that inspired the scouts in his command to actions worthy of the nation's highest military honor.[12]

On April 11, 1873, the very day that Secretary of War Belknap and General Sheridan arrived at Fort Clark,[13] a half-dozen Mexicans and Kickapoos stole thirty-six horses from Delorus Ranche about eight miles below the post. When

Black Seminole Scouts. Whitehead Memorial Museum, Del Rio, Texas.

Lieutenant Colonel Wesley Merritt learned of the raid two days later, he immediately sent fifteen Black Seminole Scouts in pursuit. Picking up the trail within four miles of Clark, the scouts tracked the band to the Devils, across to California Springs, and west to a Rio Grande ford that had provided the raiders passage into Mexico.[14] Once again, raiders had vanished with their spoils into a sanctuary nation.

General Sheridan did not learn of the incident until he had returned to Chicago, but the matter clearly infuriated him.

"There is in my opinion only one way left to settle the Mexican Frontier difficulty," he wrote on May 20, "that is, to cross the Rio Grande and recover our property, and punish the thieves."[15]

Two days before Sheridan penned those explicit words, Mackenzie took the first step toward fulfilling this mission that heretofore the general had only implied in secret conversation. With six Fourth Cavalry companies and Bullis' Black Seminoles, Mackenzie stormed Lipan and Kickapoo camps near Remolina, Coahuila, situated forty-nine miles south of the Devils' mouth. Catching the Indians off-guard in this raid that violated international treaty, the troops killed nineteen warriors and took Lipan chief Costilitos and forty women and children captive. Additionally, Mackenzie recovered fifty-six to sixty-five stolen horses.[16]

On May 25, the Texas Legislature passed a resolution recognizing Mackenzie and his command for their "*prompt action and gallant conduct in inflicting well merited punishment upon these scourges of our frontier.*"[17] Mackenzie, however, was not content to rest on his laurels. Four days later, he already was considering a second strike in a matter of weeks, provided he could secure fresh horses for his troops.[18]

General Sheridan, meanwhile, was so encouraged by Mackenzie's Remolina success that he no longer anticipated additional raids by the Indians. "In fact," he wrote on June 13, "I consider the Mexican border troubles as drawing to a close."[19]

It was wishful thinking on Sheridan's part, but raids out of Mexico did diminish for a while, even as Mackenzie held back on his plans for another invasion of Coahuila. Still, Department of Texas commander C. C. Augur seemed to prepare superiors for additional blitzes by US forces.

"It is very discouraging, and very disheartening to troops when on a trail and in hot pursuit of depredating Indians and Mexicans, to see them escape by crossing the Rio Grande and there turn and laugh at their pursuers," he wrote in his annual report on September 30. "This not unfrequently occurs."[20]

The cumulative loss of Texas property to Indians from south of the Rio Grande for 1872-1873 was a staggering $721,492. In reporting that figure to the Department of State, Secretary of State Hamilton Fish charged several warrior societies with prosecuting a "harassing predatory war" and condemned the Kickapoos and Lipans as perpetrators of the greatest atrocities.

"Their bold raids . . . have two main objects, the stealing of horses and the kidnapping of children," he stated. "Murder is an invariable accompaniment."

Particularly troubling, he added, was the fact that these tribes lived "under the protection of Mexican authorities, carrying on a trade with a circle of degraded merchants who are their accomplices. . . . The grave responsibility of the Mexican government cannot be overlooked. . . ."[21]

In the fall of 1873 and on into 1874, US and Texas forces continued to focus resources on the Devils and adjacent territories. First Lieutenant Gregory Barrett and a Fort McKavett detachment patrolled the river in late October 1873, but found no recent evidence of hostiles.[22] Four months later on February 16, 1874, the Department of Texas instructed Fort Clark to conduct another scout through the Devils country and on to the Pecos.[23]

Nevertheless, in March a large war party bloodied Howard's Well yet again. Two Colorado-bound men died and a third was wounded, and even the half-dozen who escaped harm were in dire straits. Stripped of beeves, they had no choice but to eat their mules as they struggled on toward the Trans-Pecos. By the time they reached Fort Davis, the penniless men faced the prospect of walking hundreds of miles to Santa Fe.[24]

Near Hudson three months after this latest Howard's Well cruelty, an Adams and Wickes freighter named Hernandez sighted ten Indians headed for the border with a stolen cattle herd. Leaving a six-man guard at the wagons, Hernandez set out through the hanging dust with seven men and recovered 160 animals. Thirteen days later, he turned the beeves over to G. M. Frazer at Fort Stockton.[25]

Ranger Captain Neal Coldwell and a dozen or so men, eager to make a show of force, rode west from a camp on the headwaters of the Frio or Guadalupe sometime after June. Laying a course for Beaver Lake, the company trekked across a parched divide and reached Clark's Water Hole on Dry Devils River on the third day. As the Rangers forged down-canyon, the imprisoning walls funneled the men on to the main Devils, which they crossed with difficulty.

Continuing southwest to California Springs and veering for Second Crossing, Coldwell and his command failed to locate hostiles.[26] Nevertheless, the Rangers' presence complemented a July patrol of the same region by John Bullis and his Black Seminole Scouts.[27]

Even with a military deterrent, more bloodshed was inevitable. On November 27, Kickapoos killed Juan Dias near Sycamore Creek east of the Devils and took his two small children captive.[28] Another war party cut a bloody swath along the Frio, Blanco, and Sabinal rivers two months later, driving a fatal arrow into a man's back before retreating for the Devils with forty-four stolen horses.

An eight-man citizens' force tracked the latter band for days, finally catching the Indians off-guard in a dense thicket near Beaver Lake. Squeezing off shot after shot, the riders killed two warriors and put the others to flight without their plunder. After a fifteen-day campaign, the citizens arrived back at Frio Canyon with thirty-six recovered horses and two mules.[29]

Spring brought no respite, as Indians fell upon a stagecoach in Maverick County before disappearing on a course toward the Devils and Pecos. On April 15, 1875, Fort Clark commander William R. Shafter responded to the various depredations by ordering patrols of all trails, springs, and river crossings between Clark and Fort Stockton.[30]

The next day, Lieutenant John L. Bullis headed out from Clark with three Black Seminole Scouts—Sergeant John Ward, Trumpeter Isaac Payne, and Private Pompey Factor—to reconnoiter the three-rivers area to the west. They traveled with the Twenty-Fifth Infantry's Company A as far as Beaver Lake, then parted ways with the Stockton-bound soldiers April 22. Patrolling the rugged fastness on both sides of the Pecos, Bullis and his small unit chanced upon a fresh Indian trail a few miles east of present-day Seminole Canyon State Park on the twenty-fifth. The trace bore northwest in the direction of Eagle Nest Crossing, a Rio Grande ford situated near modern Langtry.

Dismounting, Bullis and his Scouts advanced stealthily and surprised twenty-five to thirty dismounted Comanches with a sudden volley. For forty-five minutes, the four men kept up the siege, taking more fire than they could give, before finally pulling back. Bullis, trying to swing astride his spooked horse, lost the animal and faced certain death, but his scouts engineered a daring rescue that would merit all three Medals of Honor.

"Sergeant John Ward, Trumpeter Isaac Payne, and Private Pompey Factor . . . are brave and trustworthy, and are each worthy of a medal, the former of which had a ball shot through his carbine sling, and the stock to his carbine shattered," Bullis later wrote.

Leaving in their wake three dead Comanches and one wounded, Bullis and his command retreated twelve miles to Painted Cave. The next morning, they turned their horses into the sunrise and marched for Clark, the last leg of an eleven-day, 326-mile odyssey that memorialized the fighting heart of the Black Seminole Scouts.[31]

Six months later, Bullis and his scouts identified an Apache trail bearing west, prompting Tenth Cavalry troops to pursue the raiders across the Devils country. Catching the Indians in camp near the Pecos November 2, Lieutenant Andrew Geddes and detachments of G and L companies killed one hostile and took four women and a boy captive.[32]

Even as state and federal forces waged constant war to purge the Devils of warrior societies in the mid-1870s, cattlemen made inroads. The California Cattle Trail, a passageway for the last two and a half decades, continued to stay defined in 1875, as 6,400 hooves of a drove in the charge of a man named Humphreys pounded the trace en route to Arizona.[33]

Early the next year, cowmen John H. Slaughter and Billy Childress wintered a herd at Beaver Lake, thereby keeping the beeves in good flesh for a drive north in spring.[34] Sometime in the mid- to late 1870s, rancher Henry Ramsey also took advantage of the Devils' isolation and moderate climate and grazed almost 1,000 cattle at the lake. By doing so, he avoided drift and roundup problems that might result in a cowhand burning his boss' brand in the hide of another man's beef— an accepted practice that could rob a herd of its increase.[35]

Other men of the era resorted to outright cattle theft. In 1876, notorious King Fisher and his gang defiantly rustled cattle between Eagle Pass and Castroville, a stretch of rangeland southeast of the river. Initially, the outlaws held the stolen animals along the Nueces, then brazenly drove the beeves to the Devils. There, they awaited unscrupulous buyers from Kansas who took the herds north for the railheads.[36]

Meanwhile, the deterrent effect of Colonel Ranald Mackenzie's 1873 raid against Kickapoos and Lipans in Coahuila had subsided, and once again the US Army contemplated the best course of action.

CHAPTER 12

AVENGING IN MEXICO

Marshaling its forces for the spring of 1876, US Army headquarters in Texas ordered Lieutenant Colonel George Pearson Buell on March 13 to equip his command at Fort Concho for a journey to Clark and on to the Devils.[1] At abandoned Hudson, reported the *San Antonio Daily Herald,* he was to establish a "summer camp, to protect the settlers, who are filling up that section of the State very rapidly."[2]

By April 7 Buell and two cavalry companies reached Clark,[3] but the Army then revised its personnel assignments. Buell veered down the Rio Grande for distant Ringgold Barracks,[4] while First Lieutenant Louis Henry Orleman of Fort Griffin prepared to assume command of the Tenth Cavalry's B Company soon after the soldiers took station at Hudson.[5]

Lieutenant Colonel William R. Shafter, planning another campaign on the Pecos, departed Clark for Hudson April 13 in concert with not only the new Hudson garrison, but additional troops from the Tenth Cavalry and Twenty-Fourth Infantry. A day later, Lieutenant John L. Bullis saddled up at Clark to join Shafter in the field.[6]

Even as the Army strategized and deployed, Indians out of Mexico struck the settlements repeatedly. In March, hostiles attacked two men near Camp Wood and killed three people on the Nueces. In early April, a boy died in Frio River bloodshed. At Paint Rock on the Concho River northeast of the Devils, Indians wounded a man and stole sixteen horses April 19.

On the twenty-first, one day before another war party swept through Medina and Frio counties and claimed an additional life, sixteen Texas Rangers from Company F, Frontier Battalion, picked up the trail of the Paint Rock marauders. For seventy miles across an arid expanse stretching to the Devils watershed, the thirsty Rangers held their course, then finally turned back in face of certain death by dehydration. By the time they reached water, the men had endured forty-six hours without a drop touching their lips.[7]

While Company F pushed into the Devils country from the northeast, another Ranger detachment undertook its own mission to the river from east-lying Kimble County, where Indians had wounded a man and stolen horses April 21. Although the Rangers never overtook the hostiles, they discovered evidence that a separate band of perhaps thirty warriors had also ridden the Devils corridor recently.[8]

By late May, Lipan Apaches from south of the Rio Grande had killed a dozen people in spring raids,[9] and the US Army began to consider extreme measures again. By month's end, Shafter ordered a Hudson contingent into the backcountry for reconnaissance,[10] but his plans were not limited to US soil. With the consent of local Coahuilan authorities but not that of a Mexican government embroiled in revolution, Shafter crossed into Mexico above the Pecos-Rio Grande confluence in July. After pushing more than 100 miles southeast, he dispatched Lieutenant John L. Bullis, Lieutenant George H. Evans, twenty Black Seminole Scouts, and twenty men from Company B, Tenth Cavalry, on a search-and-destroy mission.

Seven miles from Saragossa (Zaragoza) on July 30, Bullis' command razed a Lipan village, killed fourteen warriors, and captured four women and ninety-six horses or mules. On Shafter's return march to the Rio Grande, his lieutenants intercepted a Lipan war party fresh from a Castroville raid and recovered more horses, although the animals' sore-footed condition left the soldiers no alternative but to kill them.[11]

Meanwhile, Texas Rangers tightened the screws on Lipan and Kickapoo passage across the Devils. Major John B. Jones, who commanded the Frontier Battalion, mustered approximately seventy men and used Beaver Lake as a staging ground for an extended scout along Johnsons Run and the Pecos.[12] On the Devils during the same general period, a Ranger unit skirmished approximately fifteen Indians who had tortured and killed a man the previous day.

"We got seven of them and the others got away," J. L. Richards recalled twenty years later. "It was said that they were led by a renegade white man."[13]

On through the fall, Texas and US forces kept up the pressure. Portions of Shafter's command stayed in the field until mid-December,[14] while companies B, E, K, and M of the Tenth Cavalry patrolled the Devils and Pecos badlands before shifting their search to the Guadalupe Mountains.[15]

Nevertheless, the year 1876 had been deadly for frontier Texas. Several predatory tribes operated out of Mexico, and Lipans alone had conducted a pair of raids that had claimed twenty-five men and one woman, reason enough to deter 250

Camp Hudson artifacts discovered in 2009. Photograph courtesy of Patrick Dearen.

families from emigrating to the region.[16]

By January 1877, the men who lodged beneath Hudson's flag had been instrumental for more than twenty years in the effort to wrest this wilderness from warrior societies. The camp's location at Second Crossing had placed it squarely in the forefront of Devils River history, but now the Army abandoned Hudson yet again, this time never to return.[17]

The fight, however, went on. After Lipan and Mescalero Apaches plundered the Fort Clark and San Felipe areas and absconded across the border in early January, approximately 200 Tenth Cavalry troops and ten Black Seminole Scouts re-entered Mexico. Across 125 miles of Coahuila they dogged the band, only to turn back January 19 without engaging their elusive enemy.[18]

A little more than two months later on March 25, Lieutenant Pat Dolan and twelve Texas Rangers from Company F, Frontier Battalion, discovered a fresh trail on the Devils and put spurs to their mounts. Riding down an Indian band, the Rangers scattered the warriors and seized thirteen horses and all their camp supplies.[19] Dolan's pivotal role in ridding the Devils of hostiles in the 1870s would earn him lasting recognition: In the river's etched defile sixteen miles downstream of Second Crossing, Dolan Falls splashes at the juncture with Dolan Creek, a southwest-trending drainage that slithers for thirty-five miles.[20]

The intensified Indian menace of 1877 persisted with the full flowering of spring. Black Seminole Scouts skirmished hostiles on the Rio Grande near the Devils' mouth April 1.[21] In a three-day span later that month, warriors killed a trio of citizens in the Fort Clark region.[22] On May 2, Company A of the Frontier Battalion struck a trace cut by ten Indians and nine ponies, and for the next three days the Rangers tracked the war party before losing the trail at the Devils' head.[23]

Although Army troops had pursued marauding Indians into Mexico with some regularity in 1876 and early 1877, Secretary of War G. W. McCrary did not expressly address the matter until June 1, 1877. Aware that Mexico fiercely opposed US operations inside its borders, McCrary instructed that Brigadier General E. O. C. Ord, commander of the Department of Texas, seek the cooperation of local Mexican officials in quelling raids on US soil by Mexican Indians. If the "lawless incursions" persisted, however, Ord's troops had the liberty to ignore the international boundary.

"When in pursuit of a band of marauders and when . . . troops are either in sight of them or upon a fresh trail," wrote McCrary, ". . . [they may] follow them across the Rio Grande, and . . . overtake and *punish them, as well as retake stolen property* taken from our citizens and found in their hands on the Mexican side of the line."

Mexico's Minister of War, Pedro Ogazon, responded June 18 by ordering General Geronimo Trevino to station troops on the Rio Grande and "repel force with force."[24] By late July, Mexican units had dug in along the border.[25] Bloodshed would have been inevitable if not for the wisdom of Mexican field commanders, who usually deployed their troops elsewhere whenever invading soldiers were in the area.[26]

Meanwhile, Mexican forces likewise ignored the Rio Grande boundary. Lieutenant Colonel William Shafter, in later testimony before Congress, indicated that he could cite numerous instances in which Mexican officers had pursued thieves into Texas prior to September 1877.[27] The most noteworthy intrusion occurred June 10, when approximately 400 Mexican regulars routed followers of Sebastian Lerdo de Tejada in Mexico and chased these *lerdistas* to a point near Painted Cave.

In a battle that erupted about noon the next day, many of the revolutionaries fell. The surviving *lerdistas*—nine officers and forty-five privates—straggled into Captain J. M. Kelley's Tenth Cavalry camp at San Felipe and surrendered to US authority.

Kelley and thirty-five men immediately rode to Painted Cave, but the Mexican regulars already had fallen back across the Rio Grande. As soon as Fort Clark commander Shafter learned of the incident, he telegraphed the Department of Texas.

"My men will be ready to start by midnight," he reported to Brigadier General Ord on the day of the Devils clash. "Shall I cross the Rio Grande in pursuit of these troops and attack them if I can overtake them?"

The ultimate decision rested with President Rutherford B. Hayes, who chose restraint. He further directed that the *lerdistas,* who had been interred at Clark, remain in custody to foster peace along the border.[28]

Two separate Indian trails stirred state and federal forces into action in late June. From the twenty-sixth until July 10, Sergeant Lamartine Pemberton Sieker and a detachment of Texas Rangers from Company D, Frontier Battalion, tracked a war party to the drouth-ravaged Devils and Pecos and recovered several horses.[29]

On June 30, Lieutenant John L. Bullis and thirty-five or so Black Seminole Scouts fell into a Trans-Pecos trace that led them across the Rio Grande—the first US strike in Mexico under Secretary of War McCrary's recent authorization. Overtaking a band of Lipans and Mescaleros July 2, Bullis and his command killed one warrior, wounded three others, and captured twenty-three horses.

In September and October, Lipans killed thirteen men and one woman in the Fort Clark region, adding to the woes of settlers east of the Devils.[30]

"There is hardly a neighborhood, hardly a family among the older settlements of Kinney, Uvalde, Medina, or Kerr Counties that have not lost members by these Indian raids," observed a congressional report.[31]

Bullis dashed into Mexico again with twenty-one men on September 26 and soon identified another Indian camp near Saragossa. In a running battle on the twenty-ninth, Bullis and his men captured three women, two children, and seventeen horses or mules.

After torching the Indians' village, Bullis joined up with Lieutenant Colonel Shafter, who had followed him into Mexico with six or seven cavalry companies. With a combined force of approximately 450 men, Shafter and Bullis fell back for Texas—a scant mile ahead of seventy-five to 100 Mexican troops who reportedly were under orders not to engage the intimidating invaders.[32]

In mid-October, Bullis and his Black Seminole Scouts patrolled the Devils and Pecos,[33] but failed to locate hostiles until a November 1 skirmish along the Rio Grande in the Big Bend.[34] Soon retreating for the Devils, Bullis took twenty-five of his best scouts into camp at Pecan Springs,[35] where he remained a couple of weeks before again riding for the border with Captain S. B. M. Young and an Eighth Cavalry detachment.

Near the Sierra del Carmen in Mexico on November 29, the joint units attacked the village of a Mescalero Apache named Alsate whom Bullis described as "the most cunning Indian on all the frontier of Texas and Mexico." Alsate escaped, but US forces killed two of his warriors, wounded three more, and decimated his village before withdrawing with approximately thirty horses and mules.[36]

Putting an end to raids out of Mexico, however, was like trying to plug a sieve. Even as the del Carmen operation was underway, an informant reported that thirty-five warriors had departed a Lipan village in Mexico November 10 and 11 to raid in Texas. Well-supplied with ammunition, the Lipans planned to cross the Devils country, spurring troops from forts Clark and Stockton to ride for the river's head to try to intercept their trail.[37]

Other marauders killed a man near Uvalde November 16 and two Mexican herders near Clark two days later,[38] while attacks on mail coaches claimed the lives of a pair of drivers elsewhere in the state by year's end.[39]

Chance was always a factor in whether a man lived or died in Indian country, and sometimes luck was better than the best armed guard. In the fall, cowhands with the Moore and West outfit successfully drove 2,500 two-year-old steers from the Eagle Pass area, through the Devils country, and on to a Colorado River spread north of Fort Concho.[40]

Still, the US government couldn't count on serendipity in making the border safe, leading Congress to hold hearings on the matter in December and January. In his December testimony before the Committee on Military Affairs, Brigadier General E. O. C. Ord reported that US forces in Texas totaled 2,941, half of which were stationed in the Fort Clark vicinity, including one company at the sub-post of San Felipe. These troops faced predatory parties of two to thirty-five warriors from Mexico who sometimes crossed the Rio Grande into Texas near the Devils mouth, a site the Army was considering for a small cantonment.[41]

One month later, Lieutenant Colonel William R. Shafter and Lieutenant John L. Bullis provided additional details to the committee. These troublesome hostiles included several bands under various chiefs:

—Washa Lobo and thirty or so Lipans from near
Saragossa, Coahuila;
—Magnus Colorado and forty to sixty Mescalero Apaches
from near El Paso del Norte (present-day Juarez);
—Tejano and warriors of an unspecified tribe from near
San Carlos, Chihuahua;
—Leon and Mescaleros from near San Carlos;
—Cheno and warriors of an unspecified tribe from near
San Carlos; and
—Alsate and Mescaleros from the Sierra del Carmen
in Coahuila.

A few bands of Kickapoos also continued to operate out of Mexico, increasing the total number of warriors to approximately 225,[42] all of whom periodically entered the United States on foot by cover of night.

"They get up into the cañons of Devil's River and the heads of those streams where there are no people living, up in the cedar brakes, and ten or fifteen men could stay there for years and not be found," noted Shafter. ". . . They lie up there and wait until a favorable opportunity occurs, until the moon gets just right, and then pitch down into one of the valleys, gather up what horses they can get as they go, and keep going until they come to the river [Rio Grande]."

Raids and citizen deaths had decreased significantly after Secretary of War McCrary's June 1877 authorization for US missions inside Mexico.[43] Nevertheless, hostiles persisted in targeting the Clark area, rendering "life and property . . . very insecure," noted Bullis.[44]

Frontier life remained fragile indeed in early 1878. "It is almost an impossibility," Shafter told the committee, "to prevent the Indians from coming into Texas."[45]

Assuredly, looming raids would keep Texas Rangers and federal soldiers astride weary mounts foaming with sweat. ✺

CHAPTER 13

LAST OF THE ARROWS

In the spring of 1878, Indians struck Kimble County and withdrew to the sunset, prompting a Texas Ranger squad that included James B. Gillett to dig boots into stirrups and take aim on the Devils. The Rangers clung to the trail for five or six days, all the way to a location near the river's head, before heavy rains obliterated the tracks and left the raid unavenged.[1]

Far from deterred, marauders soon darted into Texas again. At the Roberts Brothers Ranch five miles below the Devils' mouth, they took three horses April 5 and raced for Mexico. The next morning, US Army captain J. M. Kelley of the Tenth Cavalry traced the hoofprints a few miles down the Rio Grande to Island Crossing. Splashing across into Coahuila, Kelley and his command persevered another five miles before likewise losing the trace.[2]

Few places were as strategically important in the border war as the Devils, a point underscored May 16 when Captain Samuel B. M. Young and four Eighth Cavalry companies—A, B, K, and M—established a field camp on the river, likely about two miles below First Crossing.[3] Colonel Ranald S. Mackenzie, commanding the District of the Nueces from its headquarters at Fort Clark, rendezvoused with Young at the site, and the combined force rode for Mexico June 11.[4] The first five months of the year had seen a horrific rise in outrages, with twenty-seven citizens losing their lives,[5] and Mackenzie was determined to strike a punitive blow.

Crossing into Coahuila June 12, Mackenzie pressed on to the San Diego River and joined Lieutenant Colonel William R. Shafter and a much larger column on the seventeenth. Although the troops failed to locate marauders, they did engage in a standoff with Mexican Army troops who finally backed down in the face of greater American firepower.[6]

California Springs and Yellow Banks in 1869.
Journal of Lieutenant Colonel Thomas B. Hunt, National Archives.

Despite Captain Young's subsequent blitz into Mexico on the trail of stolen cattle August 16,[7] Indians continued to spill blood. Along Johnson Creek near present-day Mountain Home 100 miles east of Beaver Lake, raiders killed four members of a ranch family named Dowdy on October 5. Particularly heinous was the fact that the victims were all children—three girls and a boy.

Lieutenant John L. Bullis and forty-two Black Seminole Scouts had already been in the field since September 7, scouting from the Devils' mouth to Pecos Spring (near what was later Sheffield) and on up the Pecos River. Upon learning October 6 of the Dowdy killings, Bullis wheeled his command back toward the Devils to search for the perpetrators.

Two days later, two separate Tenth Cavalry contingents struck out for the river for the same purpose. From Yellow Banks to Hudson to Beaver Lake, Second Lieutenant G. H. Evans and seventeen men scoured the countryside. In the meantime, Second Lieutenant R. H. R. Loughborough and fourteen men from Camp San Felipe conducted daily patrols of the Rio Grande between the Devils confluence and a spring twenty-five miles upriver.

By the time Loughborough returned to his station October 18, and Bullis and Evans followed suit in the next two days, the detachments had ridden 892 miles without finding a single fresh track.[8] Captain Pat Dolan and ten Texas Rangers had no better success as they ranged 220 miles across the Llano River country and the Devils runs.[9]

More Devils expeditions that proved profitless, other than as deterrents, continued for the remainder of 1878. Between November 21 and November 25, Second Lieutenant Alex Rodgers and thirty men of Company A, Fourth Cavalry, patrolled from Clark to First Crossing and back. Simultaneously, First Lieutenant H. H. Crews and two other officers, along with fifteen of Bullis' Scouts and seventy-four enlisted men of the Fourth Cavalry and Twentieth Infantry, rode the three rivers wilderness.

Crews and presumably Bullis did not return to post until December 31,[10] but within weeks Bullis and his Scouts were in the Devils region again, hot on the trail of Mescaleros who had fled west past Beaver Lake with twenty-five stolen animals. Bullis picked up their spoor on the Pecos February 12, 1879, and followed it northwest for twenty-three days and hundreds of miles. Although the trace clearly ended at the Mescalero reservation in New Mexico Territory, the Indian agent refused to yield the rustled stock.[11]

Indians were not the only cattle and horse thieves plaguing the frontier; a sizable gang of outlaws reportedly operated near the head of the Devils and along the Pecos, drawing the attention of Texas Rangers by March. For three weeks, Captain Dolan and Company F, Frontier Battalion, searched between the Nueces and Beaver Lake, and from Beaver Lake to Johnsons Run,[12] while Lamartine Sieker and civilian Rollie Burns combed the upper Devils and Dry Devils.

"We saw lots of dry, rough country," recalled Burns, "but no rustlers."[13]

By the end of May, no one had died in a confirmed Indian attack anywhere in Texas since the Dowdy children the previous October. June 1, however, served as a grim reminder that life remained uncertain for even the most innocent, as Indians descended upon Nick Colson's ranch near Camp Wood in the Nueces valley and killed his wife and two daughters.

In response, the US Army organized multiple scouting parties to intercept the marauders in the Devils country. First Lieutenant J. W. Pullman and forty-four men of Company K, Eighth Cavalry, set out June 3 from Fort Clark, while four detachments of the Fourth Cavalry's E Company formed at San Felipe. First Sergeant James Logan and Sergeant Levi Bradley, each with seven-man detachments, pointed their mounts toward the Devils June 6, and after their return a week or so later, two other units of like size under sergeants William Cross and Chris. [sic] Miller, respectively, rode a similar course.

Casting a wide net anchored by far-flung military posts, the Army also dispatched three other scouting parties to the Devils four days after the killings: Second Lieutenant Theodore Mosher Jr. and a Twenty-Second Infantry detachment from Fort McKavett, First Lieutenant M. M. Maxon and a Tenth Cavalry unit from Fort Concho, and Captain S. T. Norvell from Camp Charlotte on the Middle Concho River.

The latter officer and his men, bearing south-southwest from Spring Creek, found themselves swallowed by a searing wasteland as unforgiving as it was vast. For thirty hours they rode without water, tolling off forty, sixty, a hundred miles, before finally striking Beaver Lake.

"I believe that 25 more [miles] would have caused the loss of many men and horses," reported Norvell, who subsequently related that several in his command were "out of their senses" by the time they reached water.

In all, the eight contingents spent three weeks riding a cumulative 1,821 miles between their stations, Beaver Lake, and the Rio Grande—paying particular attention to the latter—but failed to mete out justice.[14]

The US Army long had sought a more direct route across the Devils-Pecos region, and on July 5 Assistant Adjutant General Thomas M. Vincent ordered the District of the Nueces to try yet again. A flag now flew over the sub-post of Peña Blanco in present Brewster County, and a shorter road linking it to Camp San Felipe loomed important. By striking out northwest from the lower Devils, rather than tracing the winding stream north to Beaver Lake, a road might intersect the yawning gorge of the Pecos and veer upstream to the first crossing point, thereby shaving off critical miles.[15]

On July 8, Captain William Fletcher started from Fort Clark with detachments of the Twentieth Infantry and Fourth Cavalry, along with forty-two Black Seminole Scouts. After briefly camping two miles below First Crossing, Fletcher's command continued northwest to a spring within three miles of the Pecos-Rio Grande confluence. Lieutenant John L. Bullis and his Scouts identified a potential Pecos crossing a mile and a half above its mouth, and Fletcher's command set about engineering a road down the imposing bluff.

For weeks the soldiers persisted, filling arroyos and cutting through cliffs, before the Army suspended the operation August 30.[16] By year's end, District of the Pecos headquarters at Fort Concho abandoned Camp Peña Blanco, rendering the need for such a road debatable.[17] In the spring of 1880, however, the Twentieth Infantry would resume work at the crossing in order to connect east-lying posts with Fort Davis and other Trans-Pecos installations.[18]

While construction was underway in the summer of 1879, Indian forays generated more scouts to the Devils. In late July and early August, First Lieutenant L. O. Parker and twenty-five men of D Company, Fourth Cavalry, camped at Pecan Springs and patrolled the Beaver Lake road and outlying territories. Despite their best efforts to locate Indians, they found only an empty land savaged by a torturous sun.[19]

In the two years and eight months since the Army had closed Camp Hudson, troops generally had maintained only a transient presence on the Devils. On September 2, however, the Eighth Cavalry's A Company headed west from Clark to tent at Pecan Springs,[20] which remained a field camp for several months. Another Eighth Cavalry company from Clark departed for the springs November 13,[21] and although by December 10 the Department of Texas considered manning the outpost through winter, General E. O. C. Ord directed on the nineteenth that the garrison return to Clark.[22]

Already, Pecan Springs had lured more than soldiers to its life-sustaining wa-

A short distance downstream of Pecan Springs in 2009. Photograph courtesy of Patrick Dearen.

ters; a cattle outfit evidently had grazed free-ranging beeves in the adjacent valley at least since August.[23] This may have been the Ramsay (or Ramsey) operation—possibly ramrodded by Henry Ramsey[24]—which apparently had a cow camp at the springs and enough importance to warrant mail service by early winter.

The courier, bearing for Howard's Well after passing the outfit in late December, took flight from eight Indians determined to ride him down. He escaped, but returned to Ramsay's camp to secure three cowboys to escort him on to Howard's.[25]

Despite such incidents, cattle outfits were on the Devils to stay by 1880, although limited initially to areas with surface water. A windmill may have been in place along Johnsons Run by 1878,[26] but whirring blades were slow to impact the wider region. Meanwhile, the dearth of water was a critical factor for any cattleman prospecting the Devils for rangeland.

In the spring of 1880, John Young and his three partners in a cattle company combed the Devils drainage basin and the land west to the Pecos, but the lack of dependable water deterred their plans to graze 2,000 cows.[27] The following year, William Perry Hoover drove 200 longhorns from Kimble County to the Devils, where he and his family camped three months while he also searched for suitable range. Like Young and his associates, Hoover declined to accept the river's challenges, choosing instead to locate along the Pecos.[28]

As ranching made inroads, drama unfolded along what soon would be the final major front of the Indian war in Texas. On the night of March 8, 1880, a war party with five ponies crossed the Rio Grande near San Felipe village and seized twenty-five horses from a fenced pasture eleven miles above. The raiders proceeded to the head of Sycamore Creek, where they showed themselves on the morning of the ninth.

At sunrise the same day, a separate band of ten Indians—six mounted, four on foot—opened fire on a Mexican sheepherder a few miles east of the Devils and sixteen miles north of San Felipe. In a desperate fight for survival, the sheepherder took five slugs to the leg, one of them shattering bone. Gravely wounded, he took refuge in a hole and defended himself, killing one hostile and wounding another. After firing 100 rounds, he finally repelled the Indians and gained transport to Camp San Felipe.

With both bands apparently on a course for the Llano River, the District of the Nueces launched pursuit and alerted Fort McKavett and the District of the Pecos.[29] For once, Lieutenant John L. Bullis was unable to join the chase; he was busy that month escorting a party of engineers surveying the region for a railroad.[30]

The Indians went unpunished, but the incidents served to keep daily patrols underway along the border. Since the previous year, three- to five-man units had ridden from camp to camp between Eagle Pass and an unspecified point on the Devils.[31]

On October 1, General E. O. C. Ord, commanding the Department of Texas, delivered his annual report, which included an assessment of the Indian situation. In the military districts of the Pecos and the Bravo (the latter newly created from the Pecos), Indians or other marauders had claimed eight lives in the past twelve months, an increase of five over the previous year. Statewide, however, deaths had dropped by three.

"It is to be hoped, that next year," observed Ord, "with the good will and co-operation of the authorities across the Rio Grande, no report of killed &c., will be necessary."

Ord also indicated that the new road-in-progress across West Texas had been projected "from the mouth of Devil's River—crossing near the mouth of the Pecos—westward to the southern base of the Chinati Mountains, with a branch, from the post of Peña Colorado [near present Marathon], to Fort Davis."

This new route from San Antonio to Fort Davis measured 390 miles, seventy-six miles shorter than by way of the Lower Road.[32] A November 6 directive calling for an immediate pontoon bridge at the Pecos crossing promised even better passage.[33] Nevertheless, the approaching completion of the Texas and Pacific (T&P) Railway across West Texas would lead the Army to end additional road improvements by the following May.[34]

In his 1880 report, Ord stressed the importance of cooperating with railroad companies that had displayed interest in the Rio Grande borderlands downstream of the Devils juncture.

"Every railroad is not only a rapid civilizer, but a sure protector to the frontier penetrated by it," he wrote. "The sight of a locomotive, whirling along its train, is such a 'big medicine,' for the savages, that they wilt under its influence."[35]

In the spring of 1881, Indians from Mexico made a final deadly foray through the Devils region. Traveling by stealth to infiltrate a land frequented by cavalry patrols, the band of Lipans reached a settled area along the Frio River about April 24 and laid siege. By the time the marauders wheeled their mounts back for the Devils, young Allen Reiss and a woman named McLauren lay in bloody pools—the last deaths ever by confirmed Indian raid in Texas.

Lieutenant John L. Bullis and thirty-four Black Seminole Scouts picked up the trail April 27 and tracked the Indians across the Devils and on to the Rio Grande ten miles below the Pecos confluence. Entering Coahuila, Bullis and his command hounded the marauders all the way to the Burro Mountains. At daybreak on May 2, the lieutenant and twenty-seven Scouts stormed the Indians' camp and exacted terrible tribute, killing four warriors and a woman. The Scouts also recovered twenty-one horses and captured a boy and a woman who had sustained a wound.[36]

Bullis' daring strike had lasting impact.

"For this successful expedition Lieut. Bullis deserves much credit," observed C. C. Augur, new commander of the Department of Texas.[37]

Assuredly, over the last eight years Bullis and his Black Seminole Scouts had been instrumental in wresting an enormous expanse of Texas from Indian raiders. By late September, Augur would be able to boast that "it is not probable that Indian depredations will ever again be made from any point in Mexico, south of the Mouth of Pecos."[38]

Bullis soon relinquished command of the Black Seminole unit, but the Texas Legislature did not forget his exploits. An April 7, 1882 resolution recognized the "gallant and efficient services rendered by him and his command . . . in repelling the depredations of Indians and other enemies of the frontier of Texas."[39]

One challenge on the Devils may have ended, but many others still remained.

CHAPTER 14

COMING OF THE SOUTHERN PACIFIC

Despite telegraph lines connecting forts Clark and Davis by way of San Antonio and Concho in spring 1881,[1] and the daily extension of T&P track west between Fort Worth and Sierra Blanca, mail coaches continued to roll through the Devils country. The 272-mile route, which began at Brackettville (adjacent to Clark) and ended at Davis, raised the ire of Post Office Inspector John A. Galbreath in May.

"There does not seem to be the least reason for such a route," he blasted on the thirty-first. "It runs through a desolate country, uninhabited except [for] a few Mexicans and stockmen who are temporarily in that country. A crow going over it would have to take his rations along."[2]

Soon the controversy would end, for the Southern Pacific (SP) Railroad Company had projected a line across the southern part of Texas under a Galveston, Harrisburg and San Antonio (GH&SA) Railway charter. Already, the rails had reached El Paso from New Mexico Territory, and now SP construction targeted the Devils from fronts east and west.[3] By late September, the so-called Sunset Route on the east had reached D'Hanis, fifty miles down the line from San Antonio. With Indians finally vanquished on the sunrise side of the Devils-Pecos highlands, Department of Texas commander C. C. Augur could now focus his deterrence efforts on the SP line and Rio Grande between the Pecos and Presidio del Norte.[4]

While work gangs laid rails and drove spikes, the bellowing of cattle increasingly rolled through the Devils' hollows. The sharp hooves came by three means: importation, drive, and drift. By the fall of 1881 or soon after, a party named Phillips was in camp at Second Crossing, likely for the purpose of grazing beeves.[5] Meanwhile, long, thin clouds of dust still signaled passage on the old California

Ben Mayes, left front, and fellow cowhands in San Angelo in 1882. Sitting beside Mayes, left to right, are Bob Baker and Bob Haley, while Lum Hudson and Frank Gallagher stand.
N. S. Haley Memorial Library, Midland, Texas.

Cattle Trail. The most dramatic influx, however, came in the winter of 1881-1882, when beeves fled before howling blizzards that swept across northern ranges.

Ben C. Mayes, who cowboyed for T. A. Lambert in Tom Green County, recalled the challenges of riding line that season.

"Cattle were bad to drift in the winter and our work was to keep them thrown north of us," he related. "But it was hard to do. [In] real bad weather, they would come by in [a] trot, bawling and going south."

Although the cowhands did their best to ride down the beeves and turn the leaders, the tide was often too great. Falling in with herds from unfenced ranges as far north as the Panhandle, many of the Lambert cattle stormed past and eventually bunched up along the Devils.[6]

With a massive roundup indicated throughout much of Texas, cattlemen convened in spring and identified the Devils as one of seven roundup districts. As with each 10,000-square mile sector, they elected a general superintendent for the Devils and specified when work would begin. Vital in the selection of a date was the condition of the cattle, which had to put on flesh to endure extended marches back to their home pastures.

When Mayes pulled rein at the Devils that spring, he was astounded.

"You never saw the like of cattle from Beaver Lake to Pecan Spring," he remembered. "When we got down there in 'heel fly' time, the cattle would be jammed in the creek for three miles just as thick as they could be."

From Beaver Lake north, a 100-mile dry stretch loomed, and cowhands worked from "you can till you can't" to push the beeves back to first water at Dove Creek en route to their native ranges. In evening, twelve to fifteen hands would cut out 5,000 to 6,000 drift animals on the Devils, then point the herd north to drive day and night. Brutal miles later, the drove would gain Dove's dry upper reaches, where the cowhands would turn the beeves loose and let instinct prevail.

"They would string out for five miles down Dove Creek in [a] high trot for the water," related Mayes. ". . . Then we [would] go back and get another bunch the next day and have the same drive over."

Only after three weeks of steady work on the Devils did the cowboys thin the cattle enough to make the process more manageable. Still, two full months passed before cowhands started the last drift herd north.

In subsequent years, the drift events of 1881-1882 would be repeated to one degree or another, dictated by the severity of winter storms nipping at the flanks of fleeing beeves.

"You could see them going south by the thousands in bad weather," related Mayes, who continued to ride line for the Lambert outfit.[8]

While the massive roundup of 1882 was in progress, more than cowboys filled the Devils country. GH&SA track spanned San Felipe Creek by April, and from that point west to the Pecos, advance crews already slaved feverishly to cut right-of-way, build trestles, and carve tunnels through moonscape loathe to yield. Three thousand men crowded this relatively short section, sweating by day in a forsaken land and carousing by night in temporary tent cities ripe with iniquity. They were a rough lot, these Europeans, Mexicans, and Americans,[9] and being thrust upon a river named for the very epitome of wickedness did nothing to tame them.

A contemporary edition of the *San Antonio Weekly Express* recorded a late-March incident typical of coarse individuals who settled differences by their own law.

As a man named Bill Garvey assaulted a diminutive German on the Devils one evening, Fletcher Bennett of Austin objected. Angered by his intrusion, Garvey whipped out a pistol and shot Bennett through the left hand. A second round went wide, giving Bennett time to draw his own pistol and open fire. When the smoke cleared, Garvey lay dead, his body riddled with five bullet holes.

"Bennett," observed the *Express,* "is fully exonerated."[10]

The early Southern Pacific bridge over the Devils. James Cox, Historical and Biographical Record of the Cattle Industry and the Cattlemen of Texas and Adjacent Territory, 1895.

The combination of liquor and quick tempers created a situation so volatile that gang bosses carried guns for protection against their own employees.[11] Nevertheless, the rails worked inexorably up the Rio Grande from San Felipe in 1882 and turned up the cavernous mouth of the Devils. Three to four miles upstream, the GH&SA traversed the river with a 750-foot iron bridge and ascended the west-side valley of California Creek, a moderately steep grade that kept locomotives chugging.

Bearing northwest, the rails climbed hundreds of feet to present-day Comstock and turned south just past Seminole Canyon. Tunneling down into the Rio Grande chasm, the tortuous line crossed the Pecos at its mouth and climbed out again.[12]

As rails inched progressively up the Rio Grande from San Felipe, the GH&SA set up periodic stations to accommodate steam locomotive travel and permanent maintenance. The sidings included McKees at the eight-mile mark, Devil's River at fourteen miles, Feely at twenty-five miles, Comstock at thirty-five miles, Flanders at forty-six miles, and Painted Cave at Seminole Canyon (not to be confused with the Devils' Painted Cave) at fifty-four miles.[13] The station on the Devils was situated about midway between the river's mouth and the bridge.[14]

While the Sunset operation blasted and drilled that summer, western rail gangs approached the Pecos from the opposite direction. As the two divisions closed, the total work force ballooned to 8,000—all in a twenty-mile span of wilderness only a year removed from the threat of Indians.[15] Ten or so rail camps drew upon a water hole at Seminole Canyon,[16] testimony to the boom on the Devils-Pecos

The early Southern Pacific bridge across the mouth of the Pecos. James Cox, Historical and Biographical Record of the Cattle Industry and the Cattlemen of Texas and Adjacent Territory, 1895.

highlands.

On a trestle two and a half miles west of the Pecos on January 12, 1883, a ceremonial silver spike finally joined the two lines and created the transcontinental Southern Pacific Railroad.[17]

With this artery of civilization in place, stockmen increasingly flooded the Devils country with cattle and sheep. Eighteen-year-old Pope A. Presnall of San Antonio took a cattle drove through to his brother's Trans-Pecos range that year,[18] but cattlemen such as John L. Spurlin and David Baker imported beeves to the Devils to stay.

Spurlin spent early summer overseeing a roundup of 600 head on his spread near Hamilton in Central Texas. Under the charge of a Mr. Heorte and Hal Williams, the herd was to start about July 5 for the Devils, where Spurlin already had established a ranch.[19]

A few months later, Baker and his nephew, Baker Jefferies, pointed their own cattle-and-horse drove west from the Nueces and wintered the animals in an extreme lower Devils gorge known as Castle Canyon for its turret-like columns of rock. The next spring, Baker relocated to a west-bank site a half-mile upstream of Second Crossing. At the time, John Beckett owned a 107-acre tract and one-room picket house at the crossing, but Baker purchased the property for $1,000 and settled in. By doing so, he assured his association with this historic ford that henceforth would be known as Baker's Crossing.[20]

Eight and a half miles upriver at Pecan Springs, twenty-one-year-old Robert W. Prosser acquired 9,000 encompassing acres in 1883. On a spring-fed rivulet five miles closer to the crossing, he completed a headquarters with dog-run by

An early picnic inside the canyon of the Devils. Photo courtesy of Christina Tevington, Val Verde County Historical Commission.

early 1884, then set out for Mexico to purchase cattle with his partner, Herbert Fitzgerald. After a lengthy drive back to Pecan Springs, Prosser turned the animals loose to graze this fertile stretch of bottomland.[21]

Meanwhile, flocks of sheep increasingly moved across the Devils' broken landscape like gentle, white waves. Ever since 1850, when Captain Harry Love had navigated the Rio Grande by keel boat, observers had recognized the region's potential for woollybacks.

"The country and soil between Fort Duncan and the mouth of Devil's river, are represented by Captain Love as beautiful and rich beyond description . . . ," noted Assistant Quartermaster W. W. Chapman on September 5, 1850. "He describes this country as the finest in the world for grazing, and believes it capable of sustaining *almost any given number of* sheep and goats."

Chapman cited in particular the region's mild climate and year-round grazing.[22] At Painted Cave four years later, cattle drover James G. Bell specified the "poor and stony" soil as another element in making this land "fine country for sheep."[23]

Unlike beef cattle, which were prone to wild independence, free-ranging sheep required the constant supervision of sheepherders who considered factors such as

The view upstream from near Second Crossing or Baker's Crossing. Photograph courtesy of Patrick Dearen.

water, forage, weather, predators, and a location's potential for soiling wool. "The sheep," observed the April 6, 1895 *San Angelo Standard,* "is a foolish creature that needs much care."

As they drifted their flocks across the Devils wilderness, sheepherders had to remain vigilant.

"[They] literally sleep with one eye open and one ear on the alert," noted the *Standard*. "Often in the silent watches of the night they rise, build fires, fire off guns, and resort to other devices for frightening off the wolves."

Caring for such "silly" and "timid" animals was demanding enough, but sheep's tendency to graze verdure to the nub, thereby stripping an area bare if allowed,[24] fostered conflict with cattlemen. Still, woollybacks offered two modes of income—wool and mutton—and stockmen eventually realized that cattle and sheep could co-exist. Beeves generally grazed tall grasses, while sheep preferred the underlying forage.[25] By subsisting on grasses that cattle refused, a sheep could fatten in sixty days, half the time required for a steer.[26]

In 1880, few sheep ranged in soon-to-be-established Val Verde County, which now incorporates most of the Devils, but within seven years Val Verde sheep would

An early flock of sheep in the Devils country. Whitehead Memorial Museum, Del Rio, Texas.

total 102,220 and outnumber cattle four to one.²⁷

The inflow of woollybacks was gradual, however, and not always peaceful. Forty miles south of San Angelo in 1881, Ed Duggan established a sheep ranch in elevated country between the Devils, South Concho, and San Saba drainage basins.²⁸ By September 1882, a sheepman introduced a flock to the Devils with violent consequences—a rancher named Burris murdered him. The crime prompted Texas Ranger Lamartine Sieker of D Company, Frontier Battalion, to investigate.²⁹

The following year, R. R. Johnson and his thirteen-year-old son drove a herd of sheep west from Burnet County, paused on the Devils, and continued on to Howard Draw. Satisfied with the location, they spent two years drifting a flock of 1,900 head.³⁰

In July of 1883, E. K. Fawcett helped point 3,000 sheep west from Yorktown, situated seventy-five miles east of San Antonio. The drove, owned by George W. Ames, reached Del Rio in July and bore north to find permanent range on Dolan Creek, an eastside tributary of the Devils. Fawcett stayed on as a sheepherder, living in a cave while he mustered enough livestock to found his own ranch.³¹

With the advent of 1884, storm and predator attack would speak dramatically of nature's unwillingness to yield the Devils country to stockmen.

CHAPTER 15

THE BIG CATTLE DRIFT

On the night of January 15, 1884, pile-driving winds began to blanket the Devils region with one to three inches of snow. The unprecedented blizzard raged for three days, spawning bitterly cold temperatures and casting much of western Texas under an icy white shroud.

Cattle in northern territories slung their flaring nostrils away from the storm and marched south, driven mile after mile by frigid winds unrelenting in ferocity. W. H. Hiler, who ranched on the North Concho River due north of Beaver Lake, soon reported that all cattle in his section had drifted 150 miles, a distance that would have carried the beeves into the heart of the Devils country.[1]

Significantly, the January 26 *Texas Live Stock Journal* reported no sheep losses—a tribute to the resourcefulness and diligence of sheepherders.

While cattlemen organized a roundup on the Devils, a panther prowled the head of the river and stalked not only deer and livestock, but the wife of a veteran stockman named Cooper. As the woman was drawing water, the panther pounced and began to maul her savagely. Her screams alerted an employee, who bolted to her rescue and killed the animal.[2]

It would not be the last such attack on the Devils. Eight years later, a hidden panther would leap on sheepherder Will Florence as he absconded from the female cat's den with two kittens. Florence would escape injury, but only because of a shielding vest and his acquiescence in giving up the young animals.[3]

In early May of 1884, about the time the drift roundup commenced,[4] Charley Humphreys and twelve other men snaked up the drouth-stricken Devils in the dust of 3,000 yearlings. The drive had originated at George W. West's ranch in Live Oak County and would culminate at Fort Sumner, New Mexico[5]—mere months before brutal weather in the winter of 1884-1885 again focused attention on the Devils.

Down from the northeast it shrieked, a numbing, week-long blizzard that buried the South Plains in snow and set cattle marching south day after terrifying day. They came from the Cimarron and Arkansas, the Canadian and the Pease, an unstoppable avalanche of cow brutes bound for the Pecos, the Frio, the Devils. The West had seen cattle drifts before, but this was the Big Drift—the greatest winter migration in the history of the cattle industry.

One flank of this invading army poured down through the arid upper draws of the Devils and converged on Beaver Lake, the leaders barely able to quench their thirst before the trailing beeves forced them downriver. By the time the drags reached first water, cattle were strung out from Beaver Lake to Camp Hudson's ghostly walls in staggering numbers—at least 15,000 to 20,000, and perhaps as many as 200,000.[6]

Competing with native Devils stock for forage, the cattle soon grazed the valley almost bare. Nevertheless, when George Smith, boss of the Lipan Ranch near San Angelo, rode the river in early February 1885, he found the beeves in surprisingly fair condition. But the dark cloud that always seemed to hang over the Devils refused to let him depart with a smile—Mexican bandits raided his camp and fled with four horses and a mule. Smith managed to recover only the mule and one horse.[7]

With so many cattle to retrieve from the Devils, cattlemen from far-flung locales selected Kenny Mayes of Tom Green County's VP outfit to supervise.[8] Although Spring Creek cowhands were to embark for the river February 20,[9] and J. H. Ryburn and a crew from Dove Creek's Half Circle 6 soon afterward,[10] cowhands from northern territories waited until the end of March to rendezvous on the VP spread. From there, a procession of 200 to 300 men, several wagons, and hundreds of horses set a course for Beaver Lake.[11]

When they arrived, heel flies were at their liveliest, swarming about the cattle's legs and driving the bovines half-mad. Ben C. Mayes had worked the Devils roundup for several years now, but he was unprepared for the sight of so many Big Drift beeves seeking relief in Beaver Lake.

"Cattle . . . [were] standing as thick in the water as they could wedge," recalled Mayes, who arrived in late March. "They wouldn't have been closer if they had been at the feed trough. We'd . . . ride along the lake pushing them out, and sometimes form our roundups with as many cattle as we could handle in that way."[12]

Adjacent to Beaver, the cowhands established a base, the busiest cow camp that the Devils would ever see.

"There . . . [was a] preacher at the lake when we got there, and he would preach to the boys ever' night if they would listen to him," Mayes remembered. "But if

[we] could get up [a] poker game, we didn't bother him any."[13]

While cowhands worked and prayed and gambled, Nueces cowboy Charles E. Lewis, his wife Babe, and their six-month-old baby started by wagon for the Pecos. A man familiar with the country led them across the Nueces-Devils divide without incident, but as their water dwindled, the guide pushed out alone with the horses to locate a spring and lost his bearings.

On the second day of his absence, Lewis and his family headed out on foot and finally staggered upon a sheep camp. Outfitted with a fresh horse, Lewis returned to the wagon, met up with the guide, and then reunited with Babe and their child. Continuing on for the Pecos, they reached Beaver Lake and its bustling cow camp, near which a woman by the name of Young had settled with her family. After a respite, the Lewises pressed on for Second Crossing, where Lewis left his wife on the Baker Ranch while he proceeded to the Pecos.[14]

Simultaneously, cowhands slaved to round up and push beeves north to Concho tributaries, the first stop on the long journey back to the animals' home ranges. Employing a method similar to that of previous years—although on a much larger scale—the drovers had reason to celebrate every time they reached first water with a big herd after another eighty-hour drive. Recalled Ben C. Mayes:

"We turned them down the Concho draws with [a] big yell, saying, 'Go it, old heifers! We will see you in the general roundups later!"

Behind, meanwhile, festering carcasses marked the dusty trail all the way back, piling higher and higher with every drive. Indeed, the unrelenting ordeal up from Beaver Lake claimed a full thirty percent of every herd.[15]

Finally cowhands pointed the last stumbling cow north, clearing the way for Charles Lewis to return to the Nueces for his own cattle. For five days and nights, he and John Billings pushed a joint herd west for the Pecos across waterless barrens that threatened to strike down every animal. As hopes dimmed, the beeves smelled the waters of Beaver Lake and stampeded.

"No use to try to do anything with them," Lewis remembered decades later. "They ran into the lake and covered it. We only lost about 7 or 8 head but I expected to lose more."[16]

John M. Doak bossed another trail outfit that summer, a party of drovers with 800 cattle owned by Bob Chapman from the Guadalupe River headwaters thirty miles above Kerrville. En route to Antonio Creek near the present Val Verde-Terrell county line, the drove crossed the Devils beside the SP bridge, passed Comstock Station, and plodded on for the Trans-Pecos.[17]

A Kimble County drove also trekked to the Devils country in 1885, but this herd comprised not beeves but goats, animals ideally suited to the environment of present Val Verde County. The visionary behind the drive was Charles Dissler, who became the region's first stockman to make a livelihood raising goats.[18]

Within two years, 6,075 head would graze Val Verde,[19] and within fifteen years the aggregate would rise to more than 15,000. The real boom, however, would not come until the early twentieth century; by 1910, goats in the county would total 122,000, establishing goat-raising as Val Verde's chief livestock concern in terms of numbers.[20]

In this year of 1885, however, even the sheep industry sought a firm foothold on the Devils, as sheepmen came and went. Twenty-five-year-old Lemuel Bascom Cox ventured to the river and drifted a flock around Beaver Lake,[21] but Scotchman J. N. McLeod shunned the hard-scrabble life on the Devils and set up a sheep operation on the Concho.[22]

McLeod possessed either keen foresight or good fortune, for conditions soon would grow far worse on the Devils.

CHAPTER 16

HORN, FLEECE, AND DROUTH

Even as buzzards feasted on the carrion of the Big Cattle Die-Up of spring 1885, another insidious blight swept across the Devils.

This land always had been subject to a relentless drouth-rain-drouth cycle, but never before had stockmen faced it to such a degree. All that summer, the sun burned with a quiet fury, refusing to yield to rain clouds, while furnace-like winds crawled across range already devastated by the Big Drift. The Chihuahuan Desert, never more than a stone's throw away, now had a choke-hold on this river, and was loathe to let go.

Even worse, the Big Dry was not an isolated event. From Blanco County and beyond on the east to Arizona on the west, from Coahuila on the south to Fort Sumner, New Mexico, on the north, the pestilence raged like no other drouth in recorded history. Without the hope of finding pasturage elsewhere, Devils cattlemen had no choice but to watch their animals weaken and die.[1]

Despite nature's display of its awful majesty, ranching developments continued in 1885. Robert W. Prosser, who controlled Pecan Springs and miles of flowing river, stretched the region's first fence, though two years would pass before his entire ranch was under wire.[2] In the meantime, Prosser's pastures and surface water remained subject to drifting flocks of sheep and free-ranging beeves, a dilemma in this protracted drouth.

In any arid expanse, stock-raising was necessarily limited to water courses. The region later defined as Sutton County had only eleven ranches in 1885, and ten of them hugged sources of surface water. The lone exception was a spread owned by A. Winkler, who by that year tapped the Edwards-Trinity Plateau Outcrop aquifer along Dry Devils River two miles south of present Sonora. Mean-

Del Rio before 1900. Whitehead Memorial Museum, Del Rio, Texas.

while, five miles south of what was later Ozona on another Devils tributary, Johnsons Run, surveyor Joe Moss brought in his own water well in 1885.[3] Three years later, Prosser followed suit down near the Devils proper.[4]

With the discovery wells establishing the widespread availability of underground water, it was only a matter of time before ranching under fence was the accepted practice throughout the Devils country.

While ranching evolved, so did governmental designations. In 1885, authorities carved Val Verde County out of Crockett, Pecos, and Kinney counties. For county seat, citizens really had only one choice—the burgeoning railroad town of Del Rio,[5] as San Felipe del Rio was now known. By the following year, however, the community of Juno took root four miles by road downstream of Beaver Lake and a half-mile southwest of Cully Draw. A general store operated by a man named Edmundson may have already marked the 29.58-acre town site, which was not officially platted until June 1899. Folklore holds that its unusual name is a derivation of the phrase "you know," although "did you know . . . ?" might be more accurate.[6]

Among the stockmen who registered brands in Val Verde during its baptismal year were E. W. Loftin, A. F. and J. V. Dynows, H. D. Allen, W. A. Jones, Prosser and Company, J. E. Henderson, and J. H. Baker. Within another year, recorded brands would also represent individuals such as Roy Bean,[7] who would gain no-

Juno businessmen. Whitehead Memorial Museum, Del Rio, Texas.

toriety at Langtry as Judge Roy Bean, Law West of the Pecos.

Elsewhere in the Devils watershed, unorganized Crockett County had existed with expanded boundaries ever since 1875,[8] but the State of Texas hewed both Sutton and Schleicher from it in 1887.[9]

Wherever a county existed, the long arm of the tax collector was sure to find a person, even a squatter secreted on railroad land in the fortress of the Devils. But that didn't mean that nesters parted willingly with their hard-earned money, and one year in the 1880s when the county official showed up in person, some of the irate men chased him out of the country without a cent.

As tax season approached again, the tax office took precautions, arranging for Texas Ranger Ira Aten and a second man from Company D, Frontier Battalion, to accompany the collector to the squatters' homesteads.

"The only way they could be made to pay was to have the officer threaten to round up their cattle and sell them for taxes," recalled Aten.

From a camp on the San Saba, the two Rangers set out on a 100-mile ride and met up with the tax collector at Beaver Lake. For almost a month, the party combed the backcountry, as unpopular a threesome as ever traipsed the Devils.

From shack to shack, the story was usually the same: The collector requested the designated tax, an argument ensued, and the stockman finally went inside and returned with ten- and twenty-dollar gold pieces. Intimidated by the Rangers, he grudgingly paid.

Texas Ranger Ira Aten in 1887. N. S. Haley Memorial Library, Midland, Texas.

In one instance, however, the rancher entered his home and remained.

"When we went in to see what was keeping him," related Aten, "there he was, sitting on a chair with a gun across his knees, ready and willing for battle."

Only after his wife intervened could they persuade the stockman to give up his money and keep his life.

In the mid-1880s, men who had run afoul of more than tax law often denned in the most rugged canyon lands of the territory—those cut by the Sabinal and the Nueces, the Pecos and the Devils. So it was with a man who dodged a grand jury in Pennsylvania and brought his criminal ways to the Mexican border. From camp to camp he skulked throughout the Devils mountains, a thief and robber preying on hard-working stockmen.

Although Rangers generally scouted for outlaws in groups of four, Aten rode out alone from Camp Wood on the Nueces to bring him to justice.

On a dry branch thirty miles from Beaver Lake, he came upon the campfire of an elderly, gray-bearded man who could have passed for Santa Claus if not for his six-shooter and rifle. Not knowing but that this stranger was the man he sought, Aten posed as a line rider and accepted his hospitality. They made their beds across the fire from one another, each man keeping his firearms close at hand.

Soon after the wary Aten stretched out, he heard a voice. Coming to his elbow, the Ranger looked through the firelight and saw the old man kneeling.

"A more fervent prayer I never heard," Aten recalled. "He asked that the stranger in camp that night be protected and that he might be a good man. . . . A man who could pray to God like that, out in the wilds with only the blue Heavens and the stars above him, could not be the man I was hunting."

Reassured, Aten slept soundly. The next morning, he revealed his true identity and learned that the old man was a reclusive peddler of hides and jerky who spent much of his time wandering the backcountry.

On the lower Devils two days later, Aten apprehended the Pennsylvanian criminal with little trouble and struck out for Brackettville. Overtaken by dark, they stopped at a sheep camp, where Aten handcuffed himself to the felon and handed the key and his firearms to the foreman.

"I will call you if I need you," the Ranger told him.

Enduring the night, Aten and his prisoner continued down the trail at daybreak and reached Bracketville and the Kinney County sheriff's office by sundown.[10]

The drouth that had descended so grimly in 1885 continued to hold a scythe over the Devils the following year. Still, even in the driest of times, isolated showers could occur, especially in a region so expansive. On the river's headwater draws sixty-five miles south of San Angelo, the first rain in ten months fell in early spring, transforming dusty arroyos into rushing rivulets and leaving water holes sparkling in the sunlight. Sheepman M. E. Grinnell, upon freighting his 2,200-pound wool clip to San Angelo about April 20, reported his once-barren range in peak condition.[11]

Rain or not, determined stockmen clung to the Devils. When Lieutenant F. O. Johnson of the Third Cavalry traversed the Lower Road from Fort Stockton to Del Rio in June and July, he made notations of ranches at Howard's Well (Wilson's Sheep Ranch), Beaver Lake, the Juno area, the mouth of Johnsons Run, Pecan Springs, Second Crossing (Baker's Ranch and Shackelford's Ranch), and California Wells.[12]

Furthermore, ranchers from other regions continued to seek out the Devils. With the approach of fall, Perry Wilson and his son-in-law, Sam Blalock, pooled their herds in Frio County and urged the 1,200 beeves toward the sunset. As they held the herd near Brackettville one moonlit night, the animals unaccountably stampeded.

"We never could stop them cattle—just had to let 'em go," remembered Blalock, who was on night guard. "They run right through camp and this fellow, Swindler, was in bed. A little old yearling run right over him. That tickled me worse than anything that happened. Golly, he sure squalled!"

The drovers spent two days rounding up the frightened animals and forged on, only a dozen head short. Finally they reached the Devils headwaters, where Blalock set up camp for his wife Alice and infant daughters, who had accompanied

California Well in 2009. Photograph courtesy of Patrick Dearen.

the drive. They spent three months in a tent and survived a frigid winter, but it was only the start of Blalock's three-year ranching enterprise on the river.[13]

The Wilson-Blalock drove wasn't the only herd to reach the Devils in time for wintering in 1886. Veteran trail boss W. B. "Ab" Blocker pushed a herd from Tom Green County to the river's mouth, where George Berry held the Mexico-bound beeves for Blocker's brother John until the following spring.[14]

Journeying sheep also tramped across the Devils late in 1886. Martin H. Kilgore, discouraged by range conditions around Menardville, prodded his 5,000 animals southwestward in November with the help of the only drovers he could find—three outlaws, along with an elderly sheepherder who stole Kilgore's Winchester and fled the first night.

For twenty-one days between water holes, Kilgore's sheep subsisted on only scant forage laden with dew as matters grew increasingly grim. When the drovers' water dwindled to only half a bucket, one man panicked and spilled what little remained. Kilgore, however, kept his composure and located just enough moisture in scattered rock pools to see them through to the Devils.

As the sheep neared Beaver Lake, instinct overwhelmed all attempts to head them off.

"When they smelled the water, they were like crazy things," Kilgore related. "That lake covered about an acre or two but when those sheep ran into it, you couldn't see any water at all. They just covered it. They drank till . . . their paunches were just like drums."

Although Kilgore expected to lose the entire flock in the lake, not a single animal perished. Continuing on for the Pecos via the Lower Road, he crossed the herd on an improvised bridge at Lancaster Crossing (by then known as Tardy or Tarde Crossing) and found winter range below Dryden.[15]

Railroad accidents on the Devils section of the SP also marked autumn and early winter of 1886. Between the river and Del Rio on November 18, a wheel flange on an eastbound train broke, derailing the locomotive and two cars. No one suffered injury, but a sixteen-hour delay ensued.[16]

A December 31 incident two and a half miles from Devils River Station was far more serious. As a work train backed east through a sharply curving cut eight feet deep, nine Mexican laborers rode a flat car loaded with rock. The flat car was positioned next to a boxcar that served as a caboose, and when a freight train barreled into the cut from the opposite direction, the men had no escape.

Although the throttle of each locomotive was set at only six miles per hour, the grinding impact drove the caboose over the flat car and shifted its rock, crushing the men. Simultaneously, a caboose stove overturned and threw both cars into flames. By the time the firestorm ended, the victims' bodies had been incinerated.[17]

The following year, the Devils continued to spin a tale of tragedy for workers associated with the SP. On January 16, 1887, stonework contractor Thomas Cavanaugh sustained a serious fracture of his leg at the river.[18] Ten months later on November 22, a section boss died along the stream in a desperate attempt to remove a hand-car from the path of an oncoming train. As the hurtling locomotive exploded into the unit, flying shrapnel struck him in the skull.[19]

Less dramatic but equally sinister, the drouth that had seized the Devils in the summer of 1885 continued its treachery in early 1887. Once more, a vast region of Texas endured a dry, biting winter that forced cattle to retreat south.[20] Simultaneously, Albert Russell Cauthorn, seeking to save his suffering sheep, drifted his flock down to the Dry Devils country of Sutton County. Only 600 head survived the ordeal, but Cauthorn nevertheless established a sheep ranch that would endure for generations.[21]

With harsh weather eventually subsiding, San Angelo-area cowhands gigged their ponies for the Devils March 10 and found Tom Green County brands in the hides of 9,000 of the legion of cattle crowding the stream course. A thousand of the Tom Green beeves were in poor flesh or had suckling calves, so the men cut out the stronger animals and pointed them north. By early April, the drovers had turned 8,000 cattle loose on the headwaters of Dove and Spring creeks.[22]

Finally in late April, almost two years after drouth had first laid waste to the Devils and far beyond, rains began to fall. By month's end, the range from Johnsons Run to Howard's Well had sprung to life, according to the April 30 *San Angelo Standard,* and the Devils and Pecos soon reaped similar rewards.[23]

Relief had come none too soon for Val Verde County cattlemen, who now grazed 26,508 beeves valued at $181,117 and 2,260 horses and mules worth $35,624. With vigor restored to the range, losses for 1887 totaled a mere twenty-nine stock cattle and fifteen horses.

Sheepmen, however, paid a far greater price, losing 840 animals for the year. Nevertheless, they sheared 87,920 head that delivered a wool clip of 519,326 pounds, a value of $72,689.50.[24]

With the long drouth relegated to memory, Val Verde cattlemen convened in Del Rio on February 14, 1888, and planned the spring roundup. They divided the range into five districts, two of which involved the Devils. Cowhands were to meet at Camp Hudson March 15 and work upstream under Robert W. Prosser's supervision to Beaver Lake, where they would join northern outfits seeking the return of drift herds. After April 1, Val Verde cowboys would converge on upper Mud Creek, a few miles east of the Val Verde-Kinney county line, and work west to the Devils.[25]

Over on the Pecos, meanwhile, outfits from Pecos Valley Association would rendezvous April 30 at Independence Ranch to pick up drift cattle between Howard's Well and the New Mexico line.[26]

In a land absent of fences, general roundups were essential, but in spring J. B. Taylor presented a glimpse of things to come. Upon acquiring a 150,000-acre ranch by deed and lease in the Devils headwater draw country, the onetime New York physician set about making improvements. Already, he had brought in one well at a depth of 129 feet and another at 213 feet; furthermore, he had purchased an eighteen-foot Titus windmill, the largest in the region. Now, while a driller sank additional shafts, the fledgling rancher was busy fencing his entire spread, and soon 6,000 Taylor beeves would be under barbed wire.[27]

The growing number of nefarious characters who skulked about the Devils, however, would not be as easily corralled.

CHAPTER 17

BADMEN RISE UP

Whether this untamed region bearing the dark angel's name molded good men into evil figures, or whether its isolation drew individuals predisposed to wickedness, no one can say. But robbery and theft increasingly became a way of life on the Devils—and gunplay a way of death.

In spring of 1888, two Mexicans instigated trouble on a Sutton County sheep ranch managed by a man named Taylor, who proceeded to Kimble County and notified authorities. A deputy sheriff named Smith accompanied him back to the spread, where in the company of Taylor and the sheepman's boss, he attempted to arrest the Mexicans.

The suspects, however, had other ideas. They opened fire and compelled Taylor and his employer to surrender, leaving the deputy to face the smoking barrels alone. Emptying his pistol, he wounded one Mexican twice and forced the men to flee, the two riding double on Taylor's horse.

Deputy Smith quickly formed a posse and tracked the Mexicans south. On the Devils, the lawmen overtook one of the men, who evidently was now afoot, and shot him dead, then pushed on and came within gunshot range of the second Mexican. After an initial exchange of bullets, posse and fugitive engaged in a running fight all the way to Beaver Lake, where the posse finally rode the man down and killed him.[1]

Just weeks later in the Dry Devils country of Schleicher County, a party discovered two young men butchering a yearling just outside William Black's pasture fence. Tom Palmer and his cowhands, investigating in mid-June, determined that the yearling had belonged to Black. Although the beef may have strayed, the law considered the unauthorized seizure a crime, and Menard County Sheriff Dick

Russell soon arrested the suspects and escorted them to Menardville.[2]

By January 1889, the new community of Sonora had sprung up at the juncture of Dry Devils River and Lowrey Draw in Sutton County. Here where the San Angelo and Fort McKavett road forked, Charles G. Adams and an associate named Meinecke drilled a 191-foot well and erected a Perkins windmill and 500-barrel tank. The original plat included ninety-two lots, all of which Adams offered for free, and by late March thirty-two parcels had been claimed.

Although only R. W. Callahan's general store and four or five other buildings graced the town site by spring, the absence of structures was more a reflection of the delay in obtaining lumber than a lack of interest. Indeed, in this heart of a sheep kingdom of 200,000 head, reported a newspaper correspondent, the hillside and valley were "literally bedecked with tents."

By the following January, Sonora sported not only Callahan's operation, but also a saloon, beef market, barber shop, feed store and wagon yard, two-story hotel, two-teacher school with sixty-five pupils, two blacksmith shops, and at least thirty residences. In various stages of planning were a second hotel, bank, drug store, livery stable, newspaper, two additional supply stores, and ten more residences. Furthermore, a commercial hack provided tri-weekly mail-and-passenger service to and from San Angelo, sixty-eight miles distant.

Not surprisingly, in 1890 the boom town became Sutton County seat, gaining the nod over the small settlement of Wentworth four miles to the south.[3]

Despite problems with barbed wire and quarantines for Texas fever, cattle droves continued to trail across the Devils country in 1889. In spring, Coleman-Fulton Pasture Company leased 100,000 acres in Sutton and Schleicher counties above the quarantine line from J. B. Taylor. From Rockport on the Gulf Coast, the company brought in 4,000 beeves by hoof at an average cost of $1.11 per animal.[4]

Meanwhile on the Bar S—a Dry Devils outfit managed by Dave O'Keefe—fifteen-year-old Johnnie Roberts helped cut out thousands of steers and turn the herd north. Weeks later, the drove reached Amarillo on the Fort Worth and Denver City (FW&DC) Railway, culminating the first of two Bar S drives to the FW&DC shipping point in consecutive years.[5]

Net wire had yet to make inroads on the Devils, but the advent of fences encouraged sheepmen such as J. M. Campbell of Val Verde County to experiment with loose-herding in the late 1880s. By September 1889, however, Campbell returned to the shepherd system; wild animal attacks had made it infeasible to leave his flock unprotected at night.[6] Still, the predator problem did not deter the *San Angelo Standard* from soon touting the Devils River as "the sheepman's paradise"[7]—a term that quickly metamorphosed into the all-inclusive "Stockman's Paradise."[8]

In goat developments, John T. Brown had grazed a small flock of Angoras on the river since 1887.[9] In the summer of 1889, however, C. Dissler took added steps to popularize the Devils mohair industry and started west from Kendall County with 400 head. Although heat claimed many of the animals along the way, the flock flourished upon reaching the river and produced eight-inch fleeces by the following spring.[10] Within a decade or so, the Edwards Plateau nurtured many of the 100,000 Angora or Angora crossbreds in the state.[11]

In the meantime, criminal activity continued to rage along the river. In June 1889, a stockman shot a Mexican several times, the lead balls exploding into the victim's mouth and stomach. In the absence of medical care in the region, the Mexican was transported to San Angelo.[12]

Range conditions and population growth always went hand-in-hand in ranch country, and prosperity had spiked all up and down the Devils and its tributaries after the Big Dry of 1885 to 1887. Indeed, encouraged citizens organized Crockett County and chose the Johnsons Run community of Powell Well—modern Ozona—as county seat on July 7, 1891.[13] But even as splendid rains blessed isolated pastures that year,[14] wise stockmen knew to brace for the inevitable downturn in precipitation.

Juno was among the first locales crippled by empty skies in 1891. In mid-July, Beaver Lake appeared in danger of going dry, an unprecedented development that forced stockmen to consider fencing it against wandering herds to conserve the dwindling waters.[15]

The dark days on the Devils caught drovers for James Dalrymple unawares as they bore west from the Uvalde area with 2,178 two-year-old steers. Falling into the ruts of the old California Cattle Trail en route to New Mexico, the outfit negotiated First Crossing and entered a desolate land.

"The range was dry and water scarce, and many of our cattle gave out and had to be left on the trail," recalled cowhand G. W. Scott.[16]

Drouth, with its tinder box pasture conditions and low humidity, often presaged range fire, which even in periods of normal rainfall could rage unchecked at the whim of determined winds. In March 1890, in fact, flames had claimed fifteen miles of fence on a Devils ranch owned by E. R. Jackson.[17] But in a land notorious for extremes, from drouth to cattle drift, 1891 was the year of the big burn—a brimstone season when skies repeatedly boiled with smoke.

On February 5, Mexican herders careless with cigarettes reportedly ignited a fire that roared across the divide between the Devils' head draws and Dove and Spring creeks. Marching relentlessly for days, it left in its wake a twenty-by-thirty-mile path of destruction that included twenty sections on the Jackson & Aldwell spread.[18]

Five months later, another disastrous blaze charred the Newell and Mahlmann ranges between the Devils' upper reaches and the South Concho. The responsible party, a sheepherder with the Newell outfit, abandoned his flock and fled for Mexico when the early flames escaped his control. Negligent or not, he faced more than his boss' retribution; starting a prairie fire could be a penitentiary offense.[19]

Cooler temperatures in late fall brought no respite, as November wildfires blackened rangeland near the Steagall sheep ranch in the Sonora region.[20] Ironically, while some Devils outfits suffered from drouth and burn, others thrived. In mid-November D. B. Cusenbary, who ranched below Sonora, reported his sheep in better condition for the season than in the past four or five years.[21] O. T. Word, located in the Dry Devils-Elbow Lake area ten miles southwest of Sonora, soon concurred, noting that he had never been so pleased with his sheep.[22]

Still, with the prospect of outside "drifters" storming the country with flocks that winter, a sufficiency of forage and water was a concern. As early as August, the *San Angelo Standard* had foreseen the problem, citing not only extensive fires but rapid settlement as contributing factors.[23] Now as wintry winds began to howl, Devils stockmen gave drifters warning.

"We are not able to grass other people's stock free any longer," observed the *Devil's River News* of Sonora. "If people bring their stock here to winter they must expect to pay.... Free range is a thing of the past in the Stockman's Paradise as elsewhere, and it is only just and right that our stockmen should protect themselves."

W. O. Edwards even went so far as to petition neighboring ranchers to agree in writing to deny drifters water.[24]

With nerves on edge for much of 1891, a culture of violence shrouded bustling Sonora in particular. On July 30, John Q. Adams fatally shot fellow sheepman Isaac Miers (also spelled Mayers and Mires) in a dispute over watering their flocks at the well on the courthouse square. Convicted in San Angelo of murder, Adams walked free June 29, 1892, when an appellate court ruled that the presiding judge not only had allowed the introduction of illegal evidence, but had failed to instruct the jury properly.[25]

On September 17, 1891, just seven weeks after the Adams-Miers bloodshed, Adams' son Thomas C. Adams brutally murdered W. M. Wilson of Hamilton County as the two men wagoned between Sonora and Kerrville in Wilson's rig. After crushing Wilson's skull, the younger Adams torched the kerosene-saturated body and concealed it in tall grass beside the road. Within several days, a passerby discovered the remains, but Adams remained on the run with Wilson's team until authorities apprehended him in Kerrville October 5. The killing netted Adams twenty years in prison.[26]

In at least two 1891 shootings, liquor evidently played a role. John Denson shot a man over a gambling matter in Sonora's Maude S Saloon, while at outlying Lost Lake, a drunken Mexican killed a man and fled for the border. Although the party who murdered a sheepherder on a road near town also went unpunished, the guilty did not always elude retribution. That same year, gun-toting lawmen reportedly overtook a pair of horse thieves elsewhere in the region and felled them both.[27]

But even as some men contented themselves with crimes of impulse, others took note of the opportunity for ill-gotten gain along the SP Railroad.

CHAPTER 18

A POTENTIAL FOR SUDDEN DEATH

Near Samuels Station, a lonely Southern Pacific siding forty miles by rail west of the Pecos, outlaws held up a train on September 1, 1891. Identified as Thumbless Jack Wellington, John Flynt (or Flint), Tom Fields, and James Langston, the men gigged their horses east through desolate country with thousands of dollars.

In the bluff below the mouth of the Pecos, Wellington later claimed, they hid $10,000 before pressing on for the Devils with mail sacks under their saddles as blankets. At every camp, the bandits celebrated their success by tearing open another money bundle, thereby leaving a trail of Wells-Fargo packaging.

As Ranger Captain Frank Jones of Company D rode a weaving passenger train west for El Paso in October, authorities notified him that the gang was camped in the Devils country fifty miles from Comstock. Jones, his men, and their outfitted horses soon boarded an eastbound freight in Alpine and disembarked fifteen hours later at Comstock. By sundown the Rangers rode upon Hudson's forlorn walls, and a day later they stormed the band's camp and found it deserted.

For five days Jones' command and a sheriff's posse tracked the riders west to Howard's Well and on to the 7D outfit on upper Live Oak Creek, where they finally caught up with the unsuspecting fugitives October 16. Langston surrendered at once, and Fields after brief flight, but Wellington and Flynt put up a battle, even as they urged their ponies across mountainous terrain.

As the chase persisted, an off-target bullet caught Wellington's horse, forcing the train robber's submission. Twenty-eight-year-old Flynt stayed determined, however, exchanging gunfire throughout a ten-mile race before a bullet ripped through his shoulder and chest and knocked him from his horse. He may have considered the wound fatal, for he chose to commit suicide rather than give himself up.

Early Comstock. Whitehead Memorial Museum, Del Rio, Texas.

Lawmen recovered only $1,100, almost half of which was Mexican money. As Wellington languished behind bars in Del Rio, however, he revealed to Bob Beverly and Bill Welch the location of the cache near the mouth of the Pecos. Although the two cowhands combed the downstream bluff, they never uncovered the loot.

Interestingly, Captain Jones described Wellington as "a gentleman" who possessed "fine blue eyes," with a contemporary news dispatch adding that both Wellington and Fields were "rather dashing-looking"—lending credence to the notion that this brutal country sometimes hewed even the best of men in its own image. After almost ten months of incarceration at Del Rio and perhaps elsewhere, the two robbers boarded another train together, this time in shackles, in order to serve one-year sentences in federal prison.[1]

Beverly and Welch, returning to Comstock in late 1891 after their failed treasure quest, made plans to attend a wedding celebration in the section house during the Christmas season. Placing their horses in the nearby shipping pens, they spent the night in revelry, only to find their mounts and saddles gone the next morning. As they were to learn, two strangers had arrived on the evening train and stolen the animals.

Securing fresh horses, Beverly and Welch located the tracks and set out with the kind of determination that later served Beverly well as Midland County sheriff. The trail led up the divide between the Devils and Cow Creek, a Rio Grande tributary coursing north to south for twenty-one miles midway between the Devils and Pecos. The trace eventually dropped into Johnsons Run and carried the cowhands to Ozona, by now a town of 400 people.

With the help of Sam Perry, Crockett County sheriff, Beverly and Welch switched to fresh mounts and resumed the chase. Reaching the Pecos, they crossed the HAT outfit and finally reached Pecos City, where they learned that Sheriff Dave Allison of Midland and Texas Rangers had already apprehended the thieves and recovered the horses.

A few nights after Beverly and Welch returned to the Devils area, Mexican nationals robbed the Comstock store and killed a clerk. Loading pack horses with goods wrapped in red *soogans,* or bedroll quilts, the murderers escaped into the night and crossed into Mexico at the mouth of the Pecos.

A US Customs official named Cunningham quickly organized a four-man posse that included Beverly, and the tenacious riders tracked the bandits 100 miles deep into Mexico.

"We could trail them along by these red pieces of *soogan* that would be picked up by the brush as they went through," Beverly recalled.

Just outside the small village of San Felipe, the Americans found a camp abandoned in haste only minutes before. They seemed sure to overtake the Mexicans, but a San Felipe official challenged their right to be in Mexico.

"It looked like war there," related Beverly, "and we decided the best way to save our lives was through flight."

Riding only at night to escape detection by *federales,* the men reached the border and splashed their horses back across into Texas.[2]

Isolated rain finally peppered the drouth-stricken Devils in mid-December, but it served only to cause a delay on the SP that contributed to another train wreck. One after the other, four trains finally chugged west from Del Rio early on the fourteenth. About two miles shy of the Devils, the first train unaccountably stopped and flagged the second train, which in turn alerted the third unit. The fourth locomotive, however, followed too closely and roared pell-mell toward the empty caboose ahead.

Recognizing the inevitable, the engineer locked the air brakes and leaped from the locomotive with the fireman. Still, the engine barreled on, slamming into the stationary train with a wrenching of metal and splintering of wood. Personnel with both trains escaped injury, but the collision damaged the caboose and two cars, and demolished the locomotive's smokestack, headlight, and cowcatcher.[3]

Even without murder or train event, the potential for sudden death gripped the land in the 1890s like a hangman's noose. On April 2, 1891, a wagon accident on the Taylor spread claimed W. M. Mathis of Wentworth. Evidently astride a horse harnessed to a lumber-laden wagon as it negotiated a downward slope, the man fell under a wheel and was crushed.[4]

Bob Stevens near Juno. Whitehead Memorial Museum, Del Rio, Texas.

In another episode involving a horse in December of the following year, cowhand Mike Dowling narrowly escaped an equally rocky grave. As he rounded up cattle near Beaver Lake, his mount collided with a cow and he went down hard, striking his head. Unconscious for two days, he nevertheless managed to recover.[5]

A *vaquero* named Ress (possibly Reyes) wasn't so fortunate in May 1897 on William Grinnell's Buckhorn Draw ranch. When his horse returned to headquarters without him one evening, Alexander Macnabb checked the animal and discovered a stirrup missing. Realizing the situation was grim, Macnabb organized a search and found the *vaquero* dead four miles north of headquarters. No one had witnessed the accident, but the stirrup on his boot told the tragic tale of a rider dragged to death.[6]

In the cowboy's world, a bronc was always a threat, but the danger increased a thousand-fold if a thunderstorm caught him in the saddle. Lightning generally targeted a high point, and a rider's perch often placed him in just such a position. As a *vaquero* clung to his horse on storm-tossed range near Howard's Well in June 1898, a bolt exploded out of the sky and killed both rider and animal. The same blast also knocked down two men in a nearby camp.[7]

The Devils' own spawn, meanwhile, could dispatch a man with just as much certainty, as a sheepherder learned when he pursued a cottontail rabbit into a small cave in the early 1890s. As he squeezed inside, a large rattlesnake buried its fangs in his flesh. He left a young boy to tend the flock and rushed to ranch headquarters, only to die that night.

The next day, several men set out to avenge his death. Guided by the boy, they reached the cave and sent two dogs inside to locate the reptile. The rattler struck twice, killing the first dog almost instantly before hanging its fangs in the second animal's hind leg. As the dog tried to escape, it pulled the snake close enough to the entrance for a Winchester shot.

The dog survived, but by March 1892 the window of Coleman's saddle and harness shop in San Angelo showcased the reptile's skin alongside those of seven other Devils rattlers. The only specimen larger than the man-killer was a snake that had measured nine feet one inch in length and seventeen inches in girth, and had borne thirty-eight rattles and a button.[8]

Like cowboys, shepherds and goat herders frequently faced demanding situations that placed them in harm's way. In another such example, a sixty-year-old goatherd named Juan froze to death four miles northwest of Sonora in the winter of 1896-1897.[9]

Still, these laborers, typically of Mexican descent, invariably received far less pay than a cowhand's wages of twenty or more dollars a month.[10] Not until the summer of 1892 did Val Verde sheepmen convene in Del Rio and adopt a uniform monthly salary of ten dollars for sheepherders,[11] a rate that increased to between

A POTENTIAL FOR SUDDEN DEATH 153

A Devils country cowboy. Whitehead Memorial Museum, Del Rio, Texas.

twelve and fifteen dollars within five years.[12] Although their wages were modest, sheepherders remained the very backbone of an ever-growing industry with an impact that reached well beyond the Devils.

In 1888, the Santa Fe Railroad had reached San Angelo,[13] and this town at the confluence of the North and Middle Concho rivers soon became the wool center for not only the Devils but also a sprawling region. Rail cars freighted six million pounds of fleece out of San Angelo in 1891,[14] but the town's importance as a cattle shipping point was growing as well.

With connections to Indian Territory, the Santa Fe station was the destination of several cattle drives originating on the Devils in the spring of 1892. Not only did cattlemen need to reduce numbers on their drouth-stricken ranges, but the Territory was now the sole outlet for beeves from below the Texas fever quarantine line.[15]

One drove, consisting of Half Circle 6 cows and steers ready for transport to the Territory, started up the Dry Devils for San Angelo in late March,[16] while R. Prosser of Pecan Springs shipped 1,000 steers to the same location May 12.[17] Other Devils herds, including fifteen cars of cattle that a stockman named Hart loaded at San Angelo June 3, headed straight for the Chicago market. A day later, the *San Angelo Standard* praised the Hart beeves as "the best shippers out of San Angelo this season."[18]

If a longhorn avoided roundup on the Devils for a year or two, it might turn "outlaw" and even reach legendary status. Such was the case with a brindle steer branded Nine R that roamed the river's headwaters for nine years. Three times, or maybe four, cowhands threw the incorrigible animal in with a railroad-bound drove, but the steer always escaped and returned to its Devils haunt.

In 1892, Old Nine R's owner sold out, and John Custer and his hands swept the range and picked up the wild-eyed brute. By tying the steer every night, Custer managed to keep it with the drove all the way to the railroad. When cowpunchers finally secured the animal inside a cattle car, Old Nine R's freedom seemed over.

Suddenly, with a splintering of wood, the outlaw broke free and leaped to the ground, once more thundering toward the faraway Devils.

Custer, as determined as he was astounded, rode the steer down and dragged it by rope to another car. After cowhands again crowded the animal up the chute and on inside, Custer took no more chances—he tied Old Nine R in a corner for the final leg of its reluctant journey away from its beloved Devils.[19]

Meanwhile, stockmen found plenty to curse about this river with its sporadic, hit-or-miss precipitation. In early February, a nice rain blessed a ranch owned by a sheepman named Dodd, who reported the range along the Devils in excellent condition.[20] More showers in late March and early April filled water holes on the

San Angelo and Junction roads near Sonora.[21] On June 25, the *San Angelo Standard* even proclaimed the Devils "a paradise with a big P" after a "magnificent" rain a few days earlier.

Still, the Juno area suffered until late August, when drouth-breaking clouds finally drenched a broad region that encompassed not only Beaver Lake, but the Pecos all the way upstream to Pecos City.[22] Finally, stockmen throughout the Devils watershed could revel in the promise of adequate forage for winter.

While skies teased and finally delivered, men inclined to lawlessness continued to ply their perfidy. In late March, San Angelo lawman Dick Runyon investigated a sheep-rustling case at Beaver Lake reported by the owners, Western Mercantile Company and a rancher named Weisenbeck.[23] Two months later, Beaver Lake also served as stage for a deadly fray between two men vying for the affections of the same young lady.

The incident began one morning in late May when Bob Stockman, who was in his mid-thirties, called on a girl named Monroe at her father's camp. She rebuffed his advances in such a way that he placed blame on Charles Blandin, a sheepman of "quiet, unassuming disposition," according to a contemporary news article. Stockman swore to kill his rival on sight, and while he searched the premises in order to do so, Miss Monroe and her sister rode for N. G. King's ranch at Beaver Lake to alert the absent Blandin.

Halfway to the lake, Stockman overtook the girls and brandished his Winchester, warning that he would kill the two unless they stopped. The girls pulled rein, but as the younger sister engaged Stockman in conversation, the older rider let her horse saunter ahead. A hundred yards down the trail, she lashed the animal into a gallop and proceeded to outrace Stockman to the King place.

Blandin, upon hearing the girl's story, could not understand Stockman's acrimony and decided against flight. As his accuser rode up to the King house, Blandin went outside and asked the nature of the trouble. Stockman replied only that one of them had to die, and slid off his horse with his Winchester.

Blandin, however, stood too close to allow the rifle barrel to swing upward, a position he continued to hold as he tried to calm the enraged man. When Stockman lunged to one side to create room to fire, Blandin drew his six-gun and shot him in the head, killing him instantly.

Although the shooting seemed justified, a peace justice placed Blandin under $1,000 bond after he rode into Juno and reported the incident.[24]

In an era in which horse theft was considered almost as heinous as murder, purveyors of frontier justice sometimes meted out punishment at the end of a rope for either offense. Even the threat of a noose might loosen an accomplice's tongue, as a summer incident illustrated.

About July 23, Bob Glenn and his stepson, Dave Lucas, started west from Falls

County by train and foot to look for work. At Ballinger, they joined up with Glenn's brother, Jeff, who had a single horse. The three of them proceeded to the head of Kickapoo Creek, where the Glenn brothers swiped two more horses and saddles. Now that all three were mounted, they bore south into Sutton County.

On the Devils or Dry Devils, the brothers switched the stolen horses for fresh animals—a deed that led to their late-August arrest in Falls County after Lucas turned state's witness against his relatives, albeit reluctantly.

"Dave Lucas," reported the September 2 *Dallas Morning News,* "stated that his statement was first obtained by the liberal application of a rope around his neck, but was nevertheless true."

Unable to post bonds of $500 each, the Glenn brothers went directly to jail.[25]

Even the approach of Christmas failed to bring harmony to the Devils. On December 21, a fight between sheepmen Thomas McDowell and William Scholby ended with Scholby shot to death.[26]

For stockmen so recently out of drouth's clutches, the year 1893 began promisingly enough—forage was abundant, sheep were the fattest in years, and excellent mutton sales were expected.[27] Nevertheless, in distant locales brewed events that would have a devastating effect on the Devils wool industry in particular.

CHAPTER 19

FANG, CLAW, AND BUFFALO HIDES

In February 1893, the Philadelphia and Reading Railroad failed, ushering in the Panic of 1893.

By mid-May, prices on the New York Stock Exchange plummeted to all-time lows. In August, nationwide unemployment swelled to one million on the way to three times that number. Before the economy began to recover three years later, the unprecedented depression would bankrupt seventy-four railroads, 500 or more banks, and 15,000 companies.[1]

In the spring of 1892, wool had brought fourteen cents a pound in San Angelo,[2] and as late as July of the Panic year, Devils sheepman Garrett Bean sold his clip at a thirteen-cent rate.[3] Nevertheless, the crippled market of the next few months would soon lead a journalist to condemn 1893 as "the most terrible [year] ever witnessed in the American wool trade."[4] With a record decline in prices, Devils sheepmen realized a mere seven cents a pound for their fall clips,[5] down fifty percent from the year before.

During the depression's initial period, activity continued to swirl around Beaver Lake. In May 1893, its shore was the scene of another shooting, this time with a Mexican man as victim. Transported to Del Rio, he died the next month.[6] By November, J. O. Taylor and his partner Franks (likely E. S. Franks) gained control of the lake and readied to fence fifty sections. For water, they planned to use not only Beaver, but also the William I. Babb well and two wells of their own.[7]

Within a few years, the *San Angelo Standard* touted Taylor's seventy-eight-section Beaver Lake Ranch as "one of the best improved properties" in the area. Consisting of railroad and school land and a few leased sections, the spread was home to 1,600 cattle that watered at seven wells and three large lakes.[8]

Jim Taylor and Floyd Earwood at Juno in 1902. Whitehead Memorial Museum, Del Rio, Texas.

Above and beyond Taylor's success in building a ranch, he earned the admiration of his cowhands.

"Jim Taylor turned out to be one of the best friends I ever had in the world," noted Oliver Prentiss, who certainly needed a friend when he first arrived at Beaver Lake as a mere youth in the mid-1890s.

Thrown out of his Eagle Pass home at age twelve by an abusive stepfather, Oliver had no choice but to saddle an old outlaw nag and ride away. Without a nickel to his name or even a change of clothes, he drifted toward Juno.

"I would sleep wherever night overtook me if I didn't make it to a ranch house," he related.

One day a rider named Frank overtook the boy, who recognized the man as a friend of his stepfather's. What Oliver didn't realize, however, was that Frank's character was in question; only recently, he had escaped conviction in Del Rio for train robbery. Soon the aimless youth was astride a better horse and helping Frank round up and brand beeves.

"I worked hard . . . , never dreaming that they were not his, but really old man [Robert W.] Prosser's cattle," Oliver remembered.

Only after the boy took a job at Dave Baker's ranch did he learn of his role in the rustling operation. Several months later and far wiser to the ways of the Devils' lawless element, Oliver was riding for highly respected Jim Taylor on the Beaver Lake outfit.[9]

In the meantime, stockmen had grown discontent with the increasing outlaw depredations in the vicinity of the lake. In early spring of 1894, they initiated a movement to establish a Texas Rangers camp at Juno.[10] The call went unheeded, even after burglars struck Henry Stein's Juno store one night in late March or early April. The felons, possibly two Mexicans who had browsed the stock the evening before, pilfered $350 in goods, including gold watches and clothing. Before fleeing town, they also stole four horses.[11]

Only weeks later, violence bloodied the Hudspeth & Swift Ranch twenty-five miles south of Sonora when two Mexican men decided to settle a years-long feud. One actor, whose name was Anacio, wrenched a pistol from Melian Gonzales and proceeded to stab him nine times with a dagger. Gravely wounded, Gonzales fell, but managed to taunt his assailant, prompting Anacio to bludgeon him fatally with the gun.[12]

Even as economic depression raged, the Devils faced troubles born of nature—a winter forage shortage, sheep struggles, and wild animal attack. With the range too barren for effective drifting in the winter of 1893-1894, enterprising sheepmen fed their flocks sotol, a succulent with leaves ribbon-like and serrated. In early February, veteran stockman William Schupach asserted that his muttons were fattening faster on the indigenous plant than on the best grass of years past. Furthermore, cattle thrived so well on a sotol-Mexican meal mix that entrepreneurs began harvesting the plant for shipments east.[13]

Despite the promise that alternative forage might hold for the future of the Devils sheep industry, the dry winter impacted many stockmen. Wool clip weights dropped as much as twenty-five percent from the previous year. S. E. Couch of Crockett County, upon shearing 8,000 sheep near Ozona, declared his clip the lightest he could remember.[14] Furthermore, the early lamb crop in March of 1894 was down a full twenty percent.[15]

A flock's increase was partly dictated by wolves, which now roamed in greater numbers and with more daring than ever. As Antonio Lopez and a second sheepherder tended a flock on the Louis Thornton ranch in Val Verde County in late summer or early fall, a pair of lobos attacked their animals. When Lopez and his companion rushed out to drive the predators away, the wolves turned their flashing fangs upon the men.

Lopez went down, dying in the most horrible of ways. The second herder also faced the fight of his life, but he fended the wolves off with a pistol and knife, even as they mauled him severely.[16]

The Devils country seemed to breed extraordinary episodes involving wild creatures. Just fifteen months before in June of 1893, a skunk pounced on a sleeping rancher's face. Startled into awareness, H. Latham struck the animal, but it sank its teeth in his nose and held its grip. Latham finally fought free, but his nose was so severely lacerated that he sought medical attention in Del Rio.[17]

The nearly extinct buffalo, although never a threat to Devils stockmen, raised considerable interest after a spring 1894 report of a small herd in southern Val Verde.[18] To be sure, at a water hole halfway between Juno and Howard's Well in the summer of 1890, Will Wright had discovered the month-old carcass of a buffalo bull—a presumed stray from the TX Ranch at Horsehead Crossing on the Pecos.[19] This new sighting, however, engendered a sense of wonder that a handful of sequestered animals on the TX could not. Possibly, the Val Verde buffalo constituted a wild remnant of the vast herds that had ranged across the South Plains only a few decades before.

Although Mescaleros had hunted buffalo on the Devils in 1787,[20] by the late 1840s the animal had become a rarity along the river. Near Painted Cave in 1854, westbound drovers with the John James herd gathered buffalo chips for fuel,[21] and ten years later Frontier Rangers purportedly found additional buffalo signs at Pecan Springs.[22] Still, the Devils lay at the extreme southern limit of the animal's range, and actual sightings were all but unknown even before the great slaughter of the 1870s. After 1882, buffalo seemed to have vanished forever from the region.[23]

As the years passed, however, evidence indicated that stragglers still occasionally roamed the Devils. Bullets reportedly felled four buffalo along the river in 1886.[24] In late 1888 or early 1889, a cowboy killed an old bull between the Colorado and Rio Grande,[25] and a year or so later, George W. Fulton Jr.'s rifle brought down another buffalo on J. B. Taylor's Sutton County spread.

The latter animal was part of a wandering herd of about thirty that Taylor managed to place under barbed wire. The bison nevertheless escaped[26] and apparently drifted south to the lower Devils region where, in an offshoot canyon, they stirred excitement in the spring of 1894.

The frenzy began when Leal Martinez, foreman for C. H. Moreau's Val Verde sheep operation, journeyed cross-country from Mexico and chanced upon forty or fifty shaggy brutes.

"Martinez told me . . . that he found the herd in a small valley between two ranges of big hills, many miles from any settler," Moreau related to the *San Angelo Standard*. "That part of Val Verde County is very remote and it is possible that the herd has been there for several years without being seen by anybody."[27]

Taylor, hoping to capture the animals for his Sutton ranch if they truly existed,[28] set out for the rumored valley in early fall. Guided by Mexican hunters, he located the secluded glen with its recent buffalo signs, only to determine that the animals had migrated elsewhere. In the mud of recent rains, however, they had left an unmistakable trail.

Taylor followed the trace out of the valley, through a mountain pass extending to the Rio Grande, and upstream on the Texas side. Along the way, he gained reports from remote settlers who had witnessed the animals' passage only weeks before. Including ten or so calves, the herd had numbered about sixty, and if Taylor needed any additional proof of the animals' existence, a man named Gonzales displayed a robe fashioned from the hide of one of the calves.

Eventually the trail led Taylor and his guides into Mexico. Even then, they persisted long enough to determine that the buffalo seemed on course for the Santa Rosa Mountains. Turning back for Texas, Taylor soon reached Dryden and caught a Southern Pacific train east.[29]

Saturated by summer and fall showers that elevated the Rio Grande to its highest level in thirteen years,[30] the Devils range flourished in the winter of 1894-1895.[31] But even as supplemental rain the following spring similarly raised stockman's hopes,[32] it also laid the groundwork for catastrophe. With the soil soaked, any additional downpours in the near future would generate run-off.

In May, heavy rains flooded the upper Devils watershed, unleashing hellish walls of water. Johnsons Run swept down out of the north, increasing in force with every mile. By the time the torrent reached a point fifteen miles downstream of Ozona, it had swelled to almost half a mile wide, a deluge far too powerful for anyone in its path.

Five Mexicans—three men, a woman, and a small girl—failed to escape and drowned.

Conditions on the Devils, especially downstream of its confluence with Johnsons Run, were equally threatening. Rising waters chased A. W. Evans from his river camp to a lofty cave. The flood buried G. F. Ling's homestead under eight feet of water, and citizens briefly feared that the unstoppable currents may have washed away R. W. Prosser's headquarters three and a half miles above Second Crossing.[33]

The people of the Devils were nothing if not resilient, however, and by June they were singing the praises of a range graced by rain. The *Del Rio Record* observed that good forage was almost a certainty for summer and fall.[34] Sheepman H. Watts reported that grass was knee-high and still growing.[35] Another stockman claimed that his sheep and cattle had strayed into grass so tall he could no longer locate them.

"He is offering good rewards for them," noted the *Ozona Courier*, "as he is afraid the grass will become so dense that they will be unable to get out at all and they will die for water."[36]

A direct result of this "soft bed of velvet green," as the *Courier* dubbed the range,[37] was higher quality wool. With thick grass holding the soil in place, sheep had virtually no dust in their fleeces, resulting in at least ten percent less shrinkage at market. For sheepmen still facing depression prices for their clips that fall, the development should have paid dividends. Eastern buyers at San Angelo, however, maintained that the presence of needle grass lowered the wool's value enough to offset any quality considerations.[38] Sheepmen such as O. J. Woodhull, apparently judging the five- or six-cent offers comparable to the late-summer theft of two horses thirty miles south of Sonora, chose to store their clips until a subsequent season.[39]

As more of the Devils came under fence, limiting the mingling of cattle and spread of Texas fever, cowmen turned increasingly to high-grade beeves. That fall, J. B. Taylor purchased 465 Herefords from Jot Gunter of Grayson County and stocked his Sutton range. The herd included not only mature blooded bulls, but eighty bull calves that immediately realized good offers from local ranchers.

"The importation of this fine herd . . . is very important and will result in inestimable value to the cattle industry of this section," noted the *San Angelo Standard*.[40]

Two other Sutton ranchers, O. T. Word and D. J. Wyatt, followed suit late the next year, acquiring improved bulls in Fort Worth.[41] Still, blooded animals remained more susceptible to Texas fever, a costly potential consequence. In early 1898, several Durham bulls newly introduced to the Devils succumbed to this tick-borne disease.[42]

Predators, meanwhile, constituted a blight that barbed wire couldn't discourage. Day and night they continued to prey, meat-eaters with razor-like claws or powerful jaws, dragging down lambs and kids and even young cattle and horses. For 1897, sheepman R. N. Block estimated lamb losses from predators at ten percent or greater, with dogs and coyotes the chief culprits.[43] The threat of rabies among coyotes and wolves exacerbated the problem.[44]

In a flock or herd of vulnerable livestock, even a single animal of prey could wreak havoc. In late fall of 1895, a wolf wandered onto J. H. Neuman's Val Verde range and stayed, surreptitiously feasting on calves and colts. All the frustrated cattleman could do was wait for the carnivore to leave, but a full year passed before he proclaimed it out of the territory.[45]

Back in 1893, a Del Rio man named Campbell had proposed ridding the region of coyotes by exposing captured individuals to mange-carrying dogs; upon the coyotes' release, they could then spread the condition among their own, with detrimental consequences. Other stockmen, however, pointed out that coyotes sometimes suffered from mange without outside assistance, and yet remained numerous.[46]

Even as ranchers continued to experiment with traps and poison, the predator plague persisted,[47] inducing a Devils stockmen's association to levy a bounty on scalps in a small district in the winter of 1895-1896. By spring, the association had paid out $371.[48]

The following fall, Devils rancher James McLymont had reason to champion the idea of a statewide bounty; this "king sheepman of Texas," as *Texas Stockman and Farmer* crowned him, had just purchased more than 30,000 sheep.[49] Although legislators from predator-free regions proved a roadblock,[50] the proposal understandably enjoyed favor with many ranchers. In early 1897, Val Verde stockman John M. Campbell echoed McLymont's suggestion,[51] while Sol Meyer of Sutton County took the added measure of organizing a petition.[52]

"Make stock safe from wolves and thieves," observed C. G. Burbank of Menard County, "and land will advance and the country become settled and the whole people will derive a benefit."[53]

As the nineteenth century neared an end, however, the "thieves" aspect of the equation would offer challenges of its own along the Devils.

CHAPTER 20

THE DEVIL'S BROOD

The villainy of 1896 broke early. Only five or so days into the new year, a clash between a sheep boss and a Mexican herder named Peter ended with gunplay along Buffalo Draw near the Val Verde-Edwards county line.

The incident began when the foreman, Frank Caruthers of D. B. Cusenbary's outfit, reprimanded Peter for his job performance. Wielding a carbine as the confrontation escalated, Caruthers shot the herder through the jaw.

After Caruthers reported the matter at the nearby D. C. Ker Ranch, he left to inform Cusenbary and to give himself up to authorities in Rocksprings. Ker and J. D. Hudspeth, rushing to the scene of the shooting, found Peter still alive and transported him to Cusenbary's ranch. From there, concerned individuals took the victim into Sonora for medical attention. Although the ball damaged Peter's jaw bone and teeth, the attending physician anticipated that he would likely recover.[1]

Eleven months of relative harmony ensued before the Devils conjured up more sons of wickedness. About midnight on December 20, robbers hit the Southern Pacific again, this time near Comstock. As the train made a stop at the station, four men boarded in pairs: Rolly Shackleford and Frank Gobble at the engine, and Bud Newman and Alex Purviance (also known as Bill Jones) at a trailing car. Criminal activity at Comstock was nothing new to Shackleford; three years before, Mexican bandits had stolen his racing mare and sped away into Mexico.

Perhaps seeking warped justice this night, the masked Shackleford and his partner waited until the locomotive chugged a mile and a half west before ordering the engineer to stop. Their accomplices then coaxed the Wells-Fargo agent to admit them to the express car, but the safe had a time lock and held fast against their attempts to open it. The outlaws had no choice but to flee the train with only two or three packages that contained a silver watch, Christmas toys, and documents addressed to the Brewster County clerk.

Mounting horses, the robbers gave parting salutes with their pistols and rode away to the north.

Texas Rangers under Captain John R. Hughes, along with the Val Verde sheriff and a posse, quickly gave chase. On December 22, the same day that more Rangers arrived from Ysleta, the posse returned to Del Rio with news that Hughes' force had captured Gobble. The manhunt persisted another five days before the Rangers rode into Del Rio with all four fugitives in custody.

Purviance, frail with consumption, pleaded guilty in a Del Rio courtroom March 20, 1897, and received five years in the penitentiary. Forty days later, a judge also sentenced Shackleford to five years after the defendant confessed in an Eagle Pass court proceeding. Newman, however, fought the robbery charge and heard a Maverick County jury declare him not guilty on October 26, 1897. It marked the second time Newman had won acquittal on a felony charge; earlier, he had walked free after sending a stockman named Baker to an early grave in an 1895 shootout in Val Verde County.[2]

In late 1896 and early 1897, a second gang concentrated on ranches rather than railroad. The bandits initially struck James McLymont's sheep operation and other locations in Val Verde and Kinney counties, but by late February, they had moved north into Sutton and Crockett. Among the ranches victimized was the Crowl outfit.[3]

In early March of 1897, another dispute between a sheepman and a Mexican ranch hand sparked gunfire, this time with fatal consequences. At a spread twelve miles from Sonora, the angered Mexican stole up behind a man named Lockhart and shot him in the back. The sheepman fell, likely killed instantly, but his assailant made sure with a second shot through the head.

As the felon fled with seven other Mexican nationals, Lockhart's brother arrived and discovered the murder. Wagoning toward Sonora with the body, he met the perpetrator and his companions, who immediately opened fire. Rolling out of the wagon with his rifle, the brother killed two of the men and wounded two others. A Sonora peace officer soon arrested the six survivors and threw them in Sutton County jail.[4]

For the lawless brood who sought more than blood on their hands, the Wells-Fargo express cars that thundered along the SP remained sorely tempting, especially in light of the bordering wilderness into which a hunted man might disappear. In May, Tom "Black Jack" Ketchum and his gang held up a train near Lozier Station west of the Pecos and escaped with thousands of dollars.[5]

Despite the burden of criminal activity, Devils ranchers persevered, even as the last significant rains for seven months splattered the countryside in August.[6] The nation had finally recovered from the Panic of 1893, cattle were fat,[7] and a new tariff on imported wool promised to revive the river's wool industry.[8] Moreover, the Devils was now gaining the kind of national praise that belied its reputation as solely a hotbed for treachery.

"That is the finest sheep country that I have ever seen," proclaimed Hugh M. Johnson in the *Breeder's Gazette of Chicago*. ". . . Sheepmen have seemed to make money down there even during these disastrously hard times for sheepmen."[9]

Still, success didn't come easily. In mid-December, a wildfire raced between the Nueces and Devils, burning a swath twenty-five to fifty miles wide. For days it raged, destroying Devils rangeland where James McLymont and other stockmen had wintered 60,000 sheep the year before.[10]

Then as rain finally returned to the river in March of 1898, it came in concert with destructive winds and deadly hail. The previous spring, hail at Beaver Lake had killed twenty sheep and several calves, but the fury of this upheaval was even greater. Pounding down with crushing force, the hard, white rocks buried a ranch near Juno under two feet of ice and took a brutal toll on livestock, including 150 goats that perished in a pen on the Ed Glynn place. Little rain accompanied the storm at Juno, but a torrent at Comstock filled a water hole known as Little Lake Michigan.[11]

In subsequent months, the Devils witnessed another spate of lawlessness. By late March, authorities jailed Porfiro DeLeon at Del Rio after arresting him on suspicion of horse theft. Someone had stolen the animal from Marion Sawyer of the Devils and left it tied in a bottom land willow thicket.[12]

Within weeks, the outlaws who haunted this still-unbridled territory fell back on their favorite pastime—train robbery. No one seemed to enjoy it more than Black Jack Ketchum, who was again behind a bandana when Train Number 20 made a late-night stop along the Southern Pacific at Comstock April 28 or early on April 29.

As engineer Walter Jordan oiled the locomotive, two masked men with six-shooters accosted him with orders to pull out of the station immediately. Jordan complied, and the train lurched forward with the men swearing at him and brandishing their weapons.

A short distance west, the robbers forced Jordan to halt and allow two accomplices to board. With all four now crowded inside the locomotive, the engine drivers rolled for an additional mile before the men ordered another stop at a side track. At gunpoint, the gang compelled the engineer and fireman to uncouple all cars except the postal, baggage, and express coaches.

Messenger Richard Hayes, sequestered inside the express car, realized trouble was afoot and dared a glance out the door. He identified two pistol-wielding fig-

Comstock about 1901. Whitehead Memorial Museum, Del Rio, Texas.

ures by moonlight and whirled for his shotgun, a breechloader. He broke it apart and tried to slam a load of buckshot in the chamber, only to discover that the shell was the wrong gauge.

Withdrawing, he awaited the inevitable as the skeleton train proceeded down-track a few minutes more. When the cars screeched to a halt yet again, this time at Helmet where two additional confederates waited with horses, the bandits forced their way into the express coach and demanded money.

"I thought you got considerable money on your last haul," snapped Hayes, referring to the 1897 Lozier hold-up when perpetrators had escaped with thousands. "You should have money left."

"We got plenty, but that's been spent," the leader volunteered in veiled confession to the earlier heist.

The outlaws then blew the two Wells Fargo safes with dynamite, but found only $4.80 inside; the crafty messenger had concealed the money elsewhere. Frustrated, the bandits mounted up, fired a couple of parting shots, and rode away into the desert shadows.

News spread quickly down the line, and a train already bearing a Texas Rangers detachment west from Spofford Junction arrived on the scene three hours later. As the train rumbled to a stop, three brute-black shapes beside the rails raced away to a drumming of hooves. The Rangers opened fire on the riders, but the bullets whizzed harmlessly as the silhouettes faded into the night.

Unable to track the gang in the dark, the Rangers unloaded their mounts and waited for daybreak. By then, the Rangers were several hours behind, but they traced the hoofprints to the Rio Grande and on into Mexico. Upriver a short distance, the trail turned back into Texas, where the Rangers read in the tracks the story of a band fleeing north.[13] Although Ketchum escaped to plague trains elsewhere, three years later he would pay for his misdeeds at the end of a rope in Clayton, New Mexico.[14]

The timely arrival of the Ranger detachment had stemmed from a threat to the High Bridge, by which the SP rails had spanned the canyon of the lower Pecos since 1892. Poised on spidery legs 321 feet above the river, this engineering marvel was a vital link between east and west.[15] But with the Spanish-American War raging, Spanish sympathizers had targeted the structure. Indeed, intelligence indicated that "border desperadoes" would dynamite the bridge on the very night that Ketchum also had chosen to hold up Train Number 20.

Although Rangers under a Captain McCall reached the Pecos in time to deter any sabotage, railroad officials had reason to remain on alert until war's end three and a half months later.[16]

In late spring, another Devils badman planned the robbery of a train between San Angelo and Brownwood. Bud Newman of the Dry Devils of Val Verde (not to be confused with the better-known Sutton-Schleicher drainage) was only twenty-three, but his earlier roles in killing a man and robbing an SP train had already initiated him into big-time outlawry. He seemed to lead a charmed life, judging by his acquittals in the two cases, and now he enlisted two pairs of Sutton County brothers in a scheme that would focus on the Santa Fe line.

"Newman . . . talked up the plan of robbing a train, telling us how easy it was to do," related Pearce Keaton, a co-conspirator along with his brother John and the Taylor boys, Jeff and Bill, who lived on a ranch twenty-five miles southeast of Sonora.

Neither Keaton, thirty, nor Jeff Taylor, thirty-two, were angels themselves. A Gillespie County court had sentenced Keaton to three years of hard labor for rustling cattle in Kimble County, while Taylor had been free only two or three months after serving two prison terms—a total of seven years and seven months—for horse theft.

John Keaton purchased dynamite at a Sonora store and the rest of the gang rode for distant Coleman Junction to light the fuse. At eleven PM on June 9, the masked men stormed the train, only to meet a fusillade of Colt forty-five slugs from Stock Claim Agent R. E. Buchanan. One bullet shattered Newman's elbow and another ripped into Pearce Keaton's leg three inches below the knee.

Buchanan's daring actions put the bandits to flight without a return shot, but the flying lead also wreaked tragedy. A stray slug exploded into fireman Lee Johnson's abdomen, a wound from which he would die within twenty-four hours. Another bullet whizzed through the baggage car, slashing express messenger L. L. White's eyelash and grazing the bridge of his nose.

The bloodied gang fled for Sutton County, leaving behind a package of dynamite that quickly led lawmen to the Sonora store and over the divide to the Taylor place at the Llano's head. After possible gunfire on June 12, Sutton Sheriff Perry J. McConnell and his deputy Henry Decker, along with Tom Green County Sheriff Gerome W. Shield and Deputy US Marshal D. R. Hodges, arrested Newman, Jeff Taylor, and Pearce Keaton.

In mid-September, the latter two men stood trial in Coleman on the robbery charge, with jurors meting out almost equal punishment: nine years in prison for Keaton and eight for Taylor. Newman, meanwhile, continued to work the judicial system to his advantage and turned state's evidence in exchange for freedom.

Operating undercover on behalf of lawmen, Newman joined up with Bill Taylor and the two plotted to rob a train at Comstock in the spring of 1899. Newman then betrayed Taylor into the hands of Coleman County Sheriff W. T. Knox and Detective McKenzie of Wells-Fargo, who captured him in broken country near Comstock, ending the fugitive's eleven months on the run.

Jailed at Coleman, Bill Taylor sawed his way out a few months later, only to walk past the sheriff's home and lose his new-found liberty after mere moments under the sun. For his part in the robbery, a Coleman jury awarded him eight years in the state pen on September 13, 1899.

With the spring arrest of alleged accomplice John Keaton in Mexico, and Sheriff Knox's success in gaining his extradition from Juarez, Chihuahua, in September, all five gang members had now felt the bite of American handcuffs. Keaton, however, would win dismissal of all charges in a Ballinger courtroom in October 1900. Meanwhile, prosecutors pursued murder charges against three of the men in the shooting death of Santa Fe fireman Lee Johnson, even though Stock Claim Agent R. E. Buchanan may have squeezed off the deadly round. The fact that the robbers had placed Johnson in a dangerous position made it "immaterial who had fired the fatal shot," reported the *Dallas Morning News*.

With Newman testifying against his cohorts, Pearce Keaton and Jeff Taylor received life sentences.

Bill Taylor, meanwhile, was on his way to a Houdini-like career without the cheering crowds. Unlike the famous escape artist, Taylor was a large man, standing six feet one inch and weighing 200 pounds. His bulk didn't allow him to squeeze through as tight a space as Houdini, but he demonstrated considerable skill with a hacksaw blade. Awaiting trial on the murder charge in Coleman County jail, Taylor sawed his way out again on June 19, 1900, and this time wisely avoided the sheriff's residence. Lawmen, however, again enlisted the aid of Newman, who trailed Taylor to a point either thirty or seventy miles below Sonora.

On August 9, the onetime allies squared off in a gunfight from which neither would emerge unscathed. Three times now—once in a courtroom, twice in the Devils country—Newman had proven disloyal to his one-time partner, and Taylor made sure there wouldn't be a fourth. Despite doubling over from a serious wound to the groin, Taylor shot his betrayer dead. Taylor derived grim satisfaction even as lawmen snapped handcuffs on his wrists soon afterward.

"[He] says as he has killed Newman, which was his only object in life, [he] is perfectly willing for the law to take its course," reported the *Dallas Morning News*.

Authorities incarcerated Taylor at Rusk for the train robbery conviction, but in spring 1901 they released him to Brownwood jailers to face charges in the Santa Fe fireman's death. A second murder trial stemming from his shootout with Newman was also pending.

On July 11, Taylor sawed his way free for the third time, prompting the governor and Brown County sheriff to place $200 in bounties on his head. The focus of the search was on the Devils country.

"It is said he knows every foot of that part of the world," noted the August 8, 1901 *Dallas Morning News*, "and if he is there it will be hard work to get him out. It is not thought he will be ever taken alive, as he is a very desperate character."

That December, reports placed Taylor in Mexico south of Langtry, leading Texas Ranger H. G. Dubose of Comstock to seek the cooperation of Mexican authorities in capturing the fugitive. To be sure, Taylor had fled all the way to Durango to showcase the train-robbing skills he had honed in Texas. In late July 1902 at Bermejillo, 300 miles southwest of the Devils' mouth, he held up a train and packed his saddlebags with $53,000 in Wells-Fargo money. As he ventured into nearby Mapimi to buy a horse a few days later, authorities captured him and recovered $15,000.

Mexican jailers would have done well to check the blue-eyed bandit for a hacksaw blade, for in March 1903 Taylor was on the loose yet again and the object of a fruitless scout by Texas Rangers to Marfa and Shafter and up the Rio Grande. Forty-two years later, J. H. Baker, who had practiced law with the Brownwood firm that had defended Taylor and who subsequently had served as Brown County district attorney, lamented that the train robber had yet to be brought to justice.[17]

On the heels of the Santa Fe robbery of 1898 arose more criminality associated with the Devils. Seven miles east of Dryden later in June, Texas Rangers and the Brewster County sheriff overtook two Val Verde cowboys headed for the Devils with horses stolen from L. Burtrill's Big Bend pasture. Pearl Shackleford and Tom Woodruff surrendered peacefully and implicated fellow Val Verde native Dan Caldwell, whom lawmen quickly apprehended in Marathon. A peace justice charged the three men with horse theft and cast them into the Alpine jail.[18] In early October 1899, a jury convicted Woodruff and sentenced him to two years in prison.[19]

Back on the Devils, root-soaking rains in spring and fall of 1899 served as bookends to a four-month dry spell and anointed the entire region with "fat stock, good prospects, and happy stockmen," noted the *San Angelo Standard*.[20] Nevertheless, the year also brought added violence.

As two Greek peddlers traveled between Sonora and Ozona October 15, five men with concealed faces swooped down on their hack. The outlaws shot one peddler three times, killing him, but his associate managed to escape on foot. The gang robbed the dead man of all money on his person, but overlooked $275 hidden in the vehicle.[21]

In another incident five days later, eleven bullets sprayed a Juno dance and sent one man to the cemetery and a half-dozen citizens to jail.[22] Suspects in several other serious crimes in the Devils country remained at large, as the 1900 wanted list for Val Verde, Sutton, and Crockett counties made clear. Lawmen prowled the river for fugitives in ten murder indictments and one for assault with intent to murder. Also on the loose were twelve men charged with livestock theft, while numerous other felonies lingered unsolved.[23]

If this stream indeed was the river of His Satanic Majesty, then its outlaws most assuredly were his progeny.

EPILOGUE

By 1900, 365 years had elapsed since Europeans had first traipsed the Devils region, following in the steps of Indians from millennia past. Gradually, this river had yielded to exploration and settlement, but always grudgingly and with dramatic reminders of its sovereignty. Now, as the sun sank on yet another century, the stream once more asserted its defiance in face of the most noteworthy symbol of civilization's encroachment: the Southern Pacific.

Cloudbursts struck the Devils' head draws April 5, breeding flash floods that hurtled into the night. Converging on the Devils, they spawned a seething mass that grew in fury with the contribution of every passing side-canyon, thirty-two in all. Tracing a tortuous course between ever-steepening walls, this monster out of hell roared into the river's lower reaches and took dead aim at the railway bridge, destroying it in an awesome display of power.[1]

The Southern Pacific Railroad Company would rebuild, just as the people of the Devils would regroup and face anew all that tomorrow had to offer. But now they would do it in the context of a new century that would bring success at times, and failure at others, but always challenges built on all that had gone on before.

THE END

NOTES

Chapter 1 A RIVER UNIQUE

1 Length is from *Handbook of Texas Online* (hereafter *Handbook Online*), http://www.tshaonline.org/handbook/online, entry for "Devils River" (accessed 15 November 2005).
2 John E. Hart journal, entry for 8 November 1861, Texas Confederate Museum (hereafter TCM) Collection, Nita Stewart Haley Memorial Library (hereafter, Haley Library), Midland, Texas.
3 Robert Eccleston, *Overland to California on the Southwestern Trail, 1849* (Berkeley and Los Angeles: University of California Press, 1950), 62.
4 J. D. B. Stillman, *Wanderings in the Southwest in 1855* (Spokane, Washington: The Arthur H. Clark Company, 1990), 125.
5 W. W. Heartsill, *Fourteen Hundred and 91 Days in the Confederate Army* (Jackson, Tennessee: McCowat-Mercer Press, facsimile edition, 1953, originally published 1876), 48.
6 *San Angelo Standard* (hereafter, *SA St*), 11 August 1894.
7 This study of the Devils' geography is based on: United States Department of the Interior U.S.-Mexico Border Field Coordinating Committee, "Water-resources Issues in the Rio Grande–Rio Conchos to Amistad Reservoir Subarea Fact Sheet," http://www.cerc.usgs.gov/FCC/pubs/Fact_sheets/DOI_US-MX_Border_FCC_Fact_sheet_3.pdf (accessed 27 January 2009); *Handbook Online*, entries for "Devils River" (accessed 15 November 2005), "Dry Devils River (Schleicher County)" (accessed 15 November 2005), "Granger Draw" (accessed 15 November 2005), "Buckhorn Draw" (accessed 20 November 2005), "Johnson Draw" (accessed 15 November 2005), "Dry Devils River (Edwards County)" (accessed 15 November 2005); "Big Satan Creek" (accessed 15 November 2005), and "Dead Mans Creek" (accessed 15 November 2005). Distances between the Devils and Pecos, and the relief figure for the Devils, are from Google Earth, a resource I consulted frequently in producing this work.
8 Nature Conservancy website, http://www.nature.org/success/devilsriver/html (accessed 17 February 2008); "Tamaulipan Mezquital," http://www.worldwildlife.org/wildworld/profiles/terrestrial/na/na1312_full.html (accessed 27 January 2009); John R. Roberts and James P. Nash, *University of Texas Bulletin No. 1803: The Geology of Val Verde County* (Austin: University of Texas, 10 January 1918), 8; Lawrence Clayton, *Contemporary Ranches of Texas* (Austin: University of Texas Press, 2001), 128; and *1990-91 Texas Almanac* (Dallas: *Dallas Morning News*, 1989), 167, 250, 258.
9 Lewis Burt Lesley, editor, *Uncle Sam's Camels: The Journal of May Humphreys Stacey Supplemented by the Report of Edward Fitzgerald Beale* (Cambridge: Harvard University Press, 1929), 149-150.
10 Eccleston, *Overland*, 75.
11 Stillman, *Wanderings*, 174.
12 *Dallas Morning News* (hereafter *DMN*), 31 January 1898.
13 Thomas U. Taylor, *The Water Powers of Texas* (Washington: Government Printing Office, 1904), 19-20.
14 Jerry E. Mueller, *Restless River* (El Paso: Texas Western Press, 1975), 92.

Chapter 2 SPANISH ATTEMPTS AT CONQUEST
1. J. W. Williams, *Old Texas Trails* (Burnet, Texas: Eakin Press, 1979), 18-19.
2. Narrative of Cabeza de Vaca in Herbert Eugene Bolton, ed., *Spanish Exploration in the Southwest* (repr., New York: Barnes and Noble, 1952), 96.
3. Ibid., 98-99.
4. Albert H. Schroeder and Dan S. Matson, *A Colony on the Move: Gaspar Castaño de Sosa's Journal 1590-1591* (n.p.: The School of American Research, 1965), 25-35, 38-51; and Carlos E. Castañeda, *Our Catholic Heritage in Texas 1519-1936 Vol. 1: The Mission Era: The Finding of Texas 1519-1693* (Austin: Von Boeckmann-Jones Company, 1936), 181-183.
5. Castañeda, *Catholic Heritage Vol. 1*, 222, 227-230; and Francis Borgia Steck, *Forerunners of Captain De Leon's Expedition to Texas, 1670-1675* (n.p.: Preliminary Studies of the Texas Catholic Society, n.d., reprint from *Southwestern Historical Quarterly* (hereafter, *SHQ*) 36, No. 1, July 1932), 9, 12-16.
6. Steck, *Forerunners*, 24-29.
7. *Handbook Online*, entry for "La Salle, René Robert Cavelier, Sieur de" (accessed 28 January 2009).
8. Mendoza's journal in Herbert Eugene Bolton, ed., *Spanish Exploration in the Southwest* (New York: Charles Scribner's Sons, 1916), 330-332, 340-343; Victor J. Smith, "The Route of Juan Dominguez de Mendoza through the Big Bend in 1684," *West Texas Historical and Scientific Society*, No. 2 (1928), 64; Castañeda, *Catholic Heritage Vol. 1*, 215; and Carlos E. Castañeda, *Our Catholic Heritage in Texas 1519-1936 Vol. 2: The Mission Era: The Winning of Texas 1693-1731* (Austin: Von Boeckmann-Jones Company, 1936), 321-322.
9. Rosemary Whitehead Jones, ed., *La Hacienda* (Norman: University of Oklahoma Press, 1976), 412.
10. Diario y derrotero, q nros. Dn. Blas de la Garza Falcon . . . y Dn. Joseph Anto. Eca y Musquiz . . . in Testimonio de la fundacion . . . *A.G.I., Audiencia de Mexico*, 61-2-18 (Coahuila, 1733-1738), 117-132, Center for American History, The University of Texas at Austin, and Carlos E. Castañeda, *Our Catholic Heritage in Texas 1519-1936 Vol. 3: The Mission Era: The Missions at Work 1731-1761* (Austin: Von Boeckmann-Jones Company, 1938), 203-206.
11. Castañeda, *Catholic Heritage Vol. 3*, 340-344.
12. Alejo de la Garza Falcon, "Derrotero," Center for American History, The University of Texas at Austin; Jacobo de Ugarte y Loyola, "Diario de lo executado por el Destacamento mandado del Governador de la Provincia de Coahuila," 22 September-30 December 1775, Center for American History, The University of Texas at Austin; Vicente Rodriguez, "Derrotero," Center for American History, The University of Texas at Austin; Max L. Moorhead, *The Apache Frontier: Jacobo Ugarte and Spanish-Indian Relations in Northern New Spain, 1769-1791* (Norman: University of Oklahoma Press, 1968), 37-39; Jones, *Hacienda*, 414-415; Robert S. Weddle, *San Juan Bautista: Gateway to Spanish Texas* (Austin and London: University of Texas Press, 1968), 336-338; and *Handbook Online*, entry for "Garza Falcon, Alejo de la" (accessed 15 November 2005).
13. "Campaigns of Colonel Don Juan de Ugalde," translation of 1783 document, Clayton W. Williams Collection (hereafter CWW Collection), Haley Library; *Handbook Online*, entry for "Ugalde, Juan de" (accessed 16 December 2005); and Jones, *Hacienda*, 415.
14. Elizabeth A. H. John, *Storms Brewed in Other Men's Worlds: The Confrontation of Indians, Spanish, and French in the Southwest, 1540-1795* (College Station: Texas A&M University Press, 1975), 633.
15. James Manly Daniel, "The Advance of the Spanish Frontier and the Despoblado," dissertation, 1955, University of Texas at Austin, 280-283.

Chapter 3 BLAZING THE DEVILS TRAIL
1. J. Marvin Hunter, compiler, *The Bloody Trail in Texas: Sketches and Narratives of Indian Raids and Atrocities on Our Frontier* (Bandera, Texas: J. Marvin Hunter, 1931), 14-27. This account, written by survivor Virginia Webster, was originally published in *San Antonio Express*, 27 April 1913.

2   Francis Moore, Jr., *Map and Description of Texas, Containing Sketches of its History, Geology, Geography and Statistics* (n.p.: Texian Press, facsimile edition, 1965, originally published 1840), 30-31.
3   Hunter, *Bloody Trail,* 16-27.
4   Captain Samuel Highsmith's 15 December 1848 report to Colonel P. Hansborough Bell, commanding Texas frontier, printed in Maude Wallis Traylor, "Captain Samuel Highsmith, Ranger," *Frontier Times* 17, No. 7 (April 1940), 299-300; John C. Hays' report to Colonel P. Hansborough Bell, commanding Texas frontier, *The Northern Standard* (Clarkesville, Texas), 10 February 1849, typescript in CWW Collection, Haley Library; John C. Hays to W. L. Marcy, Secretary of War, 13 December 1848, in *Report of the Secretary of War,* 31st Cong., 1st sess., Senate Executive Document No. 32 (Washington, 1850), 64-65; and Samuel Maverick journal in Rena Maverick Green, ed., *Samuel Maverick, Texan: 1803-1870: A Collection of Letters, Journals and Memoirs* (San Antonio: privately printed, 1952), 333-341. Biographical information is from *Handbook Online,* entries for "Hays, John Coffee" (accessed 2 March 2009), "Maverick, Samuel Augustus" (accessed 2 March 2009), and "Highsmith, Samuel" (accessed 2 March 2009); and Ralph P. Bieber, ed., *Exploring Southwestern Trails 1846-1854* (Glendale, California: The Arthur H. Clark Company, 1938), 258. Details of Highsmith's death are from *The Texas Democrat,* 28 January 1849, reprinted in Traylor, "Captain Samuel Highsmith," 300.
5   For example, see J. Frank Dobie, "Stories in Texas Place Names" in Dobie and Mody C. Boatright, eds., *Straight Texas* (Austin: The Steck Company, 1937), 53.
6   This edition of *Western Texian* is apparently not extant, but the article was reprinted by *Corpus Christi Star,* 20 January 1849, and *The Northern Standard,* 10 February 1849.
7   Maverick journal, Green, *Samuel Maverick,* 335.
8   Lela Williamson, "How Devil's River Received Its Name," *West Texas Historical and Scientific Society: Publications,* Bulletin 21, No. 1 (1 December 1926), 43.
9   V. L. James, "The Devil's River of Texas," *Field and Stream* 24, No. 1 (May 1904), 48; Vinton Lee James, *Frontier and Pioneer Recollections of Early Days in San Antonio and West Texas* (San Antonio: privately printed, 1938), 172.
10 J. H. Young, "Map of the State of Texas from the Latest Authorities," 1852, in CWW Collection, Haley Library.
11 See Major Campbell Graham, Topographic Engineers, "Map of Topogl. Recone. of a Part of Northwestern Texas, 1859-1860, William Echols, Brevet 2nd Lieutenant," Records of the War Department, Office of the Chief of Engineers, Map Q 95, National Archives (hereafter, NA), Washington, DC, copy in Haley Library.
12 Mabelle Eppard Martin, "California Emigrant Roads Through Texas," *SHQ* 28, No. 4 (April 1925), 287; and "San Francisco Gold Rush Chronology," The Virtual Museum of the City of San Francisco," http://www.sfmuseum.org/hist/chron1.html (accessed 30 January 2009).
13 Brevet 2nd Lieutenant William F. Smith to Brevet Lieutenant Colonel J. E. Johnston, 25 May 1849, in *Reports of the Secretary of War with Reconnaissances of Route from San Antonio to El Paso,* 31st Cong., 1st sess., Senate Executive Document 64 (Washington: 1850) 4-7; Bieber, *Exploring,* 30; and A. B. Bender, "Opening Routes Across West Texas, 1848-1850," *SHQ* 37, No. 2 (October 1933), 121-122.
14 Martin, "Emigrant Roads," 299-300.
15 George W. B. Evans (diarist), *Mexican Gold Trail: The Journal of a Forty-Niner* (San Marino, California: The Huntington Library, 1945), 51.
16 This study of the Whiting expedition is drawn from: Smith to Johnston in *Reports,* 4-7; Whiting journal in Bieber, *Exploring,* 336-350; and Bender, "Opening Routes," 121-122. Length of refined Lower Road is from J. E. Johnston to Major General Brooke, 28 December 1849, in *Reports of the Secretary of War,* Senate Executive Document 64, 29; and Captain Edward S. Meyer's 1867 table of distances in Escal F. Duke, ed., "A Description of the Route from San Antonio to El Paso by Captain Edward S. Meyer," *West Texas Historical Association* (hereafter, *WTHA*) *Year Book* 49 (1973), 129. I drew upon Meyer's distance figures frequently in the course of this work. Whiting's mention of a rumored Spanish fortress known as Fort del Altar reflects certain early maps that pinpoint a "Presidio del Altar" on the

Devils. I could uncover no documentation that such a presidio ever existed on the river. See Whiting journal in Bieber, *Exploring,* 346; and the map "United States of America by John Melish" (Philadelphia: Murray Draper Fairman & Co., 1818).

17 This study of the joint travels of the Johnston, Freemont, and Eastland parties is based on: J. E. Johnston to Major General Brooke, 28 December 1849, in *Reports of the Secretary of War,* Senate Executive Document 64, 26-29; Captain S. G. French report in *Reports of the Secretary of War,* Senate Executive Document 64, 42-52; "To California Through Texas and Mexico: The Diary and Letters of Thomas B. Eastland and Joseph G. Eastland, His Son," *California Historical Society Quarterly,* Vol. 18, No. 2 (June 1939), 99-135; Eccleston, *Overland,* 22, 32, 53-54, 60-81, 117; Jose Policarpo Rodriguez, *Jose Policarpo Rodriguez: The Old Guide* (Nashville, Dallas: Publishing House of the Methodist Episcopal Church, 1897), 20-22, 37, 41-42; Harry Warren, compiler, and Ben E. Pingenot, ed., *Paso del Aguila: A Chronicle of Frontier Days on the Texas Border as Recorded in the Memoirs of Jesse Sumpter* (Austin: Encino Press, 1969), 10-11; Charles Wright, "From the El Paso Train," *Texas Democrat,* August 4, 1849, reprinted in *SHQ,* No. 1 (July 1944), 268-269; and *Handbook Online,* entry for "Seaton, William Henry" (accessed 2 March 2009). Information on the timber fronting Beaver Lake is from an 1856 description by John C. Reid. See John C. Reid, *Reid's Tramp, or a Journal of the Incidents of Ten Months Travel Through Texas, New Mexico, Arizona, Sonora, and California* (1858; repr., Austin: Steck Company, 1935), 99.

Chapter 4 DEAD MAN'S PASS

1 J. Frank Bowles, "Overland Trip to California in 1850," *Frontier Times* 4, No. 5 (February 1927), 12.
2 Ben E. Pingenot, "The Great Wagon Train Expedition of 1850," *SHQ* 98, No. 2 (October 1994), 182, 197-198.
3 M. Baldridge, *A Reminiscence of the Parker H. French Expedition through Texas & Mexico to California in the Spring of 1850* (Los Angeles: privately printed, 1959), 20-21; Charles Cardinell, *Adventures on the Plains* (San Francisco: California Historical Society, 1922), 1; William Miles, *Journal of the Sufferings and Hardships of Capt. Parker H. French's Overland Expedition to California* (Chambersburg, Pennsylvania: 1851), 14-15; Albert B. Tucker, "The Parker H. French Expedition Through Southwest Texas in 1850," *The Journal of Big Bend Studies* 6 (January 1994), 23, 28-31; and *Handbook Online,* entry for "French Expedition" (accessed 15 November 2005).
4 M. L. Crimmins, "Two Thousand Miles by Boat in the Rio Grande in 1850," particularly the 5 September 1850 report of W. W. Chapman, Brevet Major and Assistant Quartermaster, to Major General T. S. Jesup, Quartermaster General, Washington, DC, *West Texas Historical and Scientific Society: Publications,* No. 5 (1 December 1933), 44-52. The Chapman report is also in Caleb Coker, ed., *The News from Brownsville: Helen Chapman's Letters from the Texas Military Frontier, 1848-1852* (Austin: Barker Texas History Center and Texas State Historical Association, 1992), 380-389.
5 *Report on the United States and Mexican Boundary Survey,* House of Representatives Executive Document No. 135, 34th Cong, 1st sess. (Washington: Cornelius Wendell, Printer, 1857), 70-71.
6 George W. Baylor, "An Indian Raid in Mexico," *Frontier Times* 26, No. 12 (September 1948), 279-283 (originally published in *Galveston News,* 18 November 1899). This account bears similarities with an 1850 incident reported in *Testimony Taken by the Committee on Military Affairs in Relation to the Texas Border Troubles,* House of Representatives Misc. Document No. 64, 45th Cong., 2nd sess. (Washington: Government Printing Office, 1878), 30. The latter source speaks of a "raid by a force of 60 Mexican national troops and 350 citizens in Texas, a short distance above the mouth of the Pecos, and attack and capture of Indian village and 50 or 60 horses."
7 Warren and Pingenot, *Paso del Aguila,* 17-20; and Thomas T. Smith, *The Old Army in Texas: A Research Guide to the U.S. Army in Nineteenth-Century Texas* (Austin: Texas State Historical Association, 2000), 138. The two accounts, which vary in length, share common details, pointing to an identical skirmish. *Paso del Aguila,* consisting of Jesse Sumpter's reminiscences written

between 1902 and 1906, sets the date of the fight as 1851, while Smith, drawing from contemporary Army records, places it in August 1850. With contemporary records generally more reliable than recollections of a half-century, I have chosen to use the earlier date.
8 Pingenot, "Wagon Train," 219-220, 222; Warren and Pingenot, *Paso del Aguila,* 6-7; A. J. Sowell, *Early Settlers and Indian Fighters of Southwest Texas* (1900; repr., Austin: State House Press, 1986), 172-177; Stacey journal in Lesley, *Uncle Sam's Camels,* 51-54; Heartsill, *Fourteen Hundred,* 48; and R. H. Williams, *With the Border Ruffians: Memories of the Far West 1852-1868* (London: John Murray, 1908), 327-328. The *Paso del Aguila* account is from the reminiscences of Sumpter, one of the soldiers who arrived immediately after the battle. Sowell based his account on his interview with John L. Mann. The author and Joe Allen ground-searched Dead Man's Pass 1 April 2009.
9 August Santleben, *A Texas Pioneer* (1910; repr., Waco: W. M. Morrison, 1967), 99-103, 141-159, 226-227; Patrick Dearen, *Castle Gap and the Pecos Frontier* (Fort Worth: Texas Christian University Press, 1988), 69-70, 72; Deed L. Vest, "The Chihuahua Road," *Texana* 5, No. 1 (Spring 1967), 1-8; R. Franklin Hall, "Chihuahua Trail, Linked U.S. and Mexico," *Frontier Times* 8, No. 7 (April 1931), 312-317; and R. D. Holt, "Old Texas Wagon Trains," *Frontier Times* 26, No. 12 (September 1948), 269, 274-276, 278.
10 Samuel G. French, *Two Wars: An Autobiography of Gen. Samuel G. French* (Nashville: Confederate Veteran, 1901), 107-118, particularly French's 2 November 1851 report to Major General Thomas A. Jesup, Quartermaster General, 109-118.

Chapter 5 BY MAIL COACH AND HOOF
1 "To the Honorable, the Senate and House of Representatives of the United States, in Congress assembled. The memorial of George H. Giddings . . . ," in George H. Giddings v. The United States, Kiowa, Comanche, and Apache Indians, Indian Depredations Case No. 3873, Court of Claims of the United States, National Archives, Washington, DC.
2 Jack C. Scannell, "Henry Skillman, Texas Frontiersman," *The Permian Historical Annual* 18 (December 1978), 19-23; *Handbook Online,* entry for "Skillman, Henry;" W. W. Mills, *Forty Years at El Paso, 1858-1898* (El Paso: Carl Hertzog, 1962), 189-190.
3 James M. Day, "Big Foot Wallace in Trans-Pecos Texas," *WTHA Year Book* 55 (1979), 70-72; unnamed author identified as "One of the Nine, A Member of Company 'E' Texas Rangers," *Captain Jeff or Frontier Life in Texas with the Texas Rangers* (Colorado, Texas: Whipkey Printing Company, 1906), 84-88; Hilory G. Bedford, *Texas Indian Troubles: The Most Thrilling Events in the History of Texas* (Dallas: Hargreaves Printing Company, Inc., 1905), 114-117; Scannell, "Skillman," 22; Stanley Vestal, *Bigfoot Wallace: A Biography* (Boston: Houghton Mifflin Company, 1942), 43-45; and *Handbook Online,* entries for "Wallace, William Alexander Anderson" (accessed 2 March 2009), "Somervell Expedition" (accessed 2 March 2009), "Mier Expedition" (accessed 2 March 2009), "Black Bean Episode" (accessed 2 March 2009), and "Perote Prison" (accessed 2 March 2009).
4 J. Marvin Hunter, Sr., "The San Antonio-San Diego Mail Route," *Frontier Times* 25, No. 2 (November 1947), 54-55; and Scannell, "Skillman," 22.
5 The ad, dated 6 December 1851, was printed in *San Antonio Western Texan,* 23 September 1852, and almost certainly appeared in earlier editions. It was reprinted in Robert H. Thonhoff, *San Antonio Stage Lines, 1847-1881* (El Paso: Texas Western Press, 1971), figure 5.
6 Scannell, "Skillman," 23.
7 Frederick Law Olmsted, *A Journey Through Texas* (New York: Dix, Edwards & Co., 1857), 286-287.
8 Zenas R. Bliss, "Reminiscences of Zenas R. Bliss, Major General, United States Army, in Five Volumes," Vol. 1, 139, Haley Library.
9 Arrie Barrett, "Western Frontier Forts of Texas," *WTHA Year Book* 7 (June 1931), 131; Ben E. Pingenot, "Fort Clark, Texas: A Brief History," *The Journal of Big Bend Studies* 7 (January 1995), 103-104; Cephas C. Bateman, "Old Fort Clark, a Frontier Post," *Frontier Times* 2, No. 7 (April 1925), 31; and *Handbook Online,* entry for "Fort Clark" (accessed 2 March 2009).
10 John C. Duval, *The Adventures of Big-Foot Wallace* (1871; repr., Lincoln: University of Nebraska

Press, 1966), 78-80, 81-92; A. J. Sowell, *Life of "Big Foot" Wallace: The Great Ranger Captain* (Austin: State House Press, 1989), 138-139; Vestal, *Bigfoot Wallace,* 245-248; Sowell, *Early Settlers,* 87; and Wayne R. Austerman, *Sharps Rifles and Spanish Mules: The San Antonio-El Paso Mail, 1851-1881* (College Station: Texas A&M University Press, 1985), 30-31, 315.

11 Report of Captain Owen Shaw, 28 December 1852, in Dorman H. Winfrey and James M. Day, eds., *The Indian Papers of Texas and the Southwest, 1825-1916* (Austin: The Pemberton Press, 1966), 149, 150.

12 Otis E. Young, *The West of Philip St. George Cooke, 1809-1895* (Glendale, California: The Arthur H. Clark Company, 1955), 249-251.

13 Sowell, *Life of "Big Foot,"* 135; "Frontier Days of Texas," *SA St,* 27 December 1902; Sowell, *Early Settlers,* 87 (photo caption); Vestal, *Bigfoot Wallace,* 245; and Austerman, *Sharps Rifles,* 316.

14 Julius Froebel, *Seven Years Travel in Central America, Northern Mexico, and the Far West of the United States* (London: Richard Bentley, 1859), 416-422.

15 Sowell, *Life of Big Foot,"* 141-142.

16 Field return, Camp Blake, Texas, April 1854, NA.

17 *Handbook Online,* entry for "Blake, Jacob Edmund" (accessed 2 March 2009).

18 J. Evetts Haley, ed., *The Diary of Michael Erskine* (Midland: The Nita Stewart Haley Memorial Library, 1979), 47; and J. Evetts Haley, ed. "A Log of the Texas-California Cattle Trail," *SHQ* 35, No. 3 (January 1932), 216-217. Another possible location for Blake is the Juno area, where a mail station eventually would be located. The author, Wesley Dearen, Joe Allen, and Glen Ely ground-searched Beaver Lake in 1999.

19 Field returns, Camp Blake, Texas, April, May, and July 1854, NA.

20 Field return, Camp on the San Pedro, Texas, July 1854, NA. For clues to its location, see Bliss, "Reminiscences," Vol. II, 110.

21 Captain Meyer's 1867 journal in Duke, ed., "Description of the Route," 136.

22 Austerman, *Sharps Rifles,* 56, 57, 316.

23 Roy L. Swift and Leavitt Corning, Jr., *Three Roads to Chihuahua: The Great Wagon Roads that Opened the Southwest, 1823-1883* (Austin: Eakin Press, 1988), 174, citing W. H. Emory, *Report on the U.S. and Mexican Boundary Survey* (Washington: 1857-59), 1:24-25.

24 J. D. B. Stillman, *Wanderings in the Southwest in 1855* (Spokane: The Arthur H. Clark Company, 1990), 174-175.

25 Olmsted, *Journey,* 274; Haley, *Erskine,* 17-19; and Haley, "A Log," 208-210. For a detailed study of the California Cattle Trail through the Pecos country, see Patrick Dearen, *A Cowboy of the Pecos,* (Plano: Republic of Texas Press, 1997), 13-27.

26 Haley, *Erskine,* 31, 34, 47-48.

27 Haley, "A Log," 210-211, 214-217.

28 Indian Depredations Case No. 3873, including: Petition of George H. Giddings, 12 August 1891; "Brief of the case of Geo. H. Giddings;" "Report to accompany Bill S. 432, in the Senate of the United States," "Report to accompany Bill H. R. 1496, in the Senate of the United States;" and article of contract between the United States and George H. Giddings, 7 April 1855.

29 Francis J. Johnston, "Henry Skillman, a Confederate Courier," (January 1989), otherwise unidentified clipping of journal article in author's possession; and *Handbook Online,* entry for "Skillman, Henry" (accessed 2 March 2009).

30 Sowell, *Early Settlers,* 564; and *SA St,* 27 December 1902.

31 D. C. Buell, assistant adjutant general, Special Orders No. 115, Department of Texas, 30 September 1854, in Indian Depredations Case No. 3873.

32 Joseph Carroll McConnell, *The West Texas Frontier, Or A Descriptive History of Early Times in Western Texas* (Jacksboro: Gazette Print, 1933), 76.

33 The last extant Blake post return is for September 1854. See National Archives Microfilm Publications, notes on roll 1496, NA.

Chapter 6 AN ARMY POST AT SECOND CROSSING

1 David A. Clary, ed., "'I Am Already Quite a Texan': Albert J. Myer's Letters from Texas, 1854-

1856," *SHQ* 32, No. 1 (July 1978), 42, 44; Paul J. Scheips, "Albert James Myer, An Army Doctor in Texas, 1854-1857," *SHQ* 32, No. 1 (July 1978), 8; and Martin L. Crimmins, "General Albert J. Myer: the Father of the Signal Corps," *WTHA Year Book* 29 (October 1953), 47, 48.
2. Indian Depredations Case No. 3873, including Giddings petition, 12 August 1891.
3. Clary, "Myer's Letters," 41, 46.
4. Smith, *Old Army*, 84.
5. Francis B. Heitman, *Historical Register and Dictionary of the United States Army,* 57th Cong., 2nd Sess., House of Representatives Document No. 446 (Washington: Government Printing Office, 1903), 402.
6. Department of Texas Special Order No. 79, 20 July 1855, RG 94, NA; post return, August 1855, Fort Lancaster, NA; Stillman, *Wanderings,* 145-146; Bliss, "Reminiscences," Vol. II, 110; and Lawrence John Francell, *Fort Lancaster: Texas Frontier Sentinel* (n.p.: Texas State Historical Association, 1999), 38.
7. Smith, *Old Army*, 75. The names of the watering places between First and Second crossings may have been interchangeable in certain early accounts. For example, Bell, "A Log," 215, indicates that, from California Springs, Palo Blanco Springs was six miles in the direction of Second Crossing. Meanwhile, an early map shows "Palos Blancos" at the approximate location of California Well, as California Springs became known. This suggests that Palo Blanco and California Springs may have been variant names for the same site. See "Best route for the movements of troops from San Antonio to El Passo [sic]—Texas, being the one travelled by the State Geological Corps of Texas in 1860 and by Henry Skillman's party in March 23 1864. Described by A.R. Roessler," Texas State Archives (hereafter TSA). The author and Joe Allen ground-searched this area 23 April 2009.
8. Heitman, *Historical Register,* 402.
9. Sowell, *Early Settlers,* 195-197. Sowell's earlier account of the incident, in the 18 April 1897 *DMN,* has a spelling of Richaz.
10. Indian Depredations Case No. 3873, including Giddings petition, 12 August 1891.
11. M. L. Crimmins, ed.; "Colonel J. K. F. Mansfield's Report of the Inspection of the Department of Texas in 1856," *SHQ* 42, No. 3 (January 1939), 245, 247, 248; Henry T. Fletcher's list of "Battles, Actions, Combats, Skirmishes, Etc., in Texas, to July 1, 1902," in H. Bailey Carroll, "Texas Collection," *SHQ* 49, No. 1 (July 1945-April 1946), 122; Clayton Williams, *Never Again, Vol. 3: Texas 1848-1861* (San Antonio: The Naylor Company, 1969), 143; Averam B. Bender, *The March of Empire: Frontier Defense in the Southwest, 1848-1860* (Lawrence: University of Kansas Press, 1952), 140, citing New Orleans *Daily Picayune,* 22 June 1856; Smith, *Old Army,* 140; and Thomas T. Smith, *The U.S. Army and the Texas Frontier Economy, 1845-1900* (College Station: Texas A&M University Press, 1999), 125.
12. Crimmins, "Mansfield's Report, 1856," 255.
13. Ibid., 248, 255.
14. Ibid., 247, 253.
15. Bliss, "Reminiscences," Vol. II, 110.
16. Department of Texas order No. 93, issued 26 July 1856, received at Lancaster 10 August 1856, in post return, Fort Lancaster, Texas, August 1856 NA; and Headquarters, Department of Texas, to Captain Charles Gilbert, 29 September 1856.
17. Headquarters, Department of Texas, to Captain Charles Gilbert, 29 September 1856, NA.
18. Robert W. Frazer, *Forts of the West: Military Forts and Presidios and Posts Commonly Called Forts West of the Mississippi River to 1898* (Norman: University of Oklahoma Press, 1965, 1972), 152.
19. Reid, *Reid's Tramp,* 97-99.
20. Department of Texas Order No. 53, 21 August 1856, RG 94, NA. Also see post return, September 1856, Fort Lancaster, NA.
21. George F. Price, compiler, *Across the Continent with the Fifth Cavalry* (New York: D. Van Nostrand, Publisher, 1883), 50-51, 280, 281, 650, 663; and D. C. Buell, AAG, to Bvt. Lt. Col. John B. [no last name], 1st Artillery, Commanding Fort Clark, 14 August 1856, NA.
22. Buell to Bvt. Lt. Col. John B. [no last name], 14 August 1856.

23 Headquarters, Department of Texas, to Gilbert, 29 September 1856; D. C. Buell, AAG to Captain Robert S. Granger, 29 September 1856, NA; and Reid, *Reid's Tramp,* 98.
24 Headquarters, Department of Texas, to Gilbert, 29 September 1856.
25 Carroll, "Texas Collection," 122.
26 Indian Depredations Case No. 3873, including Giddings petition, 12 August 1891.
27 Heitman, *Historical Register,* 402; and Smith, *Old Army,* 141.
28 Stacey journal in Lesley, *Uncle Sam's Camels,* 55-56.
29 Indian Depredations Case No. 3873, including Giddings testimony, 3-5 October 1891. The case also reports the loss as twelve mules.
30 Beale report in Lesley, *Uncle Sam's Camels,* 154-155.
31 Post return, June 1857, Camp Hudson, NA.
32 Bliss, "Reminiscences," Vol. II, 29, 115-116, 126. The author and Joe Allen ground-searched the site of Hudson 31 March 2009.
33 Ibid., and post return, July 1857, Camp Hudson, NA.

Chapter 7 THE SAN ANTONIO TO SAN DIEGO MAIL
1 Emmie Giddings W. Mahon and Chester V. Kielman, "Giddings and the San Antonio-San Diego Mail Line," *SHQ* 61, No. 2 (October 1957), 228.
2 "Overland Mail Route Between San Antonio, Texas, and San Diego, California" in *The Texas Almanac for 1859* (Galveston: The Galveston News), 139, 142, 147.
3 *Contract for Carrying the Mails,* House Document No. 92, 35th Cong., 1st sess., 430; and undated "San Antonio and San Diego Mail-Line" advertisement reproduced in Noel M. Loomis, "Journal of I. C. Woods on the Establishment of the San Antonio & San Diego Mail Line" in *Brand Book Number One, The San Diego Corral of the Westerners* (n.p., 1968), 94. The ad represents mail company policies under the later proprietorship of G. H. Giddings and R. E. Doyle. Contract date was June 12. See Loomis, "Journal of I. C. Woods," 95.
4 Loomis, "Journal of I. C. Woods," 94, 95, 98, 123. Giddings apparently became eastern division agent by virtue of a July 29 agreement with Woods. See Loomis, "Journal of I. C. Woods," 97-98.
5 Beale report in Lesley, *Uncle Sam's Camels,* 144, 149-154. Also see Stacey's journal in Lesley, *Uncle Sam's Camels,* 50-54.
6 Loomis, "Journal of I. C. Woods," 68, 96, 97, 123; and Robert N. Mullin, *Stagecoach Pioneers of the Southwest* (El Paso: Texas Western Press, 1983), 13. "The memorial of George H. Giddings" in evidence for defense, 2 February 1893, Indian Depredations Case No. 3873, gives a departure date of 4 July 1857.
7 Loomis, "Journal of I. C. Woods," 96.
8 John B. Hood to Charles Phifer, 27 July 1857, file 189 T 1857 (filed with 203 T 1857), letters received by Adjutant General's Office, RG 94, NA; J. B. Hood, *Advance and Retreat* (Edison, New Jersey: The Blue and Grey Press, 1985 reprint), 8-15; Price, *Across the Continent,* 664; and *Handbook Online,* entry for "Hood, John Bell" (accessed 2 March 2009). Also see battle participant H. G. Rust's account in "Desperate Fight on Devil's River," *Frontier Times* 21, No. 4 (January 1944), 141-143.
9 Loomis, "Journal of I. C. Woods," 96.
10 Ibid., 98-99; Indian Depredations Case No. 3873, including typescripts of D. C. Jones, acting assistant surgeon, Camp Hudson, to Captain Withers, 2 August 1857, and D. E. Twiggs to L. Thomas, AAG, 5 August 1857; and James R. Arnold, *Jeff Davis's Own: Cavalry, Comanches, and the Battle for the Texas Frontier* (New York: John Wiley & Sons, 2000), 155-156.
11 Loomis, "Journal of I. C. Woods," 96, 97.
12 R. S. Granger to Captain (otherwise unidentified), 25 July 1857, and D. C. Jones to Captain Withers, 2 August 1857, typescripts in Indian Depredations Case No. 3873.
13 Loomis, "Journal of I. C. Woods," 97.
14 Ibid., 97-100.
15 Ibid., 96; *Texas Almanac for 1859,* 139, 148; Mahon and Kielman, "Giddings," 234; and Mullin, *Stagecoach Pioneers,* 14.

16 Indian Depredations Case No. 3873, including Giddings petition, 12 August 1891. The case also indicates the possibility of a seventh man with the party.
17 Post return, Camp Hudson, October 1857, NA.
18 Post return, Fort Lancaster, November 1857, NA.
19 Post return, Camp Hudson, December 1857, NA.
20 August Santleben, *A Texas Pioneer* (Waco: W. M. Morrison, 1967 facsimile reprint of 1910 edition), 264. Santleben's reference cannot be summarily dismissed, although a massacre of such magnitude should have been reflected in military or newspaper reports.
21 Loomis, "Journal of I. C. Woods," 114-115.
22 Indian Depredations Case No. 3873, including article of contract between United States and George H. Giddings, 9 March 1858.
23 *Texas Almanac for 1859*, 150.

Chapter 8 INDIAN TROUBLE
1 Bliss, "Reminiscences," Vol. I, 315, 337, and Vol. II, 21, 26, 92.
2 Bliss, "Reminiscences," Vol. II, 28-30, 92-93, 107.
3 William A. Duffen, ed., "Overland Via 'Jackass Mail' in 1858: The Diary of Phocion R. Way," *Arizona and the West* 2, No. 1 (Spring 1960), 46.
4 Department of Texas Special Orders No. 50, 4 June 1858, typescript in Indian Depredations Case No. 3873.
5 Description of site is from Meyer journal in Duke, "Description of the Route," 134. Location is from "Topographical Sketch of the Road from Fort Stockton to Fort Chadbourne, 192 miles, October and November 1867," map and table of distances, Brevet Lieutenant Colonel E. J. Strang, NA; and Brevet Lieutenant Colonel Thomas B. Hunt, "Journal showing the Route taken by the Government Train accompanying the 15th Regiment U.S. Infantry From Austin, Texas to Fort Craig, New Mexico and returning to San Antonio, July-December 1869," journal entry and map, 32, Q-154, Record Group 77, NA. Hunt also shows an unidentified structure quite near Beaver Lake, begging the question of whether or not it represents an 1858 station that had been relocated by the late 1860s. However, the preponderance of evidence—including the fact that a station at Beaver Lake would have added an extra 3.9 miles to the route—points solely to a site near later Juno. Cost is indicated in Giddings petition, 12 August 1891, Indian Depredations Case No. 3873. The post-June 1858 date is from Austerman, *Sharps Rifles*, 318. Evidence that the station was of native rock is from deposition of David Koney, 19 October 1894, Indians Depredations Case No. 3873. This depredations case indicates that Giddings had no stations on the Devils in 1855 and had yet to build such by 7 April 1856; see Giddings testimony, 3-5 October 1891, and copy of letter, Persifer F. Smith to AA Lockwood, 7 April 1856. In 1999, the author, Wesley Dearen, Joe Allen, and Glen Ely found evidence of the stage station near Juno.
6 Austerman, *Sharps Rifles*, 318.
7 Hunt's journal and map, 34; David Koney deposition in Indian Depredations Case No. 3873; and Sam Woolford, ed., "The Burr G. Duval Diary," *SHQ* 65, No. 4 (April 1962), 494.
8 Deposition of George H. Giddings, direct examination, 3 October-5 October 1891, Indian Depredations Case No. 3873.
9 D. E. Twiggs to Lieutenant Colonel L. Thomas, AAG, 24 August 1858, in *Protection of the Frontier of Texas: Letter from the Secretary of War*, House of Representatives Executive Document No. 27, 35th Cong., 2nd sess. (1859), 34-35.
10 D. E. Twiggs to Lieutenant Colonel L. Thomas, AAG, 17 September 1858, in *Protection of the Frontier*, 36.
11 Bliss, "Reminiscences," Vol. II, 152-157, 160; and deposition of Albert G. Brackett, 5 December 1891, examination and cross-examination, Indian Depredations Case No. 3873. Information on Yellow Banks is from Hunt's journal and map, 33, 34; Meyer journal in Duke, "A Description of the Route," 129, 133; and Williams, *Border Ruffians,* 327. Dunlop may have been John Dunlap. See Thomas T. Smith, Jerry D. Thompson, Robert Wooster, and Ben E. Pingenot, eds., *The Reminiscences of Major General Zenas R. Bliss, 1854-1876* (Austin:

Texas State Historical Association, 2007), 64.
12. Post return, Camp Hudson, December 1858, NA.
13. Giddings petition, 12 August 1891, 5, 11, and Giddings deposition, 5 October 1891, in Indian Depredations Case No. 3873.
14. D. E. Twiggs to Lieutenant Colonel L. Thomas, 22 October 1858, in *Protection of the Frontier*, 53-54. Also see Twiggs to Thomas, 18 October 1858, in *Protection of the Frontier*, 48.
15. L. Thomas to D. E. Twiggs, 9 November 1858, in *Protection of the Frontier*, 54.
16. Mahon and Kielman, "Giddings," 235. Information on where the two lines merged is from deposition of George H. Giddings, 11, 19, 20, and 21 December 1894, Indian Depredations Case No. 3873.
17. Post return, Camp Hudson, December 1858.
18. Giddings petition, 12 August 1891, 5-6, 11-12; cross-examination of Giddings, 5 October 1891; and Giddings deposition, 5 October 1891; all in Indian Depredations Case No. 3873.
19. D. E. Twiggs to Lieutenant Colonel L. Thomas, 13 January 1859, supplemented by information in Twiggs to Thomas, 5 February 1859, in *Difficulties on Southwestern Frontier*, House of Representatives Executive Document No. 52, 36th Cong., 1st sess. (1860), 5-7.
20. D. E. Twiggs to Lieutenant Colonel L. Thomas, 13 January 1859, *Difficulties*, 5.
21. *Claims of the State of Texas: Letter from the Secretary of War*, House of Representatives Executive Document No. 277, 42nd Cong., 2nd sess. (1872), 19.
22. General Orders No. 1, Department of Texas, 5 February 1859, in *Difficulties*, 7-8.
23. Williams, *Never Again III*, 193-194, citing "Letter, 5-15-1859, at Fort Davis, from Captain Brackett to Lieutenant Wood." Also see "Map of Scout made by Capt. A. G. Brackett and Sixty-Six men of Company I Second Cavalry on the Great Comanche War Trail in April and May 1859, Copied from a sketch furnished by Capt. Brackett Sep. 1876," Records of the War Department, Office of the Chief of Engineers, Map Q 287, NA. This map delineates Brackett's scout as originating at Fort Lancaster, a location that Brackett may have considered a staging ground.
24. Caleb Pirtle III and Michael F. Cusack, *The Lonely Sentinel: Fort Clark: On Texas's Western Frontier* (Austin: Eakin Press, 1985), 39-40.
25. Mahon and Kielman, "Giddings," 235.
26. D. H. Vinton to Major General T. S. Jesup, 3 September 1859; D. H. Vinton to Quartermaster's Office, Headquarters, Department of Texas, 26 April 1859; Edward L. Hartz to Major David H. Vinton, 1859 (otherwise undated, but post-April 26) and accompanying diary dated May 18, 1859-August 7, 1859; all in *Report of the Secretary of War*, 1 December 1859, Senate Executive Document No. 2, 36th Cong., 1st sess. (Washington: 1860), 422-441.
27. Bliss, "Reminiscences," Vol. II, 26, 92, 93, 105, 108.
28. "Frontier Campaign—W. R. Henry's Official Report," *San Antonio Texan*, 3 September 1859.
29. Bliss, "Reminiscences," Vol. II, 92, 185, 190.
30. Ibid., 21-23.
31. Ibid., 165-168.
32. Ibid., 162-163.
33. Barrett, *Western Forts*, 138.
34. Bliss, "Reminiscences," Vol. II, 26.
35. Williams, *Never Again III*, 198.
36. Post return, Camp Hudson, Texas, September 1859.
37. Special Orders No. 85, Headquarters, Department of Texas, 23 September 1859, in Indian Depredations Case No. 3873. Stoneman received the orders 27 September 1859. See post return, Camp Hudson, September 1859.
38. Smith, *Old Army*, 146.
39. Austerman, *Sharps Rifles*, 157-158, 319.
40. Report of William H. Echols, 10 October 1860, entries for 24 and 25 June and 5 August 1860, typescript in author's possession.
41. Morgan Wolfe Merrick, *From Desert to Bayou: The Civil War Journal and Sketches of Morgan Wolfe*

Merrick (El Paso: Texas Western Press, 1991), 38, 40. For clarity, I have edited the spelling in Hodge's statement.
42 Austerman, *Sharps Rifles*, 159, 319. Obviously, the station had been rebuilt after its January 1859 destruction.
43 Giddings petition, 12 August 1891, 6, 12; and deposition of David Koney, 19 October 1894; both in Indians Depredations Case No. 3873.

Chapter 9 GRAY REPLACES BLUE
1   *Handbook Online,* entry for "Secession Convention" (accessed 2 March 2009).
2   Special Orders No. 32, Department of Texas, 24 February 1861, *War of the Rebellion: A Compilation of the Official Records of the Union and Confederate Armies* (hereafter, *OR*), Series 1, Vol. 1 (Gettysburg: National Historical Society, reprint, 1972), 594.
3   Special Orders No. 36, Department of Texas, 27 February 1861, *OR,* 596.
4   Barrett, "Western Frontier Forts," 131, 138; and Allen W. Jones, "Military Events in Texas During the Civil War, 1861-1865," *SHQ* 64, no. 1 (July 1960), 69.
5   Jerry Thompson, introduction in Merrick, *From Desert,* i.
6   Merrick, *From Desert,* 10-11.
7   Harry McCorry Henderson, *Texas in the Confederacy* (San Antonio: The Naylor Company, 1955), 124; and Martin Hardwick Hall, "A Confederate Soldier's Letters from Fort Bliss, July 6, 1861," *Password* 25, No. 1 (Spring 1980), 17-20.
8   Giddings deposition, 5 October 1891, and Giddings deposition, 11, 19, 20, and 21 December 1894, both in Indian Depredations Case No. 3873; Charles M. Barnes, "The Overland Mail Service to the Pacific: Agitation for a Government Road Nipped by the Out break of the Civil War—Interesting Reminiscences by Col. Giddings," *The San Antonio Daily Express,* 28 June 1903; and Austerman, *Sharps Rifles,* 176. Information on stagecoach travel under Giddings' August 28, 1861 contract is from Heartsill, *Fourteen Hundred and 91 Days,* 49, 50, 51, 52, 54, 55, 75; Austerman, *Sharps Rifles,* 181, 186, 188, 320; and Wayne R. Austerman, "Giddings' Station, a Forgotten Landmark on the Pecos," *The Permian Historical Annual* 21 (1981), 7.
9   *Handbook Online,* entry for "Roberts, Daniel Webster" (accessed 15 November 2005).
10 *Depredations on the Frontiers of Texas,* House of Representatives Executive Document No. 257, 43rd Cong., 1st sess. (1874), 12.
11 Clayton Williams, *Texas' Last Frontier: Fort Stockton and the Trans-Pecos, 1861-1865* (College Station: Texas A&M University Press, 1982), 21-23; and *Handbook Online,* entry for "Pyron, Charles Lynn" (accessed 12 February 2009).
12 Heartsill, *Fourteen Hundred,* 44-46.
13 *Handbook Online,* entry for "Mesilla, Battle of" (accessed 12 February 2009).
14 Heartsill, *Fourteen Hundred,* 47.
15 Jerry D. Thompson, ed., *Westward the Texans: The Civil War Journal of Private William Randolph Howell* (El Paso: Texas Western Press, 1990), 138; *Handbook Online,* entries for "Sibley's Brigade" (accessed 12 February 2009) and "Sibley Campaign" (accessed 12 February 2009); and Williams, *Last Frontier,* 37.
16 Williams, *Border Ruffians,* 201.
17 Williams, *Last Frontier,* 37.
18 Oscar Haas, translator, "The Diary of Julius Giesecke, 1861-62," *Texas Military History* 3, No. 4 (Winter 1963), 230.
19 John E. Hart journal, entries for 6-8 November 1861, TCM Collection, Haley Library.
20 Haas, "Diary of Julius Giesecke," 228, 230.
21 Donald S. Frazier, *Blood & Treasure: Confederate Empire in the Southwest* (College Station: Texas A&M University Press, 1995), 120.
22 Howell diary in Thompson, *Westward the Texans,* 70-71.
23 Heartsill, *Fourteen Hundred,* 50, 56, 58.
24 Ibid., 56, 57, 58, 61.

25 Ibid., 53, 54.
26 Ibid., 54; and *Handbook Online,* entry for "Valverde, Battle of" (accessed 12 February 2009).
27 *Handbook Online,* entry for "Glorieta, Battle of" (accessed 12 February 2009).
28 Heartsill, *Fourteen Hundred,* 55, 75-76, 77.
29 Haas, "Diary of Julius Giesecke," 228-229, 242.
30 Austerman, *Sharps Rifles,* 186, 188.
31 November 1862 letter from H. J. Caniffe quoted in Scannell, "Henry Skillman," 28.
32 Williams, *Last Frontier,* 49. Also see James H. Carleton to Capt. Joseph Updegraff, 8 December 1862, NA.
33 A. H. Abney, *Life and Adventures of L. D. Lafferty* (New York: H. S. Goodspeed, 1875), 215-216.
34 Santleben, *Texas Pioneer,* 266. Santleben also lists the death of a Thomas Black near Beaver Lake in 1873, casting a measure of doubt on the date of the incident. See Santleben, *Texas Pioneer,* 268.
35 Carroll, "Texas Collection," 122.
36 The ensuing account, including the skirmish with Comanches, is from Williams, *Border Ruffians,* 323-335. Concerns exist about the historicity of certain aspects of Williams' recollections. See footnote 40 below.
37 Colonel John S. Ford to Capt. E. P. Turner, AAG, CSA, 22 January 1864, OR, Series 1, Vol. 53, 952.
38 Colonel John S. Ford to Capt. E. P. Turner, AAG, CSA, 8 February 1864, TCM Collection, Haley Library. The Concho River mentioned by Ford likely refers to the Middle Concho, along which the Upper Road coursed.
39 H. W. Halleck, Headquarters of the Army, Washington, D.C., to Brigadier General Carlton [sic], Santa Fe, New Mexico, evidently published in its entirety in Hunter, "Midnight Battle," 367.
40 According to Williams, *Border Ruffians,* 343-348, 363-373, Captain R. H. Williams and Texas State Troops, soon after capturing ten Confederate deserters near Beaver Lake in late winter of 1864, reconnoitered Fort Lancaster for Union hostiles and found only empty ruins. After ten weeks of chasing ghosts, however, a genuine threat supposedly materialized, although it comprised not federals but 300 to 500 lawless Californians and deserters. These renegades reportedly raided both sides of the border from a base in "difficult brushy country" between Fort Lancaster and the Rio Grande. Apprised of the situation, a Major Hunter started west along the Lower Road in April 1864 with Williams and approximately 575 Rangers. Passing through the Devils country, the Ranger force arrived in the vicinity of Lancaster after a nine-day march. At a wooded bluff before dawn on the eleventh day, they launched a surprise attack that killed thirty-five renegades, severely wounded another twenty, and drove the survivors into Mexico. Meanwhile, fourteen Rangers fell, with eight eventually dying of their wounds. Also see J. Marvin Hunter, "Midnight Battle at Fort Lancaster," *Frontier Times* 21, No. 9 (June 1944), 367-370, which is drawn from *Border Ruffians.*

No evidence has surfaced to corroborate the *Border Ruffians* story of a Fort Lancaster-area skirmish between Texas forces and lawless Californians and deserters. Moreover, R. H. Williams clearly could not have participated in an expedition to Fort Lancaster in April 1864; see "Report of Captain R. H. Williams of Frio County," dated 23 April 1864, in "Consolidated Report of Scouts against Indians and Deserters by the Texas State Troops Commanded by Major Jas. M. Hunter, 3rd Frontier Dist., Texas State Troops, at Fredericksburg, Texas, May 14, 1864,"TSA.

From the time of its publication, *Border Ruffians* was criticized for its inaccuracies; see "Book Reviews and Notices," *The Quarterly of the Texas State Historical Association* Vol. 12, No. 3 (January 1909), 240-241. For a more recent examination, see Glen Sample Ely, "Gone from Texas and Trading with the Enemy: New Perspectives on Civil War West Texas," *SHQ* Vol. 110, No. 4 (April 2007), 454-455, and Glen Sample Ely, "Skullduggery at Spencer's Ranch: Civil War Intrigue in West Texas," *Journal of Big Bend Studies* Vol. 21, (2009), 23-24.

In "Skullduggery," Ely suggests that "Major Hunter" was Major Sherod Hunter and equates Williams' account with Sherod Hunter's summer 1864 expedition west on the Lower Road. Sherod Hunter reportedly met with failure when Indians attacked his force at Fort Lancaster; see Mamie Yeary, compiler, *Reminiscences of the Boys in Gray, 1861-1865* (Dallas: Smith and Lamar, 1912), 449.

Williams died in 1904, and the level of his participation in producing the posthumously published *Border Ruffians* is unclear. The introduction, presumably by his editor (and younger brother) E. W. Williams, states that the volume was based largely on R. H. Williams' diaries and notes, supplemented by "many a yarn" he related (*Border Ruffians*, xix). Of the period incorporating the alleged Lancaster battle, the author unequivocally asserts that he was drawing upon R. H. Williams' November 1864 notes of "anything . . . [he] could remember of importance" (*Border Ruffians*, 310; also see Tony Mandara, "R. H. Williams: The English Texas Ranger," Confederate Historical Association of Belgium, http://chab-belgium.com/pdf/english/Williams.pdf, accessed 13 May 2010).

Nevertheless, it is impossible to determine how much of the battle account stems from those early notes as opposed to recollections. Moreover, E. W. Williams, in his role as editor after R. H. Williams' death, was in a position to interpolate, embellish, and even fictionalize without oversight on the part of his brother.

In regard to geographic matters, *Border Ruffians* is consistent with other nineteenth century descriptions of the Devils country, suggesting that R. H. Williams had firsthand knowledge. In his April 23, 1864 "Report of Captain R H. Williams of Frio County," he states that "the country we scout in is from the Frio to the Nueces and west of it," a region that could well have included the Devils. His report adds an intriguing comment: "This portion of the country is becoming inflicted by bands of deserters, who are generally well armed and mounted."

41 *Handbook Online*, entry for "Palmito Ranch, Battle of" (accessed 13 February 2009).

Chapter 10 THE DEVILS INDIAN WAR

1 Charles Goodnight to J. Evetts Haley, 27 February 1929, J. Evetts Haley Collection (hereafter, JEH Collection), Haley Library; J. Evetts Haley, "Charles Goodnight," original manuscript, 193, also marked 166, JEH Collection, Haley Library; Charles Goodnight, Emanuel Dubbs, John A. Hart, et al., *Pioneer Days in the Southwest from 1850 to 1879* (Guthrie, Oklahoma: The State Capital Company, 1909), 12-13; *Prose and Poetry of the Live Stock Industry of the United States* (New York: Antiquarian Press, reprint, 1959), 61; entry for 4 March 1866, diary of Susan E. Newcomb, 47-48, in Samuel P. Newcomb diaries, Haley Library; James Cox, *Historical and Biographical Record of the Cattle Industry and the Cattlemen of Texas and Adjacent Territory* (St. Louis: Woodward and Tiernan Printing Company, 1895); and David J. Murrah, *C. C. Slaughter: Rancher, Banker, Baptist* (Austin: University of Texas Press, 1981), 19-20. Of these sources, the Goodnight-to-Haley letter alone questions the Devils setting for the incident, instead placing it "probably" on the headwaters of the Guadalupe River.

2 Austerman, *Sharps Rifles*, 201, 320.
3 Post return, Fort Clark, Texas, December 1866.
4 *A Report on the Hygiene of the United States Army, with Descriptions of Military Posts*, War Department, Surgeon-General's Office Circular No. 8 (Washington: Government Printing Office, 1875), 192; *Testimony Taken*, 82-83; Kevin Mulroy, *Freedom on the Border: The Seminole Maroons in Florida, the Indian Territory, Coahuila, and Texas* (Lubbock: Texas Tech University Press, 1993), 117-118; and *Handbook Online*, entry for "Kickapoo Indians" (accessed 13 February 2009).
5 Williams, *Last Frontier*, 73, citing *San Antonio Herald*, 17 April 1867.
6 Sowell, *Early Settlers*, 372-373.
7 Post return, Fort Clark, Texas, March 1867, NA.
8 H. I. Richards to J. W. Throckmorton, 19 March 1867, in Winfrey and Day, *Indian Papers*, 177-180.

9 Post return, Camp Hudson, June 1867, NA.
10 Post return, Fort Davis, Texas, July 1867, NA.
11 Heitman, *Historical Register,* 429; and Smith, *Old Army,* 148.
12 Edward Hatch to AAG, District of Texas, 18 and 24 October and 18 November 1867, NA; post return, Camp Hudson, Texas, October 1867, NA; and Austerman, *Sharps Rifles,* 320.
13 U.S. Army report dated 15 March 1867, Fort Quitman, Texas, otherwise unidentified, NA, copy in author's possession.
14 William Frohock to John S. Loud, 27 December 1867, letters and telegrams received, Fort Stockton, Texas, NA; post return, Fort Stockton, Texas, December 1867, NA; and Edward Hatch to C. E. Morse, District of Texas, 3 January 1868 (incorrectly stated as "1867"), letters and telegrams received, Fort Stockton, NA. The bodies of the slain soldiers would not be found for three months.
15 Edward Hatch to Lieut. C. E., AAA General, 18 November 1867, letters sent, Fort Stockton, Texas, NA; post return, Camp Hudson, Texas, November 1867 (dated 12 December 1867), NA; and Loyd M. Uglow, *Standing in the Gap: Army Outposts, Picket Stations, and the Pacification of the Texas Frontier, 1866-1886* (Fort Worth: Texas Christian University Press, 2001), 50.
16 Post return, Camp Hudson, Texas, January 1868, NA.
17 Post return, Camp Hudson, Texas, March 1868, NA; and post return, Fort Clark, Texas, April 1868, NA.
18 Post return, Fort Clark, Texas, August 1868, NA.
19 Isaac Parker Metcalf, interview with J. Evetts Haley, no date, original interview notes and typescript, JEH Collection, Haley Library, Metcalf's quote is a synthesis of statements. Haley, in a margin note, calls into question the date of another of Metcalf's statements, thereby casting a measure of doubt on the accuracy of Metcalf's recollections. A May 2010 search, conducted on my behalf, of Texas Ranger records in the Texas State Archives showed an apparent absence of extant monthly returns, muster rolls, or adjutant general correspondence for the period in question, leaving open the question as to the historicity of Metcalf's account (Donaly Brice, TSA, email to author, 12 May 2010).
20 Uglow, *Standing,* 50.
21 C. Williams, *Last Frontier,* 113.
22 J. F. Wade to Captain C. E. [no last name], AAA General, Fifth Military District, letters sent, Fort Stockton, Texas, 31 May 1869, NA; and Hunt, journal and map, 32.
23 Carroll, "Collection," 123; and Ernest L. Reedstrom, *Scrapbook of the American West,* Caldwell, Idaho: The Caxton Printers, Ltd., 1991), 26. Also see *San Antonio Express,* 12 June 1869.
24 Swift and Corning, *Three Roads,* 240.
25 *Testimony Taken,* 30.
26 Hunt's journal and map, 32-35.
27 Santleben, *Texas Pioneer,* 99, 226-227.
28 C. Williams, *Last Frontier,* 129.
29 "A White Renegade at Santa Nina Waterhole," *San Antonio Express,* 28 September 1903; and C. Williams, *Last Frontier,* 130-131.
30 Uglow, *Standing,* 50.
31 Reedstrom, *Scrapbook,* 27.
32 W. R. Shafter to H. Clay Wood, 27 June 1870, in Jerry M. Sullivan, ed., "Lieutenant Colonel William R. Shafter's Pecos River Expedition of 1870," *WTHA Year Book* 47 (1971), 146-147. Shafter background is from *Handbook Online,* entry for "Shafter, William Rufus" (accessed 15 February 2009).
33 Charles B. Gaskill, scouting report, 26 August 1870, Fort Clark, Texas, NA.
34 W. R. Shafter's report to H. Clay Wood, 10 October 1870, in Sullivan, "Pecos River Expedition," 149-152.
35 Frank C. Kaiser, "Reminiscences of a Texas Ranger," manuscript, 1967, Haley Library, 18-19.
36 W. R. Shafter to H. Clay Wood, 4 December 1870, letters sent, Fort McKavett, Texas, NA;

and W. R. Shafter to Rangers: Commanding Officer, Fort Mason, Texas, 4 December 1870, letters sent, Fort McKavett, NA.
37 Post return, Fort Clark, Texas, December 1871, NA.
38 H. J. Richarz report, 9 December 1870, in W. C. Nunn, *Texas Under the Carpetbaggers* (Austin: University of Texas Press, 1962), 192-193.
39 Ibid., 194.
40 Post return, Fort Clark, Texas, January 1871, NA.
41 H. Clay Wood, AAG, to Commanding Officer, Fort Clark, Texas, letters sent, Department of Texas, 22 April 1871, NA; and post return, Fort Clark, Texas, May 1871, NA.
42 H. Clay Wood to Commanding Officer, Fort Clark, Texas, 27 April 1871, letters sent, Department of Texas, NA; and post return, Fort Clark, Texas, May 1871, NA.
43 Post return, Fort Stockton, Texas, May 1871, NA.
44 Post return, Fort Clark, Texas, June 1871, NA.
45 Post return, Fort Clark, Texas, July 1871, NA.
46 Post return, Fort Clark, Texas, September 1871, NA.
47 Post return, Fort Clark, Texas, October 1871, NA.
48 Post return, Fort Clark, Texas, November 1871, NA.
49 Post return, Fort Stockton, Texas, January 1872, NA.
50 Post return, Fort Clark, Texas, January 1872, NA.
51 Post return, Fort Clark, Texas, February 1872, NA.

Chapter 11 BLACK SEMINOLES TO THE RESCUE
1 Post return, Fort Clark, Texas, April 1872, NA.; Bliss, "Reminiscences," Vol. V, 177-184; *Testimony Taken,* 137; *Depredations,* 14; Santleben, *Texas Pioneer,* 143-144; R. S. Mackenzie to AAG, Department of Texas, 12 October 1872, in Ernest Wallace, ed., *Ranald S. Mackenzie's Official Correspondence Relating to Texas, 1871-1873* (Lubbock: West Texas Museum Association, 1967), 141-145; C. Williams, *Last Frontier,* 154-157; and *Handbook Online,* entries for "Big Bow" and "White Horse" (both accessed 16 February 2009).
2 W. Merritt to Captain Lewis Johnson, 19 March 1872, letters sent, Fort Stockton, Texas, NA; and post return, Fort Stockton, Texas, May 1872, NA.
3 Bliss, "Reminiscences," Vol. V, 184-187; and post return, Fort Stockton, Texas, May 1872, NA.
4 Bliss, "Reminiscences," Vol. II, 25.
5 Jno. P. Hatch to AAG, Department of Texas, 20 July 1872, in Wallace, *Official Correspondence, 1871-1873,* 108.
6 "Indian News," letter of 24 August 1872 from a Fort Clark citizen, *San Antonio Herald,* 1872, otherwise unidentified digital image in author's possession.
7 Michael Cooney's report to post adjutant, Fort Clark, Texas, 28 November 1872, in William H. Leckie, *The Buffalo Soldiers: A Narrative of the Negro Cavalry in the West* (Norman: University of Oklahoma Press, 1967), 103-104.
8 R. G. Carter, *On the Border with Mackenzie, or Winning West Texas from the Comanches* (Washington, DC: Eynon Printing Company, 1935), 421-423. Carter was stationed at Fort Clark at the time of the meeting and learned the details from Mackenzie. Biographical information on Mackenzie is from *Handbook Online,* entry for "Mackenzie, Ranald Slidell" (accessed 16 February 2009).
9 *Handbook Online,* entry for "Black Seminole Indians" (accessed 16 February 2009).
10 Post return, Fort Clark, Texas, August 1872, NA.
11 Bliss, "Reminiscences," Vol. V, 109.
12 Mulroy, *Freedom,* 117; Grace Lowe Butler, "General John Lapham Bullis," *The Texas History Teachers' Bulletin* 14, No. 1, University of Texas Bulletin No. 2746 (8 December 1927), 17-22; *Handbook Online,* entry for "Bullis, John Lapham" (accessed 16 February 2009); Woolford, "Duvall Diary," 491; and Jim Fenton, "John L. Bullis Always Meant Business," *The Permian Historical Annual* 33 (1993), 17.
13 Carter, *On the Border,* 421.
14 Ranald S. Mackenzie to AAG, Department of Texas, 22 April 1873, in Wallace, *Mackenzie's*

Official Correspondence 1871-1873, 162-163; and affidavit of Jerome Strickland, enclosed in Hamilton Fish to William W. Belknap, 6 June 1873, in Wallace, *Mackenzie's Official Correspondence 1871-1873,* 164-165.
15. Endorsement by P. H. Sheridan, 20 May 1873, on Mackenzie to AAG, Department of Texas, 22 April 1873, in Wallace, *Mackenzie's Official Correspondence 1871-1873,* 162-163.
16. Post return, Fort Clark, Texas, May 1873, NA; C. C. Augur, annual report to AAG, Headquarters, Military Division of the Missouri, 30 September 1873, in Ernest Wallace, ed., *Ranald S. Mackenzie's Official Correspondence Relating to Texas, 1873-1879,* 61-62; and "Record of Engagements with Hostile Indians in Texas 1868 to 1882," *WTHA Year Book* 9 (October 1933), 104-105. The latter source is excerpted from *Record of Engagements with Hostile Indians within the Military Division of the Missouri, from 1868 to 1882, Lieutenant-General P. H. Sheridan, Commanding* (Washington: Government Printing Office, 1882).
17. Roger N. Conger, et al., *Frontier Forts of Texas* (Waco: Texian Press, 1966), 69. The chapter cited is by Dorman H. Winfrey.
18. Ranald S. Mackenzie to C. C. Augur, 29 May 1873, in Wallace, *Mackenzie's Official Correspondence, 1871-1873,* 179-181.
19. Endorsement by P. H. Sheridan, 13 June 1873, on Ranald S. Mackenzie to C. C. Augur, 29 May 1873, in Wallace, *Mackenzie's Official Correspondence, 1871-1873,* 181.
20. Augur, annual report to AAG, 30 September 1873.
21. *Depredations,* 3, 12, 13, 14.
22. "Journal of the march of a detachment of Company M 9th Cavalry commanded by 1st Lieut. Gregory Barrett Jr., 10 Infantry," book of scouts vol. 1, Fort McKavett, Texas, NA.
23. Fort Clark medical ledger, vol. 1, 20, Haley Library.
24. C. Williams, *Last Frontier,* 177, citing W. C. Johnson, Fort Davis, letter, in *Denison Daily News,* 14 April 1874.
25. C. Williams, *Last Frontier,* 178.
26. Account by participant W. K. Jones, a commissary sergeant in Coldwell's command, in *Our Town: Friends and Neighbors, a bicentennial tribute* (N.p.: Comstock Study Club, 1976), 98-100. Coldwell's last name is sometimes spelled Caldwell.
27. Fort Clark medical ledger, vol. 1, 24.
28. *Report of the Secretary of War, Vol. 1,* House of Representatives Executive Document No. 1, Part 2, 44th Cong., 1st sess., (Washington: Government Printing Office, 1875), 99.
29. "Account of Engagement with Comanche Indians," 16 February 1875, letter to *San Antonio Herald,* in Winfrey and Day, *Indian Papers,* 369-372. I also consulted Sowell, *Early Settlers,* 188-194.
30. Charles M. Neal Jr., *Valor Across the Lone Star: The Congressional Medal of Honor in Frontier Texas* (Austin: Texas State Historical Association, 2002), 233.
31. John L. Bullis, report of scout, in *Hacienda,* 456-457.
32. Smith, *Old Army,* 161.
33. W. R. "Jake" Owen, interviews with J. Evetts Haley, Carlsbad, New Mexico, 12 August 1926, 2 March 1933, and 24 June 1937, Haley Library. Spellings of Humphrey and Humphries are included in the interview typescripts. I have chosen to use Humphreys in consideration of trail boss Charley Humphreys, who is known to have driven a herd across the Devils in 1884. See J. Marvin Hunter, compiler and ed., *The Trail Drivers of Texas* (Austin: University of Texas Press, 1985 reprint), 804-805.
34. Allen A. Erwin, *The Southwest of John H. Slaughter, 1841-1922* (Glendale, California: The Arthur H. Clark Company, 1965), 95.
35. Vinton Lee James, *Frontier and Pioneer Recollections of Early Days in San Antonio and West Texas* (San Antonio: Artes Graficas, 1938), 70.
36. Charles Askins, *Texans, Guns & History* (New York: Bonanza Books, 1970), 64.

Chapter 12 AVENGING IN MEXICO

1. Headquarters, Department of Texas, to Col. Buell, Concho, 13 March 1876, letters sent, Department of Texas, NA; and *San Antonio Daily Herald,* 24 March 1876.

NOTES 189

2   *San Antonio Daily Herald,* 24 March and 7 April 1876.
3   Ibid., 7 April 1876.
4   Ibid., 19 April 1876.
5   Ibid., 14 April 1876.
6   "Record for the Month of April 1876" in Fort Clark medical ledger Vol. 1; and post return, Fort Clark, Texas, April 1876, notes in CWW Collection, Haley Library.
7   Return for April 1876, Company F, Frontier Battalion, TSA, Austin, Texas; "Depredations by Indians," Austin, Texas, 1 January 1878, in Winfrey and Day, *Indian Papers,* 393.
8   Testimony of John B. Jones, 19 January 1878, in *Texas Frontier Troubles,* House of Representatives Committee on Foreign Affairs, House Report 701, Serial No. 1824, 45th Cong., 2nd sess. (Washington: Government Printing Office, 1878), 54.
9   Testimony of John L. Bullis before Committee on Military Affairs, 8 January 1878, in *Testimony Taken,* 190.
10 *San Antonio Daily Herald,* 30 May 1876.
11 Bullis testimony in *Testimony Taken,* 188, 190; testimony of William R. Shafter before Committee on Military Affairs, 7 January 1878, in *Testimony Taken,* 158-159; and Smith, *Old Army,* 161.
12 James B. Gillett, *Six Years with the Texas Rangers, 1875 to 1881* (Lincoln and London: University of Nebraska Press, 1976 reprint), 58-60.
13 "Pecos River Region," *DMN,* 16 February 1896, 18.
14 Fort Clark medical ledger, vol. 1, 91.
15 Leckie, *Buffalo Soldiers,* 151.
16 Bullis testimony in *Testimony Taken,* 190, 197. I also consulted *New York Times,* 9 January 1878.
17 Smith, *Old Army,* 68; and *Handbook Online,* entry for "Camp Hudson" (accessed 15 November 2005).
18 Bullis testimony in *Testimony Taken,* 189-190.
19 *Texas Frontier Troubles,* 105; Winfrey and Day, *Indian Papers,* 397; and return for March 1877, Company F, Frontier Battalion, TSA. Dolan set out March 24 from Camp Wood.
20 *Handbook Online,* entry for "Dolan Creek" (accessed 15 November 2005).
21 Heitman, *Historical Register,* 443.
22 "Record of Engagements," 112.
23 *Texas Frontier Troubles,* 105; and Winfrey and Day, Texas *Indian Papers,* 397.
24 George A. Schneider, "A Border Incident of 1878 From the Journal of Captain John S. McNaught," *SHQ* 70, No. 2 (October 1966), 315, 316.
25 *New York Times,* 9 January 1878.
26 Schneider, "Border Incident," 316.
27 *New York Times,* 9 January 1878.
28 Research notes (six pages) beginning "Microfilm Copy 666" in CWW Collection, Haley Library, drawn from: *Mexican Border Troubles,* House Executive Document No. 13, 45th Cong., 1st sess., 16-18; J. M. Kelley to AAAG, District of Nueces, 11 June 1877, NA; W. R. Shafter to E. O. C. Ord, 11 June 1877, NA; Philip H. Sheridan to E. F. Townsend, 12 and 15 June 1877, NA; E. F. Townsend to Philip H. Sheridan, 13 and 15 June 1877, NA; George W. McCrary to Secretary of State, n.d., NA; and E. O. C. Ord to General Drum, 11 June 1877, NA. Kelley's name is spelled "Kelly" in Wallace, *Mackenzie's Correspondence, 1873-1879,* 212.
29 Return for July 1877, Company D, Frontier Battalion, TSA; *Texas Frontier Troubles,* 106; and Winfrey and Day, *Indian Papers,* 397-398. The drouth reference is from testimony of E. O. C. Ord, 5 December 1877, in *Testimony Taken,* 78. Sieker's full name is from *Handbook Online,* entry for "Sieker, Lamartine Pemberton" (accessed 18 February 2009).
30 Bullis testimony in *Testimony Taken,* 190, 191.
31 *Texas Frontier Troubles,* 24.
32 Bullis testimony in *Testimony Taken,* 191-193. As published, Bullis' testimony gives an October date for the strike, but his subsequent testimony on pages 194-195 indicates he was elsewhere at that time. I have chosen to use the September dates specified in "Record of Engagements," 111.
33 Fort Clark medical ledger, 111, 115; and Leckie, *Buffalo Soldiers,* 154.

190 NOTES

34 John L. Bullis, dispatch, 23 October 1877 [date perhaps erroneous], in *Testimony Taken,* 85-86; and Bullis testimony in *Testimony Taken,* 194-195.
35 W. R. Shafter to Taylor, AAG, 9 November 1877, in *Testimony Taken,* 85-86.
36 Post return, Fort Clark, Texas, November 1877, NA; and Bullis testimony in *Testimony Taken,* 195.
37 W. R. Shafter dispatches, 14 and 18 November 1877, in *Testimony Taken,* 87-88.
38 "Record of Engagements," 112.
39 *Texas Frontier Troubles,* 106.
40 J. Frank Dobie, *A Vaquero of the Brush Country* (1929; repr., New York: Grosset and Dunlap, n.d.), 124, 128.
41 Testimony of Brigadier General E. O. C. Ord to Committee on Military Affairs, 5 and 6 December 1877, in *Testimony Taken,* 77, 78, 83, 103. In their testimonies, Ord, Shafter, and Bullis gave varying ranges for the number of warriors in a party. Ord, 83, indicated five to twenty-five. Shafter, 156, said "two or three up to thirty or forty." Bullis, 197, gave a low of two and observed that he had never known of a party larger than thirty-five.
42 Bullis testimony in *Testimony Taken,* 190-191, 201.
43 Shafter testimony in *Testimony Taken,* 156, 159, 164.
44 Bullis testimony in *Testimony Taken,* 197.
45 Shafter testimony in *Testimony Taken,* 164.

Chapter 13 LAST OF THE ARROWS
1 Gillett, *Six Years,* 100-102.
2 J. M. Kelly (Kelley) to AAG, District of the Nueces, 6 April 1878, in *Mackenzie's Correspondence, 1873-1879,* 212.
3 Post return, Fort Clark, Texas, May 1878, NA. An encampment soon known as "Mackenzie's Camp" was located about two miles downstream of First Crossing. See Captain William Fletcher to AAAG, District of the Nueces, 6 September 1879, letters sent, District of the Pecos, NA.
4 R. S. Mackenzie to AAG, Department of Texas, 23 June 1878, in *Mackenzie's Correspondence, 1873-1879,* 204; and Ernest Wallace, Ranald S. Mackenzie on the Texas Frontier (Lubbock: West Texas Museum Association, 1964, 1965), 55-56.
5 Schneider, "Border Incident," 316.
6 Mackenzie to AAG, Department of Texas, 23 June 1878, in *Mackenzie's Correspondence, 1873-1879,* 204-209.
7 Fort Clark medical ledger, vol. 1, 137.
8 "Record of Engagements," 114; *Report of the Secretary of War,* otherwise unidentified government publication (post-September 1879), 98, 111, 112, 114, JEH Collection, IV, A, 6, section 1, Haley Library; and *Handbook Online,* entry for "Mountain Home, Texas" (accessed 19 February 2009).
9 Return for October 1878, Company F, Frontier Battalion, TSA.
10 *Report of the Secretary of War,* otherwise unidentified government publication (post-September 1879), 98, JEH Collection, IV, A, 6, section 1, Haley Library.
11 John L. Bullis dispatch, 15 March 1879, included in E. O. C. Ord to AG, Military Division of the Missouri, 18 March 1879, letters and telegrams sent, Department of Texas, NA; *Report of the Secretary of War,* otherwise unidentified government publication (post-September 1879), 98-100, JEH Collection, IV, A, 6, section 1, Haley Library; and C. Williams, *Last Frontier,* 229.
12 Gillett, *Six Years,* 132-133.
13 W. C. Holden, *Rollie Burns, or an Account of the Ranching Industry on the South Plains* (Dallas: The Southwest Press, 1932), 65-66.
14 *Report of the Secretary of War,* otherwise unidentified government publication (post-September 1879), 100, 102, 109, 112, 114, JEH Collection, IV, A, 6, section 1, Haley Library; "Record of Engagements," 114; Frank M. Temple, "Reports of Scouts from Fort Concho, 1867-1889," including maps, typed from National Archives microfilm of RG 393," C: 118, manuscript in author's possession; and Marcos E. Kinevan, *Frontier Cavalryman: Lieutenant John Bigelow*

with the Buffalo Soldiers in Texas (El Paso: Texas Western Press, 1998), 203-204.
15 Thomas M. Vincent, AAG, to Commanding Officer, District of the Nueces, Fort Clark, Texas, 5 July 1879, letters and telegrams sent, Department of Texas, NA.
16 *Report of the Secretary of War,* otherwise unidentified government publication (post-September 1879), 101, JEH Collection, IV, A, 6, section 1, Haley Library; and Fletcher to AAAG, District of the Nueces, 6 September 1879. Fletcher's letter is unclear as to whether the identified crossing point was about a mile and a half above the Pecos' mouth, or about a mile and a half above an old Indian crossing. If the latter is the case, the new crossing would have been about one and three-quarters miles from the mouth.
17 Uglow, *Standing,* 164.
18 Fort Clark medical ledger, vol. 1, 199.
19 *Report of the Secretary of War,* otherwise unidentified government publication (post-September 1879), 112, JEH Collection, IV, A, 6, section 1, Haley Library.
20 Fort Clark medical ledger, vol. 1, 177.
21 Ibid., 182.
22 Thomas M. Vincent, AAG, to District Commander, Fort Clark, 10 and 19 December 1879, letters and telegrams sent, Department of Texas, NA.
23 James B. Gillett, who traveled up the Devils with Texas Rangers in August 1879, strongly implied that a ranch existed at Pecan Springs at that time. See Gillett, *Six Years,* 141, 145. The author and Joe Allen personally inspected Pecan Springs 31 March 2009.
24 James, *Frontier and Pioneer,* 70.
25 Blunt, commanding, to Fort Stockton, Texas, 4 January 1880, letters and telegrams sent, Department of Texas, NA.
26 "Master Story Teller is W. L. Jones of Baird," *Texas Stockman-Journal,* 7 February 1906.
27 Dobie, *Vaquero,* 184-185.
28 Mother Hoover (Laura Hoover), interview with Elizabeth Doyle, Ozona, Texas, 16 November 1937, WPA Federal Writers' Project Collection (hereafter WPA Collection), Manuscript Division, Library of Congress, Washington, D.C.; Claude Denham, "Frontier Problems and Amusements in Crockett County," *WTHA Year Book* 9 (October 1933), 36-37.
29 Thomas M. Vincent to AG, Washington, D.C., 11 March 1880, letters and telegrams sent, Department of Texas.
30 Fort Clark medical ledger, vol. 1, 192.
31 Thomas M. Vincent to District Commander, Fort Clark, 16 March 1880, letters and telegrams sent, Department of Texas, NA.
32 E. O. C. Ord to AG, Military Division of the Missouri, 1 October 1880, letters and telegrams sent, Department of Texas, NA.
33 John S. Mason to Commanding Officer, Fort Clark, Texas, 6 November 1880, letters and telegrams sent, Department of Texas, NA.
34 C. C. Augur to Division of AG, Chicago, Illinois, 12 May 1881, letters and telegrams sent, Department of Texas, NA.
35 Ord to AG, Military Division of the Missouri, 1 October 1880.
36 "Record of Engagements," 118; C. C. Augur, Department of Texas, to Division of Missouri AG, 27 September 1881, letters and telegrams sent, Department of Texas, NA; Switzer, commanding Fort Clark, to Brigadier General, 7 May 1881, letters and telegrams sent, Department of Texas, NA; and two telegrams to C. C. Augur, 6 May 1881, in Frost Woodhull, "The Seminole Indian Scouts On the Border," *Frontier Times* 15, No. 3 (December 1937), 122-123. Less than three weeks after the McLauren raid, Augur indicated that it had occurred on the Nueces, not the Frio. See Augur to Division of AG, Chicago, Illinois, 12 May 1881, NA.
37 Augur to AG, Division of Missouri, 27 September 1881, NA.
38 Ibid.
39 Resolution quoted in Butler, "General John Lapham Bullis," 21.

Chapter 14 COMING OF THE SOUTHERN PACIFIC
1 "U.S. Telegraph Lines in California, Arizona, New Mexico and Texas in Charge of the

Chief Signal Officer U.S.A.," map, Haley Library, citing U.S. Signal Corps Report, 1878-1879, opposite page 180.

2 Louise Horton, "The Star Route Conspiracies," *Texana 7*, no. 3 (Fall 1969), 229-231.
3 *Handbook Online*, entry for "Southern Pacific System" (accessed 22 February 2009).
4 Augur to AG, Division of Missouri, 27 September 1881.
5 *A History of Crockett County* (San Angelo: Crockett County Historical Society, printing by Anchor Publishing Company, 1976), 350.
6 Ben C. Mayes, "Reminiscences of Ben C. Mayes, San Angelo, Texas," 7, 8, manuscript, Haley Library.
7 Lan Franks and Seymour V. Connor, *A Biggers Chronicle* (Lubbock: Texas Technological College, 1961), 31.
8 Mayes, "Reminiscences," 9, 34.
9 *Our Town*, 23-24, quoting *San Antonio Express*, 16 and 30 March 1882.
10 *Our Town*, 24, quoting *San Antonio Express*, 30 March 1882.
11 *Our Town*, 23.
12 N. H. Darton, *Guidebook of the Western United States, Part F: The Southern Pacific Lines, New Orleans to Los Angeles*, United States Department of the Interior Bulletin 845 (Washington: Government Printing Office, 1933), 79-81; James, *Frontier and Pioneer*, 169, 179, 182; Swift and Corning, *Three Roads*; Ben C. Truman, *From the Crescent City to the Golden Gate via the Sunset Route of the Southern Pacific Company* (New York: Giles Litho. and Liberty Printing Company, 1887), 31; and my study of the original railroad bed on Google Earth.
13 "Time, Distances, Altitudes," table in E. McD. Johnstone, *West by South . . . Half South* (Buffalo: Matthews Northrup, 1890), page not numbered.
14 James, *Frontier and Pioneer*, 169, 179.
15 Patience Elizabeth Patterson, *Test Excavations at Site 41 VV199, The Jersey Lilly, Val Verde County, Texas*, Texas State Department of Highways and Public Transportation, Highway Design Division, Publications in Archaeology Report No., 33, Texas Antiquities Permit No. 332 (Austin: January 1987), 11.
16 *Our Town*, 24, quoting *San Antonio Express*, 30 March 1882.
17 "The Last Spike Driven and the Southern Pacific Route is Complete," *San Antonio Daily Express*, 13 January 1883; and Darton, *Guidebook*, 81.
18 *Handbook Online*, entry for "Presnall, Pope A.," (accessed 15 November 2005).
19 *Texas Live Stock Journal*, 14 July 1883.
20 *Our Town*, 40-41. Information on Castle Canyon is from Tom Meador, "Painted Caves," The Texas Caver (September 1966), 108, and Karl Baedeker, ed., *The United States with an Excursion into Mexico: Handbook for Travellers* (Leipsic: Karl Baedeker, Publisher, 1893), 465.
21 *Our Town*, 150-151; Clayton, *Contemporary Ranches*, 128-129; and Douglas Lee Braudaway and Val Verde County Historical Commission, *Val Verde County* (Charleston, South Carolina: Arcadia Publishing, 1999), 43.
22 Chapman report in Coker, *News from Brownsville*, appendix B.
23 Haley, "A Log," 214-215.
24 *SA St*, 6 April 1895.
25 Paul H. Carlson, *Texas Woollybacks: The Range Sheep and Goat Industry* (College Station: Texas A&M University Press, 1982), 108.
26 *SA St*, 25 July 1891.
27 L. L. Foster, *Forgotten Texas Census: 1887-88* (Austin: Texas State Historical Association, 2001), 223.
28 *SA St*, 26 October 1889.
29 *Texas Live Stock Journal*, 23 September 1882, and return for October 1882, Company D, Frontier Battalion, TSA. Sieker and five men set out for the Devils' head from Camp King in Uvalde County October 17 and conducted an 11-day, 250-mile scout, but were unsuccessful in locating Burris. The Company D return for October holds that Burris was wanted for murder in Kinney County.

Chapter 15 THE BIG CATTLE DRIFT

30 Matt Johnson, interview with J. Evetts Haley, 1 July 1946, Haley Library.
31 Jones, *Hacienda,* 167, 168.

Chapter 15 THE BIG CATTLE DRIFT
1 "The Storm in the West," *Texas Live Stock Journal,* 26 January 1884.
2 *Texas Live Stock Journal,* 3 May 1884.
3 *SA St,* 11 June 1892.
4 *Texas Live Stock Journal,* 17 May 1884.
5 Hunter, *Trail Drivers,* 802, 804-805.
6 A detailed account of the Big Drift, drawn largely from primary sources and focusing in particular on the Pecos, is in Dearen, *Cowboy of the Pecos,* 171-183. I also drew upon Don H. Biggers, *From Cattle Range to Cotton Patch* (1904; repr., Bandera, Texas: *Frontier Times,* 1944), 58-60; *SA St,* 14 February 1885; and Mayes, "Reminiscences," 84.
7 *SA St,* 14 February 1885.
8 Franks and Connor, *Biggers Chronicle,* 76.
9 "Sherwood Siftings," *SA St,* 21 February 1885.
10 *SA St,* 21 February 1885.
11 Franks and Connor, *Biggers Chronicle,* 76; Mayes, "Reminiscences," 84; and Florence Fenley, *Oldtimers: Their Own Stories* (Uvalde, Texas: Hornby Press, 1939), 177.
12 Ben C. Mayes, interview with J. Evetts Haley, San Angelo, Texas, 7 September 1931, Haley Library. Also see Ben Mayes, interview transcript, WPA Collection.
13 Mayes, "Reminiscences," 84, 85.
14 Fenley, *Oldtimers: Their Own Stories,* 176-177.
15 Mayes, "Reminiscences," 84; and Biggers, *Cattle Range,* 62.
16 Fenley, *Oldtimers: Their Own Stories,* 177.
17 R. J. (Bob) Lauderdale and John M. Doak, *Life on the Range and on the Trail,* San Antonio: The Naylor Company, 1936, 40-43.
18 Jones, *Hacienda,* 539.
19 Foster, *Forgotten Texas Census,* 223.
20 *Handbook Online,* entry for "Val Verde County" (accessed 15 November 2005).
21 *History of Crockett County,* 259.
22 *SA St,* 19 September 1885.

Chapter 16 HORN, FLEECE, AND DROUTH
1 This discussion of the 1885-1887 drouth is based on detailed accounts (drawn largely from primary sources and focusing in particular on the Pecos) in Dearen, *Cowboy of the Pecos,* 185-199; and Patrick Dearen, *Halff of Texas* (Austin: Eakin Press, 2000), 53-61.
2 *Our Town,* 151.
3 *Handbook Online,* entries for "Sutton County" (accessed 15 November 2005), "Wentworth, Texas" (accessed 15 November 2005), and "Johnson Draw" (accessed 15 November 2005).
4 *Our Town,* 151, 164.
5 Foster, *Forgotten Texas Census,* ???, 223.
6 Jones, *Hacienda,* 140; *Handbook Online,* entries for "Juno, Texas" (accessed 14 November 2005) and "Val Verde County" (accessed 15 November 2005); Fred Tarpley, *1001 Texas Place Names* (Austin: University of Texas Press, 1980), 114-115; and Juno plat map, Whitehead Memorial Museum Collection, Del Rio, Texas.
7 Jones, *Hacienda,* 20.
8 *1990-91 Texas Almanac,* 167.
9 *Handbook Online,* entries for "Schleicher County" (accessed 23 February 2009) and "Sutton County," (accessed 23 February 2009).
10 Ira Aten, *Six and One-Half Years in the Ranger Service: The Memoirs of Ira Aten, Sergeant, Company D, Texas Rangers* (Bandera, TX: *Frontier Times,* 1945), 6-7, 9-11, 13.
11 *SA St,* 24 June 1886.

12 "March from Ft. Stockton to Haymond made by Lieut. T. C. Woodbury, 16th Infantry in June 1886; March from Ft. Stockton to Del Rio made by Lieut. F. O. Johnson, 3rd Cavalry in June & July 1886," map by Engineer's Office, Department of Texas, August 1886, Haley Library.
13 S. H. Blalock, interview with Florence Angermiller, Eagle Pass, Texas, 25 April 1938, WPA Collection; and Fenley, *Oldtimers: Their Own Stories*, 121-122.
14 Hunter, *Trail Drivers*, 510-511.
15 Florence Fenley, *Oldtimers of Southwest Texas* (Uvalde, TX: Hornby Press, 1957), 30; and Fenley, *Oldtimers: Their Own Stories*, 17-21.
16 "San Antonio," *DMN*, 20 November 1886, 3.
17 *SA St*, 8 January 1887.
18 "San Antonio Siftings," *DMN*, 18 January 1887, 6.
19 "San Antonio Siftings," *DMN*, 24 November 1887, 3.
20 *SA St*, 9 April 1887.
21 *Our Town*, 67.
22 *SA St*, 9 April 1887.
23 Dearen, *Cowboy of the Pecos*, 194.
24 Foster, *Forgotten Texas Census*, 223.
25 *SA St*, 25 February 1888.
26 "Pecos Round-Ups," *SA St*, 7 April 1888.
27 *SA St*, 19 May 1888 and 26 October 1889.

Chapter 17 BADMEN RISE UP
1 "Schleicher Shots," *SA St*, 12 May 1888; and *SA St*, 2 June 1888.
2 "Schleicher Shots," *SA St*, 30 June 1888.
3 "Sonora Items," *SA St*, 6 April 1889; "Correspondence: The Sonora Outlook," *SA St*, 25 January 1890; "Still Another Baby Town," "*SA St*, 15 March 1890; "Sonora! The Trading Center of the Devil's River Country," *SA St*, 19 July 1890; and *Handbook Online,* entry for "Sonora, Texas" (accessed 15 November 2005).
4 A. Ray Stephens, *The Taft Ranch: A Texas Principality* (Austin: University of Texas Press, 1964), 89.
5 Johnnie Roberts, interview with J. Evetts Haley, Lovington, New Mexico, 8 July 1947, Haley Library.
6 *SA St*, 28 September 1889.
7 "Sonora!," *SA St*, 19 July 1890.
8 *SA St*, 4 April 1891.
9 "From the Tom Green Region," *DMN*, 14 March 1898.
10 *SA St*, 22 March 1890.
11 Carlson, *Texas Woollybacks*, 119.
12 "Shot Near San Angelo," *DMN*, 26 June 1889, 1.
13 "Voting Places in Crockett County Election Tuesday, July 7th," *SA St*, 20 June 1891; and "From the Del Rio Record," *SA St*, 25 July 1891.
14 "From the Devil's River News," *SA St*, 18 April 1891; *SA St*, 23 May 1891; and "Stock News: Stock Items From the Devil's River News," 15 August 1891.
15 "From the Del Rio Record," *SA St*, 25 July 1891.
16 Hunter, *Trail Drivers*, 116-117. The account gives a date of 1881 for the drive, but contextual evidence suggests 1891.
17 *SA St*, 8 March 1890.
18 Ibid., 14 February 1891.
19 Ibid., 25 July 1891.
20 Ibid., 28 November 1891.
21 Ibid., 21 November 1891.
22 Ibid., 19 December 1891. Location of Elbow (or Elbo) Lake is from *Sutton County History, 1887-1977* (n.p.: Sutton County Historical Society, 1979), 265.

23 *SA St,* 29 August 1891.
24 "From the Devil's River News," *SA St,* 28 November 1891.
25 "Sonora Tragedy," *DMN,* 1 August 1891; "Federal Court," *DMN,* 6 September 1891; "Change of Venue," *DMN,* 23 February 1892; and "John Quincy Adams Released," *DMN,* 30 June 1892. I also consulted *Sutton County History,* 16.
26 "Charged with Murder," *DMN,* 6 October 1891; "Change of Venue;" "Adams-Wilson Killing," *DMN,* 7 April 1892; "Change of Venue—Burglary—First Bale," *DMN,* 24 September 1892; and *Sutton County History,* 17.
27 *Sutton County History,* 17. In regard to the two horse thieves killed by a posse, the similarity with the spring 1888 incident involving a Kimble County deputy named Smith, along the absence of contemporary newspaper accounts for the 1891 incident, begs the question of whether or not these were separate episodes.

Chapter 18 A POTENTIAL FOR SUDDEN DEATH

1 "Train Robbers Captured," *The New York Times,* 22 October 1891; "Bound to Detroit with Prisoners," *New York Times,* 29 August 1892; "Train Robbers Caught," "As Told from Eagle Pass," "Flint's Relative Speaks," and "More Details of the Capture," *DMN,* 23 October 1891; Frank Jones to Pauline Baker, 1891, quoted in Skiles, *Roy Bean County,* 101-104; and W. M. "Bob" Beverly, interview with J. Evetts Haley, Lovington, New Mexico, 23 June 1937, Haley Library. Variant spellings of Langston's name in contemporary newspaper accounts include Langsford, Langsdon, Langsden, Lansford, and Langstein.
2 Beverly, interview. Ozona population is from *Handbook Online,* entry for "Ozona, Texas" (accessed 25 February 2009).
3 "A Smash-up," *DMN,* 17 December 1891.
4 *SA St,* 4 April 1891.
5 Ibid., 17 December 1892.
6 "Mexican Killed by His Horse," *SA St,* 22 May 1897.
7 "Mexican and Horses Found Dead" and "Ozona Courier," *SA St,* 2 July 1898.
8 *SA St,* 19 March 1892.
9 Ibid., 13 February 1897.
10 A cowboy's wage is from Beverly, interview.
11 "Border News," *SA St,* 10 September 1892.
12 *SA St,* 1 May 1897.
13 *Handbook Online,* entry for "San Angelo, Texas" (accessed 25 February 2009).
14 "Wool!," *SA St,* 2 January 1892.
15 Dearen, *Halff,* 85-88.
16 "From the Devil's River News," *SA St,* 2 April 1892.
17 *SA St,* 14 May 1892.
18 Ibid., 4 June 1892. The stockman's name may have been Harr, with a possible first name of Isaac.
19 J. Frank Dobie, *Up the Trail from Texas* (New York; Random House, 1955), 29-31.
20 "Devil's River Stock News," *SA St,* 13 February 1892.
21 "From the Devil's River News," *SA St,* 2 April 1892.
22 "Juno Jottings," *SA St,* 3 September 1892; and Dearen, *Halff,* 87.
23 *SA St,* 26 March 1892. Runyon is identified as a lawman in "A Bold Assassination," *SA St,* 30 April 1892, and as a deputy sheriff in "From the Ozona Courier," *SA St,* 15 February 1896.
24 "Killing at Beaver Lake," *SA St,* 4 June 1892.
25 "Arrested for Horsetheft," *DMN,* 2 September 1892, 6.
26 "Fatally Shot," *DMN,* 25 December 1892, 9.
27 "Texas Industrial Notes," *DMN,* 30 December 1892, 4; and "Damages for False Imprisonment," *DMN,* 7 January 1893.

Chapter 19 FANG, CLAW, AND BUFFALO HIDES

1 "Panic of 1893," http://www.historycentral.com/Industrialage/Panic1893.html

(accessed 2 January 2009); "Encyclopedia: Panic of 1893," http://www.nationmaster.com/encyclopedia/Panic-of-1893 (accessed 2 January 2009); and "Panic of 1893," http://www.encyclopediaofarkansas.net/encyclopedia/entry-detail.aspx?entryID=4292 (accessed 2 January 2009).

2 *SA St*, 14 May 1892.
3 Ibid., 29 July 1893.
4 Ibid., 11 January 1896.
5 "From the Devils River News," *SA St*, 12 May 1894.
6 *SA St*, 24 June 1893.
7 Ibid., 25 November 1893. An E. S. Franks is described as "the merchant prince of Juno" in *SA St*, 4 March 1899.
8 *SA St*, 24 February 1900.
9 Fenley, *Oldtimers of Southwest Texas*, 176-178. Fenley's reference to a man named Frank who had been implicated in a train robbery suggests that he may have been Frank Gobble (Goble), who was reported to have joined in the hold-up of a Southern Pacific train near Comstock in late 1896. If such is the case, the incident related by Fenley could have occurred no earlier than 1897.
10 "From the Del Rio Farm Stock Grower," *SA St*, 14 April 1894.
11 "Burglary at Juno," *SA St*, 21 April 1894.
12 "Killing in Sutton County," *SA St*, 12 May 1894.
13 *DMN*, 14 February 1894; *SA St*, 10 and 17 February and 3 March 1894; and "Stock News," *SA St*, 17 February 1894. Also see "Sotol," *SA St*, 8 March 1902.
14 "Correspondence: Trans-Pecos Sheep Notes," *Texas Live Stock and Farm Journal*, 11 May 1894.
15 *SA St*, 10 March 1894.
16 "A Mexican Killed," *SA St*, 6 October 1894; and *SA St*, 13 October 1894.
17 *SA St*, 24 June 1893.
18 "Herd of Buffalo," *SA St*, 5 May 1894.
19 *SA St*, 30 August 1890; and "Herd of Buffalo." I also consulted *SA St*, 12 May 1894.
20 Daniel, "Advance of the Spanish Frontier," 281-282.
21 Haley, "A Log," 214-215.
22 R. H. Williams, *Border Ruffians*, 328.
23 "San Antonio Siftings," *DMN*, 11 March 1889, 4.
24 *SA St*, 26 October 1889.
25 "San Antonio Siftings," *DMN*, 11 March 1889, 4.
26 *SA St*, 12 May 1894.
27 "Herd of Buffalo."
28 *SA St*, 12 May 1894.
29 "That Herd of Buffalo," *SA St*, 13 October 1894.
30 "From the Ozona Courier," *SA St*, 28 July 1894; "The 'Paradise' is 'In It,'" and "From the Ozona Courier," *SA St*, 11 August 1894; "Devil's River News Notes," *SA St*, 29 September 1894; and *SA St*, 13 October 1894.
31 *SA St*, 15 December 1894.
32 *SA St*, 4 May 1895; and "From the Devil's River News," *SA St*, 4 May 1895.
33 *San Angelo Standard*, 1 June 1895; and "From the Ozona Courier" and "From the Devil's River News," 1 June 1895.
34 "From the Del Rio Record," *SA St*, 8 June 1895.
35 *SA St*, 8 June 1895.
36 "From the Ozona Courier," *SA St*, 15 June 1895.
37 "From the Ozona Courier," *SA St*, 29 June 1895.
38 "A Great Activity in Sheep and Wool Raising—Cattle Fat," *SA St*, 21 September 1895; and "The San Angelo Wool Market," *SA St*, 19 October 1895.
39 "The San Angelo Wool Market;" "From the Del Rio Record," *SA St*, 9 May 1896; and *SA St*, 7 September 1895.
40 *SA St*, 26 October 1895.

41 "From the Texas Stockman and Farmer," *SA St*, 16 January 1897.
42 "From the Tom Green Region: Goat Raising on the Devil's River," *DMN*, 14 March 1898, 3.
43 "From the Devil's River," *DMN*, 31 January 1898, 3.
44 "May Sell the Stock Yards," *DMN*, 29 March 1898, 6; and "From West on the Santa Fe," *DMN*, 15 April 1898, 6.
45 *SA St*, 26 December 1896.
46 Ibid., 1 July 1893. This may have been John M. Campbell.
47 "May Sell the Stock Yards;" and "Coyotes on the Rio Grande," *DMN*, 15 May 1898, 7.
48 *SA St*, 12 December 1896.
49 Ibid.; and "Texas Stockman and Farmer," *SA St*, 20 February 1897.
50 "A Great Sheep Industry: The Concho and Devil's River Region of Texas," *SA St*, 23 April 1898.
51 "From the Texas Stockman and Farmer," *SA St*, 16 January 1897. Also see "A Great Sheep Industry."
52 *SA St*, 16 January 1897.
53 Ibid. Burbank's comments came in a letter and were published as an indirect quote.

Chapter 20 THE DEVIL'S BROOD

1 "Shot a Mexican," *SA St*, 18 January 1896.
2 "Got Very Little Booty," *SA St*, 26 December 1896; *SA St*, 26 December 1896; "Pursuit of Train Robbers," *SA St*, 26 December 1896; "Train Robbers Captured," *SA St*, 2 January 1897; "Store Robbed by Mexicans," *DMN*, 5 November 1893; "Train Robbers Captured," *SA St*, 18 June 1898; "Newman-Baker Killing," *DMN*, 7 December 1895, 9; "Southern Pacific Held Up," *DMN*, 22 December 1896; "Charged with Train-Robbing," *DMN*, 28 December 1896; "Put Under Bond," *DMN*, 2 January 1897; "Rangers Report," *DMN*, 9 February 1897; "Felony Convictions," *DMN*, 20 March 1897; "Pleaded Guilty," *DMN*, 29 April 1897; and "Newman Acquitted," *DMN*, 27 October 1897. Accounts of the robbery vary in certain details. Gobble's name is also spelled Goble, but the cemetery in Comstock, Texas, includes graves inscribed with the family name Gobble (author's inspection, April 2009). Shackleford's name is spelled Shackelford in "Store Robbed by Mexicans." Hughes' first name is from "John R. Hughes, 1855-1947," http://www.texasranger.org/halloffame/Hughes_John.htm (accessed 6 January 2009).
3 *SA St*, 6 March 1897, incorrectly dated 27 February 1897.
4 "Killing Near Sonora," *SA St*, 30 March 1897.
5 "Comstock Robbery: How the Southern Pacific Train was Held Up," *SA St*, 7 May 1898; and "Wells, Fargo & Co's Express 'Train Robbery' Ledger," 1870-1902, http://historical.ha.com/common/view_item.php?Sale_No=689&Lot_No=72001&src=pr (accessed 2 January 2009).
6 "A Great Sheep Industry."
7 *SA St*, 11 September 1897.
8 "Steady Slump in Wool," *SA St*, 5 January 1901.
9 "Gossip of a Texas Sheepman," *SA St*, 4 September 1897.
10 "Immense Prairie Fire: Reserve Range for Sixty Thousand Sheep Burned," *SA St*, 25 December 1897.
11 *SA St*, 19 March 1898; "Juno Jinglings in Del Rio Record," *SA St*, 19 March 1898; and *SA St*, 5 June 1897.
12 "Del Rio Record," *SA St*, 26 March 1898.
13 "Comstock Robbery: How the Southern Pacific Train was Held Up;" "Southern Pacific Hold-Up," *SA St*, 7 May 1898; "Robbers Got Nothing," *SA St*, 7 May 1898; "Account from Del Rio," *SA St*, 7 May 1898; and "Wells, Fargo & Co's Express 'Train Robbery' Ledger." The accounts vary in certain details. Helmet was three to three and one-half miles west of Comstock; see "Account from Del Rio."
14 *Handbook Online*, entry for "Ketchum Boys" (accessed 27 February 2009).
15 *Handbook Online*, entry for "Pecos High Bridge" (accessed 27 February 2009).

16 "Robbers Got Nothing;" "Account from Del Rio;" and "Wells, Fargo & Co's Express 'Train Robbery' Ledger." McCall was likely C.D. McCall. See entry for C. McCall, call number 401-161, Texas Adjutant General Service Records 1836-1935, TSA website, http://www.tsl.state.tx.us/arc/service/index.php?formType=name&lastname= McCal&firstname=&searchType =beginLike&organization_code=&call_no=&dosearch=Search+Now&page=1 (accessed 7 April 2010).

17 This account of the Santa Fe train robbery and ensuing events is based on: "Train Hold-Up," *SA St*, 11 June 1898; "Train Robbers Captured," *SA St*, 18 June 1898; *SA St*, 25 June 1898; "A Train Robber Confesses," *SA St*, 15 October 1898; "Alleged Train Robber," *SA St*, 20 May 1899; *SA St*, 13 October 1900; "Bill Taylor Going to Pen," *SA St*, 6 October 1900; "Train Robbers Located," *SA St*, 21 December 1901; "Alleged Robbers Captured," *DMN*, 19 June 1898; "Fort Worth Budget: Given Examining Trials," *DMN*, 1 July 1898; "Convicted of Train Robbing," *DMN*, 17 September 1898; "Keaton Gets Ten Years," *DMN*, 18 February 1899; "Bill Taylor Convicted," *DMN*, 15 September 1899; "Sheriff Knox Returns," *DMN*, 22 September 1899; "Keeton Now at Coleman," *DMN*, 24 September 1899; "Reversed Death Penalty: Opinions of Court of Appeals," *DMN*, 1 March 1900; "Sawed Their Way to Liberty," *DMN*, 21 June 1900; "Bill Taylor Is in Custody," *DMN*, 13 August 1900; "Capture of Bill Taylor," *DMN*, 14 August 1900; "Fort Worth Budget: Bill Taylor in Fort Worth," *DMN*, 3 October 1900; "Escaped Prisoner Killed," *DMN*, 22 November 1900; "Belton Court Cases: Jeff Taylor, Charged with Train Robbery, to Be Tried There," *DMN*, 13 January 1901; "Jeff Taylor's Trial," *DMN*, 4 February 1901; "Jeff Taylor Murder Trial," *DMN*, 6 March 1901; "Life Sentence for Taylor," *DMN*, 8 March 1901; "The Higher Courts: Criminal Appeals," *DMN*, 16 May 1901; "Taylor Case Continued," *DMN*, 6 June 1901; "'Bill' Taylor Breaks Jail," *DMN*, 13 July 1901; "Sheriffs' Department: Brown County," *DMN*, 14 July 1901; "An Additional Reward," *DMN*, 8 August 1901; "Nothing Heard of 'Bill' Taylor," *DMN*, 3 October 1901, 5; "Robber Was Bill Taylor," *DMN*, 31 July 1902; "Pursuing a Texas Outlaw," *New York Times*, 14 July 1901; "Taylor v. State, Court of Criminal Appeals of Texas, Feb. 28, 1900," *The Southwestern Reporter* 55 (St. Paul: West Publishing Company, 1900), 961-966; "Keaton v. State, Court of Criminal Appeals of Texas, April 11, 1900," *The Southwestern Reporter* 57 (St. Paul: West Publishing Company, 1900), 1125-1130; "Pearce Keaton v. The State, No. 1938, Decided April 11, 1900," *The Texas Criminal Reports* 41 (Austin: Gammel-Statesman Publishing Company, 1902), 621-634; "Taylor v. State, Court of Criminal Appeals of Texas, May 22, 1901," *The Southwestern Reporter* 63 (St. Paul: West Publishing Company, 1901), 330-331; and Frank S. Gray, *Pioneering in Southwest Texas: True Stories of Early Day Experiences in Edwards and Adjoining Counties* (Austin: Steck Company, 1949), 177-207. Gray was personally acquainted with Pearce Keaton and Bud Newman. Included in Gray's account are the circa 1945 recollections of J. H. Baker, an attorney with the Brownwood law firm of Jenkins & McCartney that defended Pearce Keaton and Bill Taylor in their trials. Some of the newspaper accounts differ on certain details.

18 "Horse Thieves Arrested," *SA St*, 25 June 1898.
19 "District Court at Del Rio," *DMN*, 16 October 1899.
20 "The Ozona Courier," *SA St*, 22 April 1899; *Texas Stock and Farm Journal*, 10 May 1899; *SA St*, 16 September 1899; "It Has Rained," *SA St*, 28 October 1899; *SA St*, 2 December 1899; and "Del Rio Record," *SA St*, 30 December 1899.
21 *SA St*, 21 October 1899.
22 "Devil's River News," *SA St*, 11 November 1899.
23 *List of Fugitives From Justice for 1900* (Austin: Von Boeckmann, Moore & Schutze, State Contractors, 1900), 36-38, 152.

EPILOGUE

1 "Floods in the Southwest," *DMN*, 7 April 1900; and "Tourists Caught in Storm," *DMN*, 9 April 1900.

BIBLIOGRAPHY

Books

Abney, A. H. *Life and Adventures of L. D. Lafferty.* New York: H. S. Goodspeed, 1875.

Arnold, James R. *Jeff Davis's Own: Cavalry, Comanches, and the Battle for the Texas Frontier.* New York: John Wiley & Sons, 2000.

Askins, Charles. *Texans, Guns & History.* New York: Bonanza Books, 1970.

Aten, Ira. *Six and One-Half Years in the Ranger Service: The Memoirs of Ira Aten, Sergeant, Company D, Texas Rangers.* Bandera, TX: *Frontier Times,* 1945.

Austerman, Wayne R. *Sharps Rifles and Spanish Mules: The San Antonio-El Paso Mail, 1851-1881.* College Station: Texas A&M University Press, 1985.

Baedeker, Karl, ed. *The United States with an Excursion into Mexico: Handbook for Travellers.* Leipsic: Karl Baedeker, Publisher, 1893.

Baldridge, M. *A Reminiscence of the Parker H. French Expedition through Texas & Mexico to California in the Spring of 1850.* Los Angeles: privately printed, 1959.

Bedford, Hilory G. *Texas Indian Troubles: The Most Thrilling Events in the History of Texas.* Dallas: Hargreaves Printing Company, 1905.

Bender, Averam B. *The March of Empire: Frontier Defense in the Southwest, 1848-1860.* Lawrence: University of Kansas Press, 1952.

Bieber, Ralph P., ed. *Exploring Southwestern Trails 1846-1854.* Glendale, CA: Arthur H. Clark Company, 1938.

Biggers, Don H. *From Cattle Range to Cotton Patch.* 1904. Reprint, Bandera, TX: *Frontier Times.*

Bolton, Herbert Eugene, ed. *Spanish Exploration in the Southwest 1542-1706.* New York: Charles Scribner's Sons, 1916.

Brand Book Number One, The San Diego Corral of the Westerners. N.p., 1968.

Braudaway, Douglas Lee, and Val Verde County Historical Commission. *Val Verde County.* Charleston, SC: Arcadia Publishing, 1999.

Burton, Jeffrey. *The Deadliest Outlaws: The Ketchum Gang and the Wild Bunch.* 2nd ed. Denton: University of North Texas Press, 2009.

Captain Jeff or Frontier Life in Texas with the Texas Rangers. Colorado, TX: Whipkey Printing Company, 1906.

Cardinell, Charles. *Adventures on the Plains.* San Francisco: California Historical Society, 1922.

Carlson, Paul H. *Texas Woollybacks: The Range Sheep and Goat Industry.* College Station: Texas A&M University Press, 1982.

Castañeda, Carlos E. *Our Catholic Heritage in Texas 1519-1936.* Vol. 1, *The Mission Era: The Finding of Texas 1519-1693.* Austin: Von Boeckmann-Jones Company, 1936.

———. *Our Catholic Heritage in Texas 1519-1936.* Vol. 2, *The Mission Era: The Winning of Texas 1693-1731.* Austin: Von Boeckmann-Jones Company, 1936.

———. *Our Catholic Heritage in Texas 1519-1936*. Vol. 3, *The Mission Era: The Missions at Work 1731-1761*. Austin: Von Boeckmann-Jones Company, 1938.
Clayton, Lawrence. *Contemporary Ranches of Texas*. Austin: University of Texas Press, 2001.
Coker, Caleb, ed. *The News from Brownsville: Helen Chapman's Letters from the Texas Military Frontier, 1848-1852*. Barker Texas History Center Series. Austin: Texas State Historical Association, 1992.
Conger, Roger N., James M. Day, Joe B. Frantz, Kenneth F. Neighbours, W. C. Nunn, Ben Procter, Harold B. Simpson, and Dorman H. Winfrey. *Frontier Forts of Texas*. Waco: Texian Press, 1966.
Cox, James. *Historical and Biographical Record of the Cattle Industry and the Cattlemen of Texas and Adjacent Territory*. St. Louis: Woodward and Tiernan Printing Company, 1895.
Darton, N. H. *Guidebook of the Western United States, Part F: The Southern Pacific Lines, New Orleans to Los Angeles*, United States Department of the Interior Bulletin 845. Washington, DC: Government Printing Office, 1933.
Dearen, Patrick. *Castle Gap and the Pecos Frontier*. Fort Worth: Texas Christian University Press, 1988.
———. *A Cowboy of the Pecos*. Plano: Republic of Texas Press, 1997.
———. *Crossing Rio Pecos*. Fort Worth: Texas Christian University Press, 1996.
———. *Halff of Texas*. Austin: Eakin Press, 2000.
Dobie, J. Frank, and Mody C. Boatright, eds. *Straight Texas*. Austin: Steck Company, 1937.
Dobie, J. Frank. *A Vaquero of the Brush Country*. 1929. Reprint, New York: Grosset and Dunlap, n.d.
———. *Up the Trail from Texas*. New York: Random House, 1955.
Duvall, John C. *The Adventures of Big-Foot Wallace*. 1871. Reprint, Lincoln: University of Nebraska Press, 1966.
Eccleston, Robert. *Overland to California on the Southwestern Trail, 1849*. Berkeley: University of California Press, 1950.
Erwin, Allen A. *The Southwest of John H. Slaughter, 1841-1922*. Glendale, CA: Arthur H. Clark Company, 1965.
Evans, George W. B. *Mexican Gold Trail: The Journal of a Forty-Niner*. San Marino, CA: Huntington Library, 1945.
Fenley, Florence. *Oldtimers: Their Own Stories*. Uvalde, TX: Hornby Press, 1939.
———. *Oldtimers of Southwest Texas*. Uvalde, TX: Hornby Press, 1957.
Foster, L. L. *Forgotten Texas Census: 1887-88*. Austin: Texas State Historical Association, 2001.
Francell, Lawrence John. *Fort Lancaster: Texas Frontier Sentinel*. N.p.: Texas State Historical Association, 1999.
Franks, Lan, and Seymour V. Connor. *A Biggers Chronicle*. Lubbock: Texas Technological College, 1961.
Frazer, Robert W. *Forts of the West: Military Forts and Presidios and Posts Commonly Called Forts West of the Mississippi River to 1898*. Norman: University of Oklahoma Press, 1972.
Frazier, Donald S. *Blood & Treasure: Confederate Empire in the Southwest*. College Station: Texas A&M University Press, 1995.
French, Samuel G. *Two Wars: An Autobiography of Gen. Samuel G. French*. Nashville: Confederate Veteran, 1901.
Froebel, Julius. *Seven Years Travel in Central America, Northern Mexico, and the Far West of the United States*. London: Richard Bentley, 1859.
Gillett, James B. *Six Years with the Texas Rangers, 1875 to 1881*. Lincoln: University of Nebraska Press, 1976.
Goodnight, Charles, Emanuel Dubbs, John A. Hart, et al. *Pioneer Days in the Southwest from 1850 to*

1879. Guthrie, OK: State Capital Company, 1909.

Green, Rena Maverick, ed. *Samuel Maverick, Texan: 1803-1870: A Collection of Letters, Journals and Memoirs*. San Antonio: privately printed, 1952.

Gray, Frank S. *Pioneering in Southwest Texas: True Stories of Early Day Experiences in Edwards and Adjoining Counties*. Austin: Steck Company, 1949.

Haley, J. Evetts, ed. *The Diary of Michael Erskine*. Midland: Nita Stewart Haley Memorial Library, 1979.

Heartsill, W. W. *Fourteen Hundred and 91 Days in the Confederate Army*. 1876. Facsimile of the first edition. Jackson, TN: McCowat-Mercer Press, 1953.

Henderson, Harry McCorry. *Texas in the Confederacy*. San Antonio: Naylor Company, 1955.

A History of Crockett County. San Angelo: Crockett County Historical Society, printing by Anchor Publishing Company, 1976.

Holden, W. C. *Rollie Burns, or an Account of the Ranching Industry on the South Plains*. Dallas: Southwest Press, 1932.

Hood, J. B. *Advance and Retreat*. 1880. Reprint, Edison, NJ: Blue and Grey Press, 1985.

Hunter, J. Marvin, comp. *The Bloody Trail in Texas: Sketches and Narratives of Indian Raids and Atrocities on Our Frontier*. Bandera, TX: J. Marvin Hunter, 1931.

———, comp. and ed. *The Trail Drivers of Texas*. 1925. Reprint, Austin: University of Texas Press, 1985.

James, Vinton Lee. *Frontier and Pioneer Recollections of Early Days in San Antonio and West Texas*. San Antonio: Artes Graficas, 1938.

John, Elizabeth A. H. *Storms Brewed in Other Men's Worlds: The Confrontation of Indians, Spanish, and French in the Southwest, 1540-1795*. College Station: Texas A&M University Press, 1975.

Johnstone, E. McD. *West by South . . . . Half South*. Buffalo: Matthews Northrup, 1890.

Jones, Rosemary Whitehead, ed. *La Hacienda*. Norman: University of Oklahoma Press, 1976.

Kinevan, Marcos E. *Frontier Cavalryman: Lieutenant John Bigelow with the Buffalo Soldiers in Texas*. El Paso: Texas Western Press, 1998.

Lauderdale, R. J. (Bob), and John M. Doak. *Life on the Range and on the Trail*. San Antonio: Naylor Company, 1936.

Leckie, William H. *The Buffalo Soldiers: A Narrative of the Negro Cavalry in the West*. Norman: University of Oklahoma Press, 1967.

Lesley, Lewis Burt, ed. *Uncle Sam's Camels: The Journal of May Humphreys Stacey Supplemented by the Report of Edward Fitzgerald Beale*. Cambridge: Harvard University Press, 1929.

List of Fugitives From Justice for 1900. Austin: Von Boeckmann, Moore & Schutze, State Contractors, 1900.

Merrick, Morgan Wolfe. *From Desert to Bayou: The Civil War Journal and Sketches of Morgan Wolfe Merrick*. El Paso: Texas Western Press, 1991.

Miles, William. *Journal of the Sufferings and Hardships of Capt. Parker H. French's Overland Expedition to California*. Chambersburg, PA, 1851.

Mills, W. W. *Forty Years at El Paso, 1858-1898*. El Paso: Carl Hertzog, 1962.

Moore, Francis, Jr. *Map and Description of Texas, Containing Sketches of its History, Geology, Geography and Statistics*. 1840. Facsimile of the first edition. N.p.: Texian Press, 1965.

Moorhead, Max L. *The Apache Frontier: Jacobo Ugarte and Spanish-Indian Relations in Northern New Spain, 1769-1791*. Norman: University of Oklahoma Press, 1968.

Mueller, Jerry E. *Restless River*. El Paso: Texas Western Press, 1975.

Mullin, Robert N. *Stagecoach Pioneers of the Southwest*. El Paso: Texas Western Press, 1983.

Mulroy, Kevin. *Freedom on the Border: The Seminole Maroons in Florida, the Indian Territory, Coahuila, and Texas*. Lubbock: Texas Tech University Press, 1993.

Murrah, David J. *C. C. Slaughter: Rancher, Banker, Baptist*. Austin: University of Texas Press, 1981.

Neal, Charles M. Jr. *Valor Across the Lone Star: The Congressional Medal of Honor in Frontier Texas.* Austin: Texas State Historical Association, 2002.
The New Handbook of Texas. 6 vols. Austin: Texas State Historical Association, 1996.
Nunn, W. C. *Texas Under the Carpetbaggers.* Austin: University of Texas Press, 1962.
Olmsted, Frederick Law. *A Journey Through Texas.* New York: Dix, Edwards, 1857.
Our Town: Friends and Neighbors, a bicentennial tribute. N.p.: Comstock Study Club, 1976.
Patterson, Patience Elizabeth, *Test Excavations at Site 41VV199, The Jersey Lilly, Val Verde County, Texas.* Texas State Department of Highways and Public Transportation, Highway Design Division, Publications in Archaeology Report No. 33, Texas Antiquities Permit No. 332. Austin: January 1987.
Pirtle, Caleb III, and Michael F. Cusack. *The Lonely Sentinel: Fort Clark: On Texas's Western Frontier.* Austin: Eakin Press, 1985.
Price, George F., comp. *Across the Continent with the Fifth Cavalry.* New York: D. Van Nostrand, Publisher, 1883.
Prose and Poetry of the Live Stock Industry of the United States. 1904. Reprint, New York: Antiquarian Press, 1959.
Reedstrom, Ernest L. *Scrapbook of the American West.* Caldwell, ID: Caxton Printers, 1991.
Reid, John C. *Reid's Tramp, or a Journal of the Incidents of Ten Months Travel Through Texas, New Mexico, Arizona, Sonora, and California.* Austin: Steck Company, 1935.
A Report on the Hygiene of the United States Army, with Descriptions of Military Posts. War Department, Surgeon-General's Office Circular No. 8. Washington, DC: Government Printing Office, 1875.
Roberts, John R., and James P. Nash. *University of Texas Bulletin No. 1803: The Geology of Val Verde County.* Austin: University of Texas, January 10, 1918.
Rodriguez, Jose Policarpo. *Jose Policarpo Rodriguez: The Old Guide.* Nashville: Publishing House of the Methodist Episcopal Church, 1897.
Santleben, August. *A Texas Pioneer.* 1910. Facsimile reprint of the first edition. Waco: W. M. Morrison, 1967.
Schroeder, Albert H., and Dan S. Matson. *A Colony on the Move: Gaspar Castaño de Sosa's Journal 1590-1591.* N.p.: School of American Research, 1965.
Skiles, Jack. *Judge Roy Bean Country.* Lubbock: Texas Tech University Press, 1996.
Smith, Thomas T. *The Old Army in Texas: A Research Guide to the U.S. Army in Nineteenth-Century Texas.* Austin: Texas State Historical Association, 2000.
―――. *The U.S. Army and the Texas Frontier Economy, 1845-1900.* College Station: Texas A&M University Press, 1999.
Smith, Thomas T., Jerry D. Thompson, Robert Wooster, and Ben E. Pingenot, eds. *The Reminiscences of Major General Zenas R. Bliss, 1854-1876.* Austin: Texas State Historical Association, 2007.
The Southwestern Reporter 55. St. Paul: West Publishing Company, 1900.
The Southwestern Reporter 57. St. Paul: West Publishing Company, 1900.
The Southwestern Reporter 63. St. Paul: West Publishing Company, 1901.
Sowell, A. J. *Early Settlers and Indian Fighters of Southwest Texas.* Austin: State House Press, 1986.
―――. *Life of "Big Foot" Wallace: The Great Ranger Captain.* Austin: State House Press, 1989.
Steck, Francis Borgia. *Forerunners of Captain De Leon's Expedition to Texas, 1670-1675.* N.p.: Preliminary Studies of the Texas Catholic Society, n.d.
Stephens, A. Ray. *The Taft Ranch: A Texas Principality.* Austin: University of Texas Press, 1964.
Stillman, J. D. B. *Wanderings in the Southwest in 1855.* Spokane, WA: Arthur H. Clark Company, 1990.
Sutton County History, 1887-1977. N.p.: Sutton County Historical Society, 1979.
Swift, Roy L., and Leavitt Corning Jr. *Three Roads to Chihuahua: The Great Wagon Roads that Opened*

the Southwest, 1823-1883. Austin: Eakin Press, 1988.
Tarpley, Fred. *1001 Texas Place Names.* Austin: University of Texas Press, 1980.
Taylor, Thomas U. *The Water Powers of Texas.* Washington, DC: Government Printing Office, 1904.
The Texas Almanac for 1859. Galveston: Galveston News, 1858.
Texas Almanac 1990-91. Dallas: Dallas Morning News, 1989.
The Texas Criminal Reports 41. Austin: Gammel-Statesman Publishing Company, 1902.
Thompson, Jerry D., ed. *Westward the Texans: The Civil War Journal of Private William Randolph Howell.* El Paso: Texas Western Press, 1990.
Thonhoff, Robert H. *San Antonio Stage Lines, 1847-1881.* El Paso: Texas Western Press, 1971.
Truman, Ben C. *From the Crescent City to the Golden Gate via the Sunset Route of the Southern Pacific Company.* New York: Giles Litho. and Liberty Printing Company, 1887.
Uglow, Loyd M. *Standing in the Gap: Army Outposts, Picket Stations, and the Pacification of the Texas Frontier, 1866-1886.* Fort Worth: Texas Christian University Press, 2001.
Vestal, Stanley. *Bigfoot Wallace: A Biography.* Boston: Houghton Mifflin, 1942.
Wallace, Ernest. *Ranald S. Mackenzie on the Texas Frontier.* Lubbock: West Texas Museum Association, 1964.
―――, ed. *Ranald S. Mackenzie's Official Correspondence Relating to Texas, 1871-1873.* Lubbock: West Texas Museum Association, 1967.
―――, ed. *Ranald S. Mackenzie's Official Correspondence Relating to Texas, 1873-1879.* Lubbock: West Texas Museum Association, 1968.
Warren, Harry, comp., and Ben E. Pingenot, ed. *Paso del Aguila: A Chronicle of Frontier Days on the Texas Border as Recorded in the Memoirs of Jesse Sumpter.* Austin: Encino Press, 1969.
Weddle, Robert S. *San Juan Bautista: Gateway to Spanish Texas.* Austin: University of Texas Press, 1968.
Williams, Clayton. *Texas' Last Frontier: Fort Stockton and the Trans-Pecos, 1861-1865.* College Station: Texas A&M University Press, 1982.
―――. *Never Again.* Vol. 3, *Texas 1848-1861.* San Antonio: Naylor Company, 1969.
Williams, J. W. *Old Texas Trails.* Burnet, TX: Eakin Press, 1979.
Williams, R. H. *With the Border Ruffians: Memories of the Far West, 1852-1868.* Edited by E. W. Williams. London: John Murray, 1908.
Winfrey, Dorman H., and James M. Day, eds. *The Indian Papers of Texas and the Southwest, 1825-1916.* 5 vols. Austin: Pemberton Press, 1966.
Woodhouse, S. W. *From Texas to San Diego in 1851: The Overland Journal of Dr. S. W. Woodhouse.* Edited by Andrew Wallace and Richard H. Hevley. Lubbock: Texas Tech University Press, 2007.
Young, Otis E. *The West of Philip St. George Cooke, 1809-1895.* Glendale, CA: Arthur H. Clark Company, 1955.

Collections
Clayton W. Williams Collection. Nita Stewart Haley Memorial Library, Midland, Texas.
J. Evetts Haley Collection. Nita Stewart Haley Memorial Library, Midland, Texas.
Monthly Returns, Texas Ranger Frontier Battalion, companies D, E, and F, 1874-1882.
Texas State Library and Archives Commission, Austin.
National Archives, Washington, DC.
Texas Confederate Museum Collection. Nita Stewart Haley Memorial Library, Midland, Texas.
Whitehead Memorial Museum. Del Rio, Texas.

Congressional Reports and Documents
Claims of the State of Texas: Letter from the Secretary of War. House of Representatives Executive

Document No. 277, 42nd Cong., 2nd sess. 1872.
Contract for Carrying the Mails. House of Representatives Document No. 92, 35th Cong., 1st sess.
Depredations on the Frontiers of Texas. House of Representatives Executive Document No. 257, 43rd Cong., 1st sess. 1874.
Difficulties on Southwestern Frontier. House of Representatives Executive Document No. 52, 36th Cong., 1st sess. 1860.
Heitman, Francis B. *Historical Register and Dictionary of the United States Army.* House of Representatives Document No. 446, 57th Cong., 2nd sess. Washington, DC: Government Printing Office, 1903.
Mexican Border Troubles. House of Representatives Executive Document No. 13, 45th Cong., 1st sess. Washington, DC, 1877-1878.
Protection of the Frontier of Texas: Letter from the Secretary of War. House of Representatives Executive Document No. 27, 35th Cong., 2nd sess. 1859.
Report of the Secretary of War. Senate Executive Document No. 32, 31st Cong., 1st sess. Washington, DC, 1850.
Report of the Secretary of War, Vol. 1. House of Representatives Executive Document No. 1, Part 2, 44th Cong., 1st sess. Washington, DC: Government Printing Office, 1875.
Report on the United States and Mexican Boundary Survey. House of Representatives Executive Document No. 135, 34th Cong, 1st sess. Washington, DC: Cornelius Wendell, Printer, 1857.
Reports of the Secretary of War with Reconnaissance of Route from San Antonio to El Paso. Senate Executive Document No. 64, 31st Cong., 1st sess. Washington, DC, 1850.
Testimony Taken by the Committee on Military Affairs in Relation to the Texas Border Troubles. House of Representatives Misc. Document No. 64, 45th Cong., 2nd sess. Washington, DC: Government Printing Office, 1878.
Texas Frontier Troubles. House of Representatives Committee on Foreign Affairs, House Report 701. Serial No. 1824, 45th Cong., 2nd sess. Washington, DC: Government Printing Office, 1878.

Indian Depredations Case
George H. Giddings v. The United States, Kiowa, Comanche, and Apache Indians.
Indian Depredations Case No. 3873, Court of Claims of the United States. National Archives: Washington, DC, December Term, 1891.

Interview Transcripts, Nita Stewart Haley Memorial Library, Midland, Texas.
Beverly, W. M. "Bob," interview by J. Evetts Haley. Lovington, New Mexico, June 23, 1937.
Johnson, Matt, interview by J. Evetts Haley. July 1, 1946.
Mayes, Ben C., interview by J. Evetts Haley. San Angelo, Texas, September 7, 1931.
Metcalf, Isaac Parker, interview by J. Evetts Haley. No date.
Owen, W. R., interview by J. Evetts Haley. Carlsbad, New Mexico, August 12, 1926, March 2, 1933, and June 24, 1937.

Interview Transcripts, WPA Federal Writers' Project Collection
(Manuscript Division, Library of Congress, Washington, DC)
Blalock, S. H., interview by Florence Angermiller. Eagle Pass, Texas, April 25, 1938.
Hoover, Mother (Laura Hoover), interview by Elizabeth Doyle. Ozona, Texas, November 16, 1937.
Mayes, Ben. "Range Lore."

Journal and Magazine Articles
Austerman, Wayne R. "Giddings' Station, a Forgotten Landmark on the Pecos." *The Permian*

Historical Annual, no. 21 (1981): 3-12.

Barrett, Arrie. "Western Frontier Forts of Texas." *West Texas Historical Association Year Book* 7 (June 1931): 115-139.

Bateman, Cephas C. "Old Fort Clark, a Frontier Post." *Frontier Times* 2, no. 7 (April 1925): 31-32.

Baylor, George W. "An Indian Raid in Mexico." *Frontier Times* 26, no. 12 (September 1948): 279-283.

Bender, A. B. "Opening Routes Across West Texas, 1848-1850." *Southwestern Historical Quarterly* 37, no. 2 (October 1933): 116-135.

Bowles, J. Frank. "Overland Trip to California in 1850." *Frontier Times* 4, no. 5 (February 1927): 12-16.

Butler, Grace Lowe. "General John Lapham Bullis." *The Texas History Teachers' Bulletin* 14, no. 1. University of Texas Bulletin no. 2746 (8 December 1927): 17-22.

Carroll, H. Bailey. "Texas Collection," *Southwestern Historical Quarterly* 49, no. 1 (July 1945-April 1946): 120-173.

Clary, David A., ed. "'I Am Already Quite a Texan': Albert J. Myer's Letters from Texas, 1854-1856." *Southwestern Historical Quarterly* 32, no. 1 (July 1978): 25-76.

Crimmins, Martin L., ed. "Colonel J. K. F. Mansfield's Report of the Inspection of the Department of Texas in 1856." *Southwestern Historical Quarterly* 42, no. 3 (January 1939): 351-387.

———. "General Albert J. Myer: the Father of the Signal Corps." *West Texas Historical Association Year Book* 29 (October 1953): 47-66.

———. "Two Thousand Miles by Boat in the Rio Grande in 1850." *West Texas Historical and Scientific Society: Publications,* no. 5 (December 1, 1933): 44-52.

Day, James M. "Big Foot Wallace in Trans-Pecos Texas." *West Texas Historical Association Year Book* 55 (1979): 70-80.

Denham, Claude. "Frontier Problems and Amusements in Crockett County." *West Texas Historical Association Year Book* 9 (October 1933): 35-47.

"Desperate Fight on Devil's River." *Frontier Times* 21, no. 4 (January 1944): 140-143.

Duffen, William A., ed. "Overland Via 'Jackass Mail' in 1858: The Diary of Phocion R. Way," *Arizona and the West* 2, no. 1 (Spring 1960): 35-53.

Duke, Escal F., ed. "A Description of the Route from San Antonio to El Paso by Captain Edward S. Meyer." *West Texas Historical Association Year Book* 49 (1973): 128-141.

Fenton, Jim. "John L. Bullis Always Meant Business." *The Permian Historical Annual* 33 (December 1993): 15-24.

Haas, Oscar, trans. "The Diary of Julius Giesecke, 1861-62." *Texas Military History* 3, no. 4 (Winter 1963): 228-242.

Haley, J. Evetts, ed. "A Log of the Texas-California Cattle Trail," *Southwestern Historical Quarterly* 35, no. 3 (January 1932): 208-237.

Hall, Martin Hardwick. "A Confederate Soldier's Letters from Fort Bliss, July 6, 1861." *Password* 25, no. 1 (Spring 1980): 17-20.

Hall, R. Franklin. "Chihuahua Trail, Linked U.S. and Mexico." *Frontier Times* 8, no. 7 (April 1931): 312-317.

Holt, R. D. "Old Texas Wagon Trains," *Frontier Times* 26, no. 12 (September 1948): 269-278.

Horton, Louise. "The Star Route Conspiracies," *Texana* 7, no. 3 (Fall 1969): 220-233.

Hunter, J. Marvin. "Midnight Battle at Fort Lancaster." *Frontier Times* 21, no. 9 (June 1944): 366-370.

Hunter, J. Marvin, Sr. "The San Antonio-San Diego Mail Route." *Frontier Times* 25, no. 2 (November 1947): 54-58.

James, V. L. "The Devil's River of Texas." *Field and Stream* 24, no. 1 (May 1904): 45-48.

Jones, Allen W. "Military Events in Texas During the Civil War, 1861-1865." *Southwestern Historical*

Quarterly 64, no. 1 (July 1960): 64-70.

Mahon, Emmie Giddings W. and Chester V. Kielman. "Giddings and the San Antonio-San Diego Mail Line." *Southwestern Historical Quarterly* 61, no. 2 (October 1957): 220-239.

Martin, Mabelle Eppard. "California Emigrant Roads Through Texas." *Southwestern Historical Quarterly* 28, no. 4 (April 1925): 287-301.

Meador, Tom. "Painted Caves." *The Texas Caver.* (September 1966): 107-110.

Pingenot, Ben E. "Fort Clark, Texas: A Brief History," *The Journal of Big Bend Studies* 7 (January 1995): 103-122.

———. "The Great Wagon Train Expedition of 1850." *Southwestern Historical Quarterly* 98, no. 2 (October 1994): 182-225.

"Record of Engagements with Hostile Indians in Texas 1868 to 1882." *West Texas Historical Association Year Book* 9 (October 1933): 101-118.

Scannell, Jack C. "Henry Skillman, Texas Frontiersman." *The Permian Historical Annual* 18 (December 1978): 19-31.

Scheips, Paul J. "Albert James Myer, An Army Doctor in Texas, 1854-1857." *Southwestern Historical Quarterly* 32, no. 1 (July 1978): 1-24.

Schneider, George A. "A Border Incident of 1878 From the Journal of Captain John S. McNaught." *Southwestern Historical Quarterly* 70, no. 2 (October 1966): 314-320.

Smith, Victor J. "The Route of Juan Dominguez de Mendoza through the Big Bend in 1684." *West Texas Historical and Scientific Society,* no. 2 (1928): 55-68.

Sullivan, Jerry M., ed. "Lieutenant Colonel William R. Shafter's Pecos River Expedition of 1870." *West Texas Historical Association Year Book* 47 (1971): 146-152.

"To California Through Texas and Mexico: The Diary and Letters of Thomas B. Eastland and Joseph G. Eastland, His Son." *California Historical Society Quarterly* 18, no. 2 (June 1939): 99-135.

Traylor, Maude Wallis. "Captain Samuel Highsmith, Ranger." *Frontier Times* 17, no. 7 (April 1940): 291-302.

Tucker, Albert B. "The Parker H. French Expedition Through Southwest Texas in 1850." *The Journal of Big Bend Studies* 6 (January 1994): 23-36.

Vest, Deed L. "The Chihuahua Road." *Texana* 5, no. 1 (Spring 1967): 1-10.

Williamson, Lela. "How Devil's River Received Its Name." *West Texas Historical and Scientific Society: Publications* 21, no. 1 (December 1, 1926): 43.

Woodhull, Frost. "The Seminole Indian Scouts on the Border." *Frontier Times* 15, no. 3 (December 1937): 118-127.

Woolford, Sam, ed. "The Burr G. Duval Diary." *Southwestern Historical Quarterly* 65, no. 4 (April 1962): 487-511.

Wright, Charles. "From the El Paso Train." *Southwestern Historical Quarterly*, no. 1 (July 1944): 268-269.

Manuscripts and Maps

"Best route for the movements of troops from San Antonio to El Passo-Texas[sic], being the one travelled by the State Geological Corps of Texas in 1860 and by Henry Skillman's party in March 1864. Described by A.R. Roessler," (map) Texas State Archives, Austin.

Bliss, Zenas R. "Reminiscences of Zenas R. Bliss, Major General, United States Army." 5 vols. Unpublished manuscript, 1886-1894. Nita Stewart Haley Memorial Library, Midland, Texas. Carbon copy typescript.

"Campaigns of Colonel Don Juan de Ugalde." Unpublished manuscript, translation. Clayton W. Williams Collection, Nita Stewart Haley Memorial Library, Midland, Texas. Typescript.

Daniel, James Manly. "The Advance of the Spanish Frontier and the Despoblado." PhD diss.,

University of Texas at Austin, 1955.
Echols, William H. "Report of 10 October 1860." Typescript in author's possession.
"Fortunately a very delightful record . . ." (ms) Clayton W. Williams Collection, Nita Stewart Haley Memorial Library, Midland, Texas.
Garza Falcon, Alejo de la. "Derrotero." (ms) Center for American History, University of Texas at Austin.
Garza Falcon, Blas de la. "Diario y derrotero, q nros. Dn. Blas de la Garza Falcon . . . y Dn. Joseph Anto. Eca y Musquiz . . . in Testimonio de la fundacion." (ms) *A.G.I., Audiencia de Mexico,* 61-2-18 (Coahuila, 1733-1738), 117-132. Center for American History, University of Texas at Austin.
Graham, Major Campbell, Topographic Engineers. "Map of Topogl. Recone. of a Part of Northwestern Texas, 1859-1860, William Echols, Brevet 2nd Lieutenant." Records of the War Department, Office of the Chief of Engineers, Map Q-095, National Archives, Washington, DC, copy in Nita Stewart Haley Memorial Library.
Hart, John E. Diary. Unpublished manuscript. Texas Confederate Museum Collection, Nita Stewart Haley Memorial Library, Midland, Texas.
Hunt, Brevet Lieutenant Colonel Thomas B. "Journal showing the Route taken by the Government Train accompanying the 15th Regiment U.S. Infantry From Austin, Texas to Fort Craig, New Mexico and returning to San Antonio, July-December 1869." (ms with maps) Q-154, RG 077, National Archives, Washington, DC.
Kaiser, Frank C. "Reminiscences of a Texas Ranger." Unpublished manuscript, 1967. Nita Stewart Haley Memorial Library, Midland, Texas.
"Map of Scout made by Capt. A. G. Brackett and Sixty-Six men of Company I Second Cavalry on the Great Comanche War Trail in April and May 1859, Copied from a sketch furnished by Capt. Brackett Sep. 1876." Records of the War Department, Office of the Chief of Engineers, Map Q-287, National Archives, Washington, DC.
"March from Ft. Stockton to Haymond made by Lieut. T. C. Woodbury, 16th Infantry in June 1886; March from Ft. Stockton to Del Rio made by Lieut. F. O. Johnson, 3rd Cavalry in June & July 1886." Map by Engineer's Office, Department of Texas, August 1886. Nita Stewart Haley Memorial Library, Midland, Texas.
Mayes, Ben C. "Reminiscences of Ben C. Mayes, San Angelo, Texas." Unpublished manuscript, 1932. Nita Stewart Haley Memorial Library, Midland, Texas. Typescript.
"Microfilm Copy 666." Research notes. Clayton W. Williams Collection, Nita Stewart Haley Memorial Library, Midland, Texas.
Newcomb, Samuel P. Diary from 1 January 1865 to 21 December 1865. Nita Stewart Haley Memorial Library, Midland, Texas.
Rodriguez, Vicente. "Derrotero." Unpublished manuscript. Center for American History, University of Texas at Austin.
Strang, Brevet Lieutenant Colonel E. J. "Topographical Sketch of the Road from Fort Stockton to Fort Chadbourne, 192 miles, October and November 1867." (map) National Archives, Washington, DC.
Temple, Frank M. "Reports of Scouts from Fort Concho, 1867-1889, including maps, typed from National Archives microfilm of RG 393," copy in author's possession.
Ugarte y Loyola, Jacobo de. "Diario de lo executado por el Destacamento mandado del Governador de la Provincia de Coahuila" (ms) (September 22-December 30, 1775). Center for American History, University of Texas at Austin.
"United States of America by John Melish." (map) Philadelphia: Murray Draper Fairman, 1818.
"U.S. Telegraph Lines in California, Arizona, New Mexico and Texas in Charge of the Chief Signal Officer U.S.A." (map) Nita Stewart Haley Memorial Library, Midland, Texas.

Young, J. H. "Map of the State of Texas from the Latest Authorities," 1852, Clayton W. Williams Collection, Nita Stewart Haley Memorial Library, Midland, Texas.

Newspapers
Corpus Christi Star. January 20, 1849.
Dallas Morning News. 1886-1902.
Galveston News. November 18, 1899.
New York Times. January 9, 1878; October 22, 1891; August 29, 1892; and July 14, 1901.
The Northern Standard (Clarkesville, Texas). February 10, 1849.
San Angelo Standard. 1885-1902.
San Antonio Express. June 12, 1869; March 16 and 30, 1882; January 13, 1883; May 18, 1902; September 28, 1903; and June 28, 1903.
San Antonio Herald. 1869-1872; February 16, 1875; March 24, 1876; April 7, 14, 17, and 19, 1876; and May 30, 1876.
San Antonio Texan. September 3, 1859.
San Antonio Western Texan. September 23, 1852.
Texas Live Stock Journal (sometimes styled *Texas Stock and Farm Journal* and *Texas Stockman-Journal*). 1882-1906.

Online Sources
The Handbook of Texas Online. http://www.tshaonline.org/handbook/online/. Accessed 2005-2009.
Heritage Auction Galleries. "Wells, Fargo & Co's Express 'Train Robbery' Ledger," 1870-1902. http://historical.ha.com/common/view_item.php?Sale_No=689& Lot_No=72001&src= pr. Accessed January 2, 2009.
The Nature Conservancy. "Devils River." http://www.nature.org/success/devilsriver.html. Accessed February 17, 2008.
Texas Rangers Hall of Fame and Museum. "John R. Hughes, 1855-1947." http://www.texas-ranger.org/halloffame/Hughes_John.htm. Accessed January 6, 2009.
United States Department of the Interior U.S.-Mexico Border Field Coordinating Committee. "Water-resources Issues in the Rio Grande—Rio Conchos to Amistad Reservoir Subarea Fact Sheet." http://www.cerc.usgs.gov/FCC/pubs/Fact_sheets/DOI_US-MX_Border_FCC _Fact_sheet_3.pdf. Accessed January 27, 2009 (page discontinued).
World Wildlife Fund. "Tamaulipan Mezquital." http://www.worldwildlife.org/wildworld/ profiles/terrestrial/na/na1312_full.html. Accessed January 27, 2009.

US Army Military Records
Fort Clark medical ledger. 2 vols. Nita Stewart Haley Memorial Library, Midland, Texas.
Journal of the march of a detachment of Company M 9th Cavalry commanded by 1st Lieut. Gregory Barrett Jr., 10 Infantry. Fort McKavett microfilm roll 373714-No. 6, National Archives, Washington, DC.
Letters and telegrams sent and received. Adjutant General's Office, Department of Texas, District of the Nueces, District of the Pecos, Division of the Missouri, Fort McKavett, Fort Stockton. National Archives, Washington, DC.
Post and field returns, Texas. Camp Blake, Camp Hudson, Camp on the San Pedro, Fort Clark, Fort Lancaster, Fort Stockton. National Archives, Washington, DC.
Records of the War Department. Office of the Chief of Engineers. National Archives, Washington, DC.
U.S. Department of War, Civil Works Map File, Q-154, RG 77, National Archives, Washington, DC.

INDEX

Adams and Wickes (freighters), 92-94, 104
Adams, Charles G., 144
Adams, John Q., 146
Adams, Thomas C., 146
Adams, William C., 82
Albuquerque, New Mexico, 85
Allen, H. D., 135
Allison, Dave, 150
Alpine, Texas, 148, 170
Alsate, 111-112
Amarillo, Texas, 144
Ames, George W., 129
Amlung Family, 67
Anacio (assailant), 159
Andres, Nick, 39
Antonio Creek, 132
Apache Indians, 18-21, 57, 89, 106
Apache Indians, Lipan, 19-20, 22, 36-37, 47-48, 57-59, 64, 74, 86, 89, 101, 103-104, 106, 108, 109, 111-112, 120
Apache Indians, Mescalero, 20, 21, 58, 109, 111-112, 116, 160
Arkansas River, 131
Aten, Ira, 136-137, 137 (photo), 138
Augur, C. C., 104, 120, 122
Austin, Texas, 124
Babb, William I., 157
Bacon, John M., 90
Baker (stockman), 165
Baker Ranch, 132, 138
Baker, Bob, 123 (photo)
Baker, Dave, 158
Baker, David, 126
Baker, J. H., 135, 170
Baker's Crossing, 126, 128 (photo)
Baldridge, Michael, 35
Ballinger, Texas, 156, 169

Bar S Ranch, 144
Barrett, Gregory, 104
Barry, William, 64-65
Bastrop County, Texas, 22
Battle of Glorieta, 85
Battle of Mesilla, 82-83, 85
Battle of Palmito Ranch, 87
Battle of Sacramento, 43
Bautista de Elguezabal, Juan, 19
Bayard, William, 90
Baylor, John Robert, 82-83, 85
Beale, Edward Fitzgerald, 14, 60-63
Bean, Garrett, 157
Bean, Roy, 135-136
Beaver Lake, 31-32, 32 (photo), 33, 39-40, 45, 50, 57, 64, 67, 73, 79, 83-86, 91-96, 99, 104-106, 108, 115-117, 124, 130-133, 135-138, 140-141, 143, 145, 152, 155, 157-159, 166, 184
Beaver Lake Ranch, 157-158
Beaver Lake Station, 70, 70 (map), 73, 80, 80 (map), 181
Beckett, John, 126
Belknap, William W., 101-102
Bell, James G., 53, 127
Bell, P. Hansborough, 24
Bennett, Fletcher, 124-125
Bermejillo, Durango, Mexico, 170
Berry, George, 140
Beverly, Bob, 149-150
Bexar County, Texas, 89
Big Bend, Texas, 79, 111, 170
Big Bow, 98
Big Cattle Die-Up, 132, 134
Big Drift, 131-134
Big Dry, 134, 138, 141, 145
Big Satan Creek, 12

209

Billings, John, 132
Birch, James, 62, 66
Birch, Mrs. James, 67
Black Seminole Scouts, 101-103, 103 (photo), 105-106, 108-111, 115-117, 120-121
Black, Tom, 86
Black, William, 143
Blake, Jacob E., 50
Blalock, Alice, 138, 140
Blalock, Sam, 138, 140
Blanco County, Texas, 134
Blanco River, 105
Blandin, Charles, 155
Blas, de la Garza Falcon, 18
Blawinsky, Charles, 39
Bliss, Zenas R., 46, 61, 68, 75-77, 95, 98-99, 102
Block, R. N., 162
Blocker, John, 140
Blocker, W. B. "Ab," 140
Bobole Indians, 16, 17
Bosque, Fernando del, 17
Bowles, J. Frank, 34
Brackett, Albert G., 72, 74
Brackettville, Texas, 122, 138
Bradley, Levi, 116
Brazos River, Clear Fork of, 66
Breeder's Gazette of Chicago, 166
Brewington (Gruington) (freighter), 93-94
Brewster County, Texas, 74, 117, 165, 170
Brown (Indian fighter), 39
Brown County, Texas, 170
Brown, John T., 145
Brownsville, Texas, 87
Brownwood, Texas, 168, 170
Brushy Creek, 22
Buchanan, R. E., 168-169
Buckhorn Draw, 12, 152
Buell, D. C., 59-60
Buell, George Pearson, 107
Buffalo Draw, 164
buffalo, 20-21, 160-161
Bull-Head Lake, 61
Bullis, John L., 101-103, 105-108, 111-113, 115-117, 119-121
Burbank, C. G., 163
Burnet County, Texas, 22, 129
Burns, Rollie, 116

Burris (rancher), 129
Burro Mountains, Mexico, 120
Burtrill, L., 170
Butterfield Overland Mail, 73, 82
Cabeza, de Vaca, 16
Caldwell, Dan, 170
California Cattle Trail, 52, 106, 122-123, 145
California Creek, 125
California Springs, 29, 47, 50, 52-53, 59, 83, 84 (photo), 99, 103, 105, 115, 138, 139 (photo), 179
California Well (see "California Springs")
Callahan, R. W., 144
Camels, 62-63, 74-75, 79
Camp Blake, 50, 52-53, 55
Camp Charlotte, 116
Camp Cooper, 66
Camp Davis, 59
Camp Hudson Times, 84-85
Camp Hudson, 59-61, 61 (map), 65-69, 69 (map), 71-75, 76 (photo), 77-78, 78 (map), 79, 81-85, 89-92, 96-100 (photo), 104, 107-109, 109 (photo), 115, 117, 131, 141, 148
Camp King, 192
Camp Lancaster (also see "Fort Lancaster"), 57-58, 58 (map), 59-60, 65
Camp Leon, 81
Camp Llano, 23-24
Camp on the Rio San Pedro, 56-57
Camp on the San Pedro, 51, 55, 57
Camp Palo Blanco, 57
Camp Peña Blanco, 117
Camp Peña Colorado, 120
Camp San Felipe, 109-110, 112, 115-117, 119
Camp Stockton, 78, 78 (map)
Camp Uvalde, 75
Camp Van Camp, 78
Camp Wood, 107, 116, 137
Campbell (Del Rio stockman), 162
Campbell, John M., 144, 163, 197
Canadian River, 131
Cape Hatteras, North Carolina, 66
Carleton, James H., 86-87
Carpenter, S. D., 57
Carter, Kit, 88
Caruthers, Frank, 164
Castaño, Gaspar de Sosa, 16

Castle Canyon, 126
Castroville, Texas, 106, 108
Cattle, 11, 52-53, 57-59, 92, 106, 112, 119, 122-124, 126-134, 138, 140-141, 143-145, 152, 154, 157, 159-162, 166
Cauthorn, Albert Russell, 141
Cavanaugh, Thomas, 141
Central America (steamship), 66
Chapman, Bob, 132
Chapman, W. W., 36, 127
Cheno, 112
Chihuahua City, Mexico, 43, 73, 93
Chihuahua Trail, 40-41, 48, 67
Chihuahua, Mexico, 23, 25, 40, 43, 73
Chihuahuan Desert, 12, 25, 79, 134
Childress, Billy, 106
Chinati Mountains, 120
Cibola Creek, 95
Cimarron River, 131
Civil War, 81-87, 102
Clark's Water Hole, 104
Clifford, William, 65
Coahuila, Mexico, 16-20, 74, 89, 99, 101, 104, 106, 108-109, 114, 120, 134
Coldwell, Neal, 104-105
Coleman County, Texas, 169
Coleman Junction, 168
Coleman, Texas, 169
Coleman's (saddle and harness shop), 152
Coleman-Fulton Pasture Company, 144
Collins, Tom, 37
Colorado River, 18, 79, 112, 160
Colson, Nick, 116
Columbus, Texas, 79
Comanche Indians, 18, 20-23, 27, 46-47, 56, 64-65, 69, 86, 91, 95, 98, 67, 71, 73, 105-106
Comanche War Trail, Great, 24, 74
Committee on Military Affairs, US Congress, 112
Comstock Station, 125, 132
Comstock, Texas, 125, 148-149, 149 (photo), 150, 164, 166, 167 (photo), 169-170
Concho River, 18-19, 87, 107, 132-133
Confederate States of America Forces, 82, 86
Confederate States of America Forces, Texas Cavalry, Fifth Regiment, 83-84
Confederate States of America Forces, Texas

Cavalry, Fourth Regiment, 83, 85
Confederate States of America Forces, Texas Cavalry, Seventh Regiment, 83-84
Cook, Philip St. George, 47
Cooney, Michael, 98-101
Coons, Ben, 35
Cooper (stockman), 130
Cooper, Mrs. (wife of stockman), 130
Coopwood, Bethel, 88
Costilitos, 103
Couch, S. E., 159
Cow Creek, 149
Cowboys, 11, 52-53, 57-58, 92, 106, 112, 119, 122-124, 126, 130-132, 138, 140-141, 144-145, 152, 153 (photo), 154, 158, 160, 170
Cox, Lemuel Bascom, 133
Creek Indians, 101
Crews, H. H., 115-116
Crockett County, Texas, 11-12, 135-136, 145, 150, 159, 165, 171
Cross, William, 116
Crowder, John, 39
Crowl Ranch, 165
Cully Draw, 135
Cunningham (US Customs official), 150
Cusenbary, D. B., 146, 164
Custer, John, 154
D'Hanis, Texas, 122
Dacate Mountains, 16-17
Dacate River (Devils River), 17
Dallas Morning News, 156, 169-170
Dallas News, 14
Dalrymple, James, 145
Dark Canyon, 12
Davis, Jefferson, 83
Davis Mountains, 33
De Elguezabal, Juan Bautista, 19
De la Cruz, Manuel, 16-17
de la Garza Falcon, Alejo, 19
De San Buenaventura, Dionisio, 17
De Sosa, Gaspar Castaño, 16
de Ugalde, Juan, 19, 20
De Vaca, Cabeza, 15
Dead Man's Creek, 12
Dead Man's Pass, 36-37, 37 (map), 38 (photo), 39-40, 53, 63, 67-68, 71, 96
Decker, Henry, 169

212 INDEX

Del Bosque, Fernando, 17
Del Rio Record, 161
Del Rio, Texas, 16, 18-19, 28, 91, 129, 135, 135 (photo), 138, 140-141, 149-150, 152, 157-158, 160, 162, 165-166
Delaware Indians, 24, 33
DeLeon, Porfirio, 166
Delorus Ranche, 102
Dennin, Thomas G., 79
Denson, John, 147
Devil's River News, 146
Devil's River Station (railroad station), 125, 140
Devils River Station (US Army camp), 50
Devils River, origin of name, 24-25
Devils River, other names for, 16-17, 19, 24-25
Dias, Juan, 105
Dionisio de San Buenaventura, 17, 18
Dissler, C., 145
Dissler, Charles, 132
Doak, John M., 132
Dodd (sheepman), 154
Dodge, Francis, 91
Dolan Creek, 110, 129
Dolan Falls, 110
Dolan Falls, 74, 74 (photo)
Dolan, Pat, 109-110, 115-116
Dominguez, de Mendoza, 18
Doniphan, Alexander P., 43
Dove Creek, 124, 131, 141, 145
Dowdy Family, 115-116
Dowling, Mike, 152
Dry Devils River (Edwards-Val Verde counties), 12, 15, 104, 168
Dry Devils River (Schleicher-Sutton counties), 11-12, 12 (photo), 116, 134, 141, 143-144, 146, 154, 156
Dryden, Texas, 18, 140, 161, 170
Dubose, H. G., 170
Duggan, Ed, 129
Dunlap, John, 57
Dunlop (sutler), 71-72
Dutchover, Dedrich, 45
Dynows, A. F., 135
Dynows, J. D., 135
Eagle Nest Crossing, 105

Eagle Pass, Texas, 36-37, 78, 86, 106, 112, 119, 158, 165
Earwood, Floyd, 158 (photo)
Eastland, Thomas B., 28-33
Eccleston, Robert, 11, 14, 29-30
Echols, William H., 74-75, 79
Edmundson (merchant), 135
Edwards County, Texas, 12, 164
Edwards Plateau, Texas 12, 145
Edwards, W. O., 146
El Paso del Norte, Mexico, 43, 112
El Paso, Texas 23, 25, 27, 33-34, 36, 38, 41-42, 45, 47, 50, 60, 66, 70-71, 82, 85-86, 88, 122, 148
Elbow Lake, 146
Eldorado, Texas, 11-12
Elguezabal, Juan Bautista de, 19
Emory, William H., 36
Enchanted Rock, 23
Erskine, Michael, 52
Evans, A. W., 161
Evans, G. H., 115
Evans, George H., 108
Factor, Pompey, 105-106
Falcon, Alejo de la Garza, 19
Falls County, Texas, 155-156
Fawcett, E. K., 129
Feely Station, 125
fencing, 134-135, 142, 144-145, 157
Ficklin mail line, 90-91
Ficklin, Ben, 90
Fields, Tom, 148-149
Fink, Theodore, 61, 65, 68
First Crossing, 27-30, 30 (map), 34, 36, 46-47, 49-50, 52, 57-58, 60, 62, 70, 74-76, 81, 83, 85, 91, 96, 98-99, 114-115, 117, 145
Fish, Hamilton, 104
Fisher, King, 106
Fisk, Jim, 40
Fitzgerald, Herbert, 127
Flanders Station, 125
Fletcher, William, 117
Floods, 14, 35, 161, 172
Florence, Will, 130
Flow, Devils River, 14
Flynt (Flint), John, 148

Ford, John S., 86-87
Fort Bliss, 82, 85
Fort Clark, 44 (map), 46-47, 50, 56-60, 65, 70-74, 78 (map), 81-82, 85-86, 88-91, 95-107, 109-117, 122
Fort Concho, 99, 107, 112, 116-117, 122
Fort Craig, New Mexico, 85
Fort Davis, 55-57, 60, 68, 73, 81, 90, 104, 117, 120, 122
Fort Duncan, 37, 101-102, 127
Fort Griffin, 107
Fort Inge, 34, 38, 41, 45, 47, 89, 95-96
Fort Lancaster (also see "Camp Lancaster"), 66-67, 73, 78 (map), 81-82, 86, 89, 91, 96-97, 99, 184-185
Fort Leaton, 24
Fort Mason, 63
Fort McIntosh, 74
Fort McKavett, 95, 104, 116, 119, 144
Fort Quitman, 70
Fort Riley, 46
Fort Stockton, 89, 91, 96, 98-99, 104-105, 112, 138
Fort Sumner, New Mexico, 130, 134
Fort Sumter, South Carolina, 81
Fort Terrett, 47
Fort Worth and Denver City Railway, 144
Fort Worth, Texas, 92, 122
Franklin Mountains, 82
Franks, E.S., 157, 196
Frazer, G. M., 104
Freeman, W. G., 46
Freemont Association, 28-31
French, Parker H., 35-36
French, S. G., 28, 41-42
Frio Canyon, 105
Frio County, Texas, 138
Frio River, 15, 28, 104-105, 107, 120, 131, 185
Froebel, Julius, 48-50
Frohock, William, 91
Fry, Adolph, 46
Fulton Jr., George W., 160
Gadsden Purchase, 59
Galbreath, John A., 122
Gallagher, Frank, 123 (photo)
Gallagher, Ned, 71-72

Galveston, Harrisburg and San Antonio Railway, 122, 124-125
Garner (expressman), 79
Garvey, Bill, 124
Garza Falcon, Alejo de la, 19
Garza Falcon, Blas de la, 18
Garza Falcon, Miguel de la, 18
Gaskill, Charles B., 95
Geddes, Andrew, 97, 106
Geniocane Indians, 17
Giddings Company, 57, 60, 69, 73-74, 82
Giddings, George H., 54, 54 (photo), 55, 62, 66-67, 70
Giesecke, Julius, 83, 85
Gilbert, Charles, 59-60
Gillespie County, Texas, 168
Gillett, James B., 114
Givins, Emory, 39
Glenn, Bob, 155-156
Glenn, Jeff, 156
Glynn, Ed, 166
goats, 127, 132-133, 145, 166
Gobble, Frank, 164-165, 196
Goliad, Texas, 44
Gonzales (settler), 161
Gonzales, Anastacio, 98
Gonzales, Melian, 159
Goodnight, Charles, 88
Granger Draw, 12
Grant, Ulysses S., 101
Grayson County, Texas, 162
Grinnell, M. E., 138
Grinnell, William, 152
Gruington (Brewington) (freighter), 93-94
Guadalupe Mountains, 108
Guadalupe River, 48, 104, 132
Gulf Coast, Texas, 15, 144
Gunter, Jot, 162
Guyquechale Indians, 16, 17
Haley, Bob, 123 (photo)
Half Circle 6 Ranch, 131, 154
Hall (wagoner), 71
Hall, Martin Hardwick, 82
Halleck, H. W., 87
Hamilton, Texas, 126, 146
Hamner, H. A., 82
Hart (Harr) (stockman), 154

214 INDEX

Hart, John E., 11, 83
Hartz, Edward L., 74-75
Haskell, Alex M., 67
HAT Ranch, 150
Hatch, John P., 99
Hayes, Richard, 166-167
Hayes, Rutherford B., 111
Hays, John C., 23-25, 28, 44
Hays-Highsmith Expedition, 23-25, 27, 40
Heartsill, W. W., 11, 85
Helmet, Texas, 167, 197
Henderson, J. E., 135
Henry, W. R., 75-76
Heorte (drover), 126
Hernandez (freighter), 104
Highsmith, Samuel, 23-25
Hiler, W. H., 130
Hill Country, Texas, 12
Hill, Charley, 40
Hill, Henry, 57
Hinkley, Private, 73
Hodge, Jack, 79
Hodges, D. R., 169
Hood, John B., 63-65
Hooker, A. E., 96
Hoover, William Perry, 119
Horsehead Crossing, 78, 86-87, 160
Howard Draw, 52, 96, 129
Howard, Richard, 27-28, 33
Howard's Canyon, 60
Howard's Spring, 33, 45, 50, 51 (map), 52-53, 60, 62-63, 70, 79, 80-81, 83, 86, 90-92, 96, 98-99, 104, 119, 138, 141, 148, 152, 160
Howard's Well (see "Howard's Spring")
Hudson, Lum, 123 (photo)
Hudson, Walter W., 59
Hudspeth & Swift Ranch, 159
Hudspeth, J. D., 164
Hughes, John R., 165
Humphreys (drover), 106
Humphreys, Charley, 130
Hunt, Thomas B., 92
Hunter, James M., 55
Hunter, Sherod, 185
Independence Ranch, 141
Indianola, Texas, 40-41, 81, 93
Indians, Tonkawa, 59, 64
Indians (also see individual tribes), 15-19, 30, 33-34, 36-40, 42, 44, 46, 48-50, 52-53, 55-57, 59-60, 63, 65-68, 71, 73-76, 78-80, 82-83, 86, 89-101, 104-105, 107-108, 110-116, 119-120, 172
Irvin, Wardlow, 90-91
Irwin, A., 89
Island Crossing, 114
Jacksboro, Texas, 92
Jackson & Aldwell Ranch, 145
Jackson, E. R., 145
Jacobo, de Ugarte y Loyola, 19
James, John, 52-53, 78, 160
Jediondo Indians, 18
Jeffries, Baker, 126
Jesup, Thomas S., 41
Jett, William G., 82
Joel, Richard, 88
Johnson Creek, 115
Johnson, Albert, 91
Johnson, F. O., 138
Johnson, Hugh M., 166
Johnson, Lee, 168-170
Johnson, Lewis, 98
Johnson, R. R., 129
Johnsons Run, 12, 16, 19, 33, 91-93, 108, 116, 119, 135, 138, 141, 145, 150, 161
Johnston, J. E., 27, 28, 33, 43
Jones (Indian victim), 86
Jones, Bill (see "Purviance, Alex")
Jones, Eldridge, 90
Jones, Frank, 148-149
Jones, John B., 108
Jones, W. A., 135
Jordan, Walter, 166
Juan (goatherd), 152
Juarez, Chihuahua, Mexico, 169
Juarez, Mexico, 112
Junction, Texas, 155
Juno, Texas, 19, 70, 135, 136 (photo), 138, 145, 151 (photo), 155, 158 (photo), 159-160, 166, 171
Keaton, John, 168-169
Keaton, Pearce, 168-169
Kelley, J. M., 110, 114
Kendall County, Texas, 145
Ker Ranch, D. C., 164
Kerr County, Texas, 111
Kerrville, Texas, 132, 146
Ketchum, Tom "Black Jack," 165-168

Kickapoo Creek, 156
Kickapoo Indians, 71, 89, 99, 101-106, 108, 112
Kilgore, Martin H. , 140
Kimble County, Texas, 108, 114, 119, 132, 143, 168
King, N. G. , 155
Kingsbury Falls, 36
Kinney County, Texas, 17, 111, 135, 138, 141, 165
Kiowa Indians, 98
Knox, W. T., 169
La Salle, René Robert Cavelier, Sieur, 18
Lafferty, L. D., 86
Lambert, T. A., 123
Lancaster Crossing, 27, 48, 56, 66, 77, 140
Lancaster Station, 73
Lane Rangers, W. P., 82, 84-85
Lane, Albert, 88
Lane, W. P., 82
Langston, James, 148
Langtry, Texas, 105, 136, 170
Laredo, Texas, 44, 59
Larios, Juan, 17
Larkin, Smith, 68
Las Moras Springs, 45 (photo), 46
Latham, H., 159-160
Leander, Texas, 22
Lemley, George, 88
Leon, 112
Leona River, 34
Lerdistas, 110-111
Lewis, Babe, 132
Lewis, Charles E., 132
Lincoln, Abraham, 85
Lindsay, A. J., 58
Ling, G. F., 161
Lipan Ranch, 131
Little Lake Michigan, 166
Live Oak Creek, 16, 24, 48, 57, 89, 91, 130, 148
Llano River, 95, 115, 119, 169
Llano, Texas, 23
Lockhart (sheepman), 165
Loftin, E. W., 135
Logan, James, 116
Lopez, Antonio, 159
Los Angeles, California, 82
Lost Lake, 147

Loughborough, R. H. R., 115
Love, Harry, 36, 127
Lower Road, 27, 33-34, 36, 40, 42-43, 50-52, 55-56, 59-60, 66, 71, 73, 81, 82-83, 86-88, 90 (map), 92-93, 96-97, 99, 117, 120, 138, 140, 175, 184-185
Lowrey Draw, 144
Loyola, Jacobo de Ugarte y, 19
Lozier Station, 165, 167
Lucas, Dave, 155-156
Mackenzie, Ranald S., 101, 102 (photo), 103-104, 106, 114
Mackenzie's Camp, 190
Macnabb, Alexander, 152
Magnus Colorado, 112
Mahlmann Ranch, 145-146
Mahon, M. M., 116
Mann, John L., 39
Mansfield, J. K. F., 58-59
Manuel, de la Cruz, 16, 17
Mapimi, Durango, Mexico, 170
Marathon, Texas, 120, 170
Marfa, Texas, 170
Marrufo, Ramon, 19
Martinez, Leal, 160
Mason, James, 63
Matagorda Bay, Texas, 18
Mathis, W. M., 150
Maude S Saloon, 147
Maverick County, Texas, 17, 36, 105, 165
Maverick, Samuel, 24-25
Mayes, Ben C., 123, 123 (photo), 124, 131-132
Mayes, Kenny, 131
McCall, Captain, 168
McComb (wagoner), 71
McConnell, Perry J., 169
McCrary, G W., 110-111, 113
McDowell, Thomas, 156
McKees Station, 125
McKenzie, Detective, 169
McLauren (Indian raid victim), 120
McLeod, J. N., 133
McLymont, James, 163, 165-166
Medina County, Texas, 89, 107, 111
Meehan (soldier), 77
Meinecke (entrepreneur), 144
Menard County, Texas, 143, 163
Menard, Texas, 19

Menardville, Texas, 140, 144
Mendoza, Dominguez de, 18
Merrick, Morgan Wolfe, 81
Merritt, Wesley, 98, 103
Mesilla, New Mexico, 73, 82
Mesilla Valley, New Mexico, 82
Metcalf, Isaac Parker, 91-92
Mexican War, 36, 43-44, 50
Meyer, Sol, 163
Middle Concho River, 116, 154
Midland County, Texas, 149
Midland, Texas, 150
Mier Expedition, 44
Miers (Mayers, Mires), Isaac, 146
Miguel, de la Garza Falcon, 18
Miles, William, 36
Miller, Chris. [sic], 116
Monroe, Miss, 155
Moore and West (cattle partnership), 112
Moreau, C. H., 160
Mosher Jr., Theodore, 116
Moss, Joe, 135
Mountain Home, Texas, 115
Mud Creek, 89, 141
Muzquiz, Jose, 20
Myer, Albert J., 56
Neuman, J. H., 162
Newell Ranch, 145-146
Newman, Bud, 164-165, 168-170
Nichols, W. A., 81
North Concho River, 130, 154
North San Gabriel River, 22
Norvell, S. T., 116-117
Nueces River, 15, 19, 33, 41, 48, 75, 86, 95, 99, 106-107, 116, 126, 132, 137, 166, 185
O'Keefe, Dave, 144
Oakes, James, 59-60
Ogazon, Pedro, 110
Old Nine R, 154
Olmsted, Frederick Law, 45, 52
Ord, E. O. C., 110-112, 117, 120
Orleman, Louis Henry, 107
Outlaws, 140, 159, 165, 171
Outlaws, burglars, 159
Outlaws, gunmen, 143, 145-147, 155-157, 164-165, 170-171
Outlaws, robbers, 137-138, 150
Outlaws, stock thieves, 106, 116, 131, 143-144, 147, 149-150, 155-156, 158-159, 162, 166, 168, 170-171
Outlaws, thieves, 137-138, 140, 163
Outlaws, train robbers, 147-149, 158, 164-170
Ozona Courier, 161
Ozona, Texas, 135, 150, 159, 161, 171
Paint Rock, Texas, 107
Painted Canyon (near Devils River), 27, 46, 49-50, 52, 57
Painted Cave (near Devils River), 27, 28 (map), 29, 36, 52-53, 71, 83, 86, 106, 110, 127, 160
Painted Cave (Seminole Canyon) Station, 125
Palmer, Tom, 143
Palo Blanco Springs, 57, 179
Palo Pinto, Texas, 88
Palos Blancos, 179
Panhandle, Texas, 123
Panic of 1893, 157, 159, 161, 166
Parker, L. O., 117
Payne, Isaac, 105-106
Pease River, 131
Pecan Springs, 26 (photo), 27, 31, 40, 86-87, 87 (photo), 111, 117-118 (photo), 119, 124, 126-127, 134, 138, 154, 160
Pecos City, Texas, 150, 155
Pecos County, Texas, 135
Pecos High Bridge, 168
Pecos River, 11-12, 15-16, 18-20, 24-25, 32-33, 40, 48, 52, 56-60, 66, 75, 77-78, 86, 89, 92, 95, 104-108, 111, 115-117, 119-120, 122, 124-126, 126 (photo), 131-132, 137, 140-141, 148-150, 155, 160, 165, 168
Pecos Spring, 115
Pecos Valley Association, 141
Perez, Juan de los Rios, 16
Perote Prison, 44
Perry, Sam, 150
Perry, W. H., 82
Peter (sheepherder), 164
Pettie, Samuel, 96
Philadelphia and Reading Railroad, 157
Phillips (cattleman), 122
Piedra Pinta, 86
Piedras Negras, Mexico, 18
Polk, James K., 25
Port Lavaca, Texas, 28, 36, 40

Powell Well (Ozona), Texas, 145
Powell, E. C., 89
Predators, 144, 159, 162-163
Predators, coyotes, 162
Predators, dogs, 162
Predators, panthers, 130
Predators, wolves, 159, 162-163
Prentiss, Oliver, 158
Presidio de Aguaverde, Coahuila, 19
Presidio de San Juan Bautista, 18-19
Presidio de San Saba, 19
Presidio del Altar, 175-176
Presidio del Norte, Mexico, 23-24, 40, 122
Presnall, Pope A., 126
Price, Sterling, 43
Priest, Jerry, 39
Prosser and Company, 135
Prosser, R., 154
Prosser, Robert W., 126-127, 134-135, 141, 158, 161
Pullman, J. W., 116
Purviance, Alex (Bill Jones), 164-165
Quitman Mountains, 25
Railroad Accidents, 140-141, 150
Ramsay (Ramsey) cattle operation, 119
Ramsey (Ramsay) cattle operation, 119
Ramsey, Henry, 106, 119
Range fire, 36, 41, 145-146, 166
Red's Water Hole, 95
Reid, John C., 59
Reinhart, John, 57
Reiss, Allen, 120
Remolina, Coahuila, Mexico, 103
Ress (Reyes) *(vaquero)*, 152
Reynolds, Samuel H., 50
Richards, H. I., 89-90
Richards, J. L., 108
Richarz (Richaz), Joseph, 57
Richarz, H. J., 96
Ringgold Barracks, 36, 74, 107
Rio de las Lajas (Devils River), 16
Rio Grande City, Texas, 36
Rio Grande, 11, 12, 16-19, 24-25, 30, 36, 40, 43, 46, 57, 59-60, 73, 85, 89, 91, 95-96, 100-101, 103-105, 107-108, 110-115, 117, 119-120, 122, 125, 127, 149, 160-161, 168, 170, 184
Rio Salado (Pecos River), 16
Rio San Pedro (Devils River), 19, 24-25, 50

River of Rocks (see "Devils River")
Roberts Brothers Ranch, 114
Roberts, Johnnie, 144
Rockport, Texas, 144
Rocksprings, Texas, 164
Rodgers, Alex, 115
Ruggles, Daniel, 57
Runyon, Dick, 155
Rusk, Texas, 170
Russell, Dick, 143-144
Ryan, Thomas, 64-65
Ryburn, J. H., 131
Sabinal River, 92, 105, 137
Samuels Station, 148
San Angelo Standard, 11, 14, 141, 144, 146, 154-155, 157, 160, 162, 171
San Angelo, Texas, 131, 138, 141, 144-146, 152, 154-155, 157, 162, 168
San Antonio, Texas 23-25, 27-29, 33, 35, 38, 41-44, 50, 52-55, 60, 62-63, 65-67, 81-83, 85, 88-89, 92, 120, 122, 126, 129
San Antonio Daily Herald, 107
San Antonio to San Diego Mail, 62-63, 65-70, 73-74, 79
San Antonio Weekly Express, 124-125
San Antonio-El Paso stage line, 82, 85
San Antonio-Santa Fe Mail, 43-48, 50, 53-55
San Carlos, Chihuahua, Mexico, 112
San Carlos, Mexico, 24
San Diego River, Coahuila, 18-19, 114
San Diego, California, 62, 66-67
San Elizario, Texas, 43, 70
San Felipe Creek, 28, 124
San Felipe del Rio (Del Rio), Texas, 92, 119, 125, 135
San Felipe Springs, 19, 28, 29 (photo), 83, 92, 93 (map)
San Felipe, Mexico, 150
San Fernando, Mexico, 27
San Juan de Endes, Mexico, 36-37
San Pedro Creek, 16, 27
San Pedro River (Devils River), 19, 24-25, 50
San Saba River, 19, 136
Sanford, Ben, 48
Sansom, John, 95
Santa Fe, New Mexico, 23, 43, 45, 85, 104
Santa Fe Railroad, 154, 168-170
Santa Fe Trail, 43
Santa Nina Waterhole, 93

Santa Rosa, Coahuila, 21
Santa Rosa de Santa Maria, Coahuila, 16
Santa Rosa Mountains, Mexico, 161
Santleben, August, 67, 93
Saragossa (Zaragoza), Mexico, 108, 111-112
Sawyer, Marion, 166
Sawyer, Risher, and Hall (mail contractor), 88
Schleicher County, Texas, 11, 136, 144, 168
Scholby, William, 156, 159
Scott, G. W., 145
Second Crossing, 30-31, 35, 37, 40, 49, 51-53, 57-61, 61 (map), 63, 67, 74, 90-91, 105, 109-110, 122, 126, 128 (photo), 132, 138, 161
Seminole Canyon, 125-126
Seminole Canyon State Park, Texas, 105
Seminole Indian Negro Scouts (see "Black Seminole Scouts")
Seminole Indians, 101
Seminole Wars, 101
Seven D (7D) Ranch, 148
Shackelford Ranch, 138
Shackleford, Pearl, 170
Shackleford, Rolly, 164-165
Shafter, Texas, 170
Shafter, William Rufus, 95, 105, 107-108, 110-114
Sharp, George, 91
Shaw, Owen, 47
Sheep, 126-129, 129 (photo), 130, 132-134, 138, 140-141, 143-144, 146, 154-157, 159-166
Sheepherders, 128-130, 140, 144, 146-147, 152, 159, 164
Sheffield, Texas, 115, 140
Sheffield, Texas, 27
Sheridan, Philip H., 101-104
Shield, Gerome W., 169
Sibley, Henry H., 83-85
Sibley's Brigade, 83-85
Sieker, Lamartine Pemberton, 111, 116, 129
Sierra Blanca, Texas, 122
Sierra Dacate (see "Dacate Mountains")
Sierra del Carmen, Mexico, 74, 111-112
Skillman, Henry, 27, 30, 43, 45, 53, 55, 63, 65-66
Slaughter, C. C., 88
Slaughter, John H., 106
Smith (deputy sheriff), 143

Smith, Clint, 95
Smith, George, 131
Smith, Jeff, 95
Smith, William F., 25, 27
Somervell, Alexander, 44
Sonora, Texas, 134, 144, 146-147, 152, 155, 159, 162, 164-165, 168-171
South Concho River, 129, 146
South Plains, Texas, 131, 160
Southern Pacific Railway Company, 122, 125, 125 (photo), 126, 126 (photo), 127 (photo), 132, 140-141, 147-148, 150, 161, 164-169, 172
Spanish-American War, 168
Spofford Junction, 167
Sprague, John T., 34-35, 38
Spring Creek, 116, 131, 141, 145
Spurlin, John L., 126
Steagall Ranch, 146
Stein, Henry, 159
Stevens, Bob, 151 (photo)
Stillman, J. D. B., 11, 14
Stockman, Bob, 155
Stoneman, George, 75-76, 78
Sumpter, Jesse, 38
Sunset Route, 122, 125
Sutton County, Texas, 11-12, 134, 136, 141, 143-144, 156, 160, 162, 163
Sutton County, Texas, 165, 168-169, 171
Swindler (drover), 138
Sycamore Creek, 105, 119
Tamaulipan Thornscrub, 12
Tardy (Tarde) Crossing (see "Lancaster Crossing")
Taylor (sheepman), 143
Taylor Ranch, 150
Taylor, Bill, 168-170
Taylor, Henry, 92
Taylor, J. B., 142, 144, 160-162
Taylor, J. O. "Jim," 157-158, photo (158)
Taylor, Jeff, 168-169
Tejada, Sebastian Lerdo de, 110
Tejano, 112
Terrell County, Texas, 132
Texas and Pacific Railway, 120, 122
Texas Legislature, 121
Texas Live Stock Journal, 130
Texas Rangers, 23-24, 47, 75-76, 94-96, 104-105, 107-108, 113-115, 150, 159, 165,

167-168, 170
Texas Rangers, Frontier Battalion, Company A, 110
Texas Rangers, Frontier Battalion, Company D, 111, 129, 136-138, 148
Texas Rangers, Frontier Battalion, Company F, 107-109, 116
Texas Rangers, Second Texas Rangers, Company B, 91-92
Texas State Forces, 81, 86, 91
Texas State Forces, Frontier Rangers, 83, 86, 160
Texas State Forces, Second Texas Mounted Rifles, 81-82
Texas State Forces, Second Texas Mounted Rifles, Company A, 82
Texas State Forces, Second Texas Mounted Rifles, Company B, 82
Texas State Forces, Second Texas Mounted Rifles, Company C, 82
Texas State Forces, Second Texas Mounted Rifles, Company D, 82
Texas State Forces, Second Texas Mounted Rifles, Company E, 82
Texas State Forces, Second Texas Mounted Rifles, Company F, 82, 84-85
Texas State Forces, Second Texas Mounted Rifles, Company H, 82
Texas State Forces, Texas Militia, Twenty-Sixth Brigade, 82
Texas State Forces, Texas Mounted Volunteers, 47
Texas State Forces, Texas State Troops, 184
Texas Stockman and Farmer, 163
Thornton, Louis, 159
Thorpe, Corporal, 77
Throckmorton, J. W., 89
Tom Green County, Texas, 123, 131, 140-141, 169
Tonkawa Indians, 30
Tracy, E., 58
Train Accidents (see "Railroad Accidents")
Trans-Pecos, Texas, 12, 111, 132
Treaty of Guadalupe Hidalgo, 36
Trevino, Geronimo, 110
Tucson, Arizona, 82
Turkey Creek, 29
Twiggs, D. E., 71, 73, 78-79
TX Ranch, 160

Ugalde, Juan de, 19, 20
Ugarte y Loyola, Jacobo de, 19
Upper Road, 27, 33, 73, 86-87
US Army (also see individual units), 25, 27, 29, 31, 33-38, 40, 43, 45-47, 52, 62, 71, 76, 82-83, 85, 88-89, 94, 102, 106, 110-113
US Army Mounted Rifles, 58
US Army Ninth Cavalry, Company E, 96-97
US Army Ninth Cavalry, Company H, 98
US Army Second Cavalry, Company C, 57
US Army, Company K, 73
US Army, Department of New Mexico, 86
US Army, Department of Texas, 57, 59, 61, 69, 73, 78-79, 81, 91, 96-97, 104, 107, 110, 117, 120-122
US Army, District of the Bravo, 120
US Army, District of the Nueces, 114, 117, 119
US Army, District of the Pecos, 117, 119-120
US Army, Eighth Cavalry, 111
US Army, Eighth Cavalry, Company A, 114, 117
US Army, Eighth Cavalry, Company B, 114
US Army, Eighth Cavalry, Company K, 114, 116
US Army, Eighth Cavalry, Company M, 114
US Army, Eighth Infantry, 48, 65-66
US Army, Eighth Infantry, Company A, 51, 60
US Army, Eighth Infantry, Company C, 60
US Army, Eighth Infantry, Company E, 35
US Army, Eighth Infantry, Company F, 60
US Army, Eighth Infantry, Company G, 60, 61, 68
US Army, Eighth Infantry, Company H, 51, 60
US Army, Eighth Infantry, Company Seven A, 68, 77
US Army, Fifteenth Regiment, 92
US Army, Fifth Infantry, Company A, 57
US Army, Fifth Infantry, Company I, 56
US Army, First Artillery, 59, 73
US Army, First Artillery, Company D, 74
US Army, First Artillery, Company F, 74
US Army, First Artillery, Company I, 57
US Army, First Colorado Volunteers, 85
US Army, First Infantry, 28, 41-42, 50, 55, 57, 59, 66, 68
US Army, First Infantry, Company B, 57, 59-60

220 INDEX

US Army, First Infantry, Company K, 79
US Army, Fourth Cavalry, 89, 101, 103, 115, 117
US Army, Fourth Cavalry, Company A, 115
US Army, Fourth Cavalry, Company C, 88, 90
US Army, Fourth Cavalry, Company D, 117
US Army, Fourth Cavalry, Company E, 116
US Army, Headquarters of the Army, 59
US Army, Mounted Riflemen, Company A, 56
US Army, Mounted Riflemen, Company G, 56
US Army, Mounted Riflemen, Company H, 57
US Army, Ninth Cavalry, 95
US Army, Ninth Cavalry, Company A, 98-100
US Army, Ninth Cavalry, Company C, 90, 96
US Army, Ninth Cavalry, Company D, 90-91
US Army, Ninth Cavalry, Company F, 95
US Army, Ninth Cavalry, Company G, 90-92
US Army, Ninth Cavalry, Company I, 90
US Army, Ninth Cavalry, Company K, 91
US Army, Ninth Cavalry, Company L, 92
US Army, Ninth Cavalry, Company M, 91-92, 95
US Army, One Hundred Twenty-Sixth New York Volunteer Infantry, 102
US Army, Second Cavalry, 65, 75
US Army, Second Cavalry, Company G, 63-65
US Army, Second Dragoons, Company A, 48
US Army, Second Dragoons, Company G, 48
US Army, Tenth Cavalry, 109-110, 114-116
US Army, Tenth Cavalry, Company B, 107-108
US Army, Tenth Cavalry, Company E, 108
US Army, Tenth Cavalry, Company G, 106
US Army, Tenth Cavalry, Company K, 108
US Army, Tenth Cavalry, Company L, 106
US Army, Tenth Cavalry, Company M, 108
US Army, Third Cavalry, 138
US Army, Third Infantry, 28
US Army, Twentieth Infantry, 115, 117
US Army, Twenty-Fifth Infantry, 95
US Army, Twenty-Fifth Infantry, Company A, 97, 105
US Army, Twenty-Fifth Infantry, Company C, 96
US Army, Twenty-Fifth Infantry, Company D, 97
US Army, Twenty-Fifth Infantry, Company F, 96-99
US Army, Twenty-Fifth Infantry, Company H, 97

US Army, Twenty-Fifth Infantry, Company I, 98-99
US Army, Twenty-Fourth Infantry, 95, 98, 107
US Army, Twenty-Fourth Infantry, Company F, 96
US Army, Twenty-Fourth Infantry, Company I, 96
US Army, Twenty-Second Infantry, 116
Uvalde County, Texas, 95, 111
Uvalde, Texas, 112, 145
Val Verde County, Texas, 12, 17, 128, 132, 133, 135, 141, 144, 152, 159-160
Val Verde County, Texas, 163-165, 168, 170-171
Valois, Lieutenant, 99-100
Van Horne, Jefferson, 28
Van Valzah, D. D., 97
Vera Cruz, Mexico, 44
Victoria, Texas, 25
Vincent, F. R., 98
Vincent, Thomas M., 117
Vinton, D. H., 78
VP Ranch, 131
Wade, Ben, 46
Wallace, William "Bigfoot," 43-48, 50, 65-66
Waller, Edwin, 81-82
Ward, John, 105-106
Warner's Ranch, California, 52
Washa Lobo, 112
Wasson, David, 53-55
Watts, H., 161
Way, Phocion R., 68-69
Webster, E. P., 45
Webster, John, 22
Webster, Mrs. John, 22-23
Webster, Virginia, 22-23
Weisenbeck (rancher), 155
Welch, Bill, 149-150
Wellington, Thumbless Jack, 148-149
Wells-Fargo, 148, 164-165, 167, 169-170
Wentworth, Texas, 144, 150
West, George W., 130
Western Mercantile Company, 155
Western Texian, 24
White Horse, 98
White, L. L., 169
Whiting, Charles J., 65
Whiting, William H. C., 25, 27, 43
Wilcox, John A., 88-89

Williams, E. W., 185
Williams, Hal, 126
Williams, R. H., 83, 184-185
Wilson, Perry, 138, 140
Wilson, W. M., 146
Wilson's Sheep Ranch, 138
Winkler, A., 134
Woll, Adrian, 44
Woodhull, O. J., 162
Woodruff, Tom, 170-171
Woods, I. C., 62-63, 66-67
Word, O. T., 146, 162
Wright, Samuel, 90
Wright, Will, 160
Wyatt, D. J., 162
Xaviercillo, 20
Yellow Banks, 53 (photo), 71, 72 (photo), 86, 115, 115 (map)
Yellow Tank, 53 (photo), 72 (photo)
Yorktown, Texas, 129
Young, John, 119
Young, Mrs. (settler), 132
Young, Samuel B. M., 111, 114-115
Ysleta, Texas, 165
Yuma, Arizona, 73
Zaragoza (Saragossa), Mexico, 108, 111-112

ABOUT THE AUTHOR

The author of nine nonfiction books and nine novels, Patrick Dearen is a recognized authority on the lower Pecos River country. He grew up in Sterling City, Texas, and earned a bachelor of journalism from the University of Texas at Austin.

His nonfiction works include *Castle Gap and the Pecos Frontier*, *Portraits of the Pecos Frontier*, *Crossing Rio Pecos*, *A Cowboy of the Pecos*, and *Halff of Texas*. Through his books *The Last of the Old-Time Cowboys* and *Saddling Up Anyway*, Dearen has also preserved the stories of the last generation of cowhands who plied their trade before mechanization. His novels include *Perseverance*, set along the rails in Depression-era Texas.

Dearen has been honored by Western Writers of America, West Texas Historical Association, and Permian Historical Association. A backpacking enthusiast and ragtime pianist, he makes his home in Midland, Texas, with his wife Mary and son Wesley.

Devils River: Treacherous Twin to the Pecos, 1535-1900
ISBN 978-0-87565-423-2
Paper. $22.95.